Good Morning,
I'm Joan Lunden

Good Morning,

G. P. PUTNAM'S SONS   NEW YORK

I'm Joan Lunden

JOAN LUNDEN
with
Ardy Friedberg

I want to dedicate this book to my husband, Michael, who has given me three wonderful constants: love, friendship, and support. And he's given me another thing too. Something we have come to call "a sense of human."

And to Paul Thompson, Harry Geise and Bill De-Blonk for giving me my start at KCRA-TV in Sacramento.

And to my mother, not only for giving me my start in life, but for her love and for encouraging me always to reach for the stars.

G. P. Putnam's Sons
Publishers Since 1838
200 Madison Avenue
New York, NY 10016

Library of Congress Cataloging-in-Publication Data

Lunden, Joan.
Good morning, I'm Joan Lunden.

1. Lunden, Joan.   2. Journalists—United States—
Biography.   3. Television personalities—United States—
Biography.   I. Friedberg, Ardy.   II. Title.
PN4874.L85A34   1986   791.45´092´4   [B]   86-1690
ISBN 0-399-13126-4

Printed in the United States of America
1   2   3   4   5   6   7   8   9   10

CONTENTS

PROLOGUE

6:59:50 A.M.

"Quiet on the set please, everybody," Barry, one of the stage managers, says, as he echoes the warning from the director in the control room, and begins the ten-second countdown. David Hartman and I settle into our chairs and put our notes on the coffee table in front of us. A few feet away, Vice-President George Bush sips some coffee as he waits for his interview, and outside, the limousines are arriving with the morning's other guests.

"Now in ten . . . five, four, three . . ."

At home the audience sees the *Good Morning America* symbol of the rising sun and hears our theme music. The *"GMA* face," the person or group that gives a friendly greeting from somewhere in America, comes on the monitor: "Hello, I'm Charlie Adams in Kansas City, Missouri. Good Morning, America."

7:00:12 A.M.

Our other stage manager, Sandy, points her finger at us, the red light on Camera 2 goes on, and we're on the air.

"Good morning. I'm David Hartman."

"And I'm Joan Lunden. It's Tuesday, the fifteenth of March."

CHAPTER ONE

━━◆〉〉〉◆━━

Good Morning America

When the *Good Morning America* audience sees David Hartman and me for the first time each weekday morning it's 7:00:12, twelve seconds after the hour. Though it's only 7:00 A.M., both David and I are sitting there wide awake with bright smiles on our faces as if we'd been up for hours. The truth is, we have. *GMA* may go on the air at 7:00 A.M. but our workday starts some three hours earlier, at 4:00 A.M. to be exact.

You may have noticed it before but I can verify the fact for you. Four o'clock in the morning comes around very early. And for me, it doesn't seem to make a bit of difference what I did the day before or what time I went to bed (rarely later than 10:00 P.M. and even earlier when I can), the alarm buzzer is always a shock at that hour. You might think that after all these years on the same schedule one would get used to getting up in the middle of the night, that one might adjust to the "early to bed, early to rise" ritual. It isn't true for me. I'm never ready to get up at that ungodly hour.

When the alarm goes off, never mind that I might be in the middle of my favorite dream, the one in which I get to sleep as late as I want to; that incessant buzz is the signal that starts my body's semiautomatic morning routine. Usually I reach over and push the off button so it won't wake my husband, Michael, though he has learned to sleep through my early-morning noise in the same way I've learned to sleep when he comes to bed at midnight or 1:00 A.M.

Occasionally, however, I'll hit the snooze button instead and use that four-minute respite to try to reason out why I'm doing this to myself five mornings a week. I mentally weigh the options of the normal life—a nine-to-five job, grocery shopping, cooking, playing with the kids, entertaining in the evening, watching the late movie, and all the rest—versus a schedule that has me finishing the workday just about the time most people are getting back to the office from lunch. Still, I have to confess that even on the worst mornings, even when I was pregnant, even on those very rare days when I'm sick, the imaginary scales come out weighted in favor of what I'm doing. This realization usually sinks in about the time the alarm goes off the second time and it's enough to lift me almost magically out of bed and point me toward the bathroom and the dawning of a new day. Now I am acutely aware that I have to get moving. I give Michael a peck on the cheek and head for the bathroom.

In that first half hour out of bed my routine is truly robotlike. After showering I'm usually pretty much awake but as a hedge against the disaster of oversleeping I always lay out the clothes I'm going to wear into the studio the night before. These are casual clothes, not those I'll wear on the air. I stack them in the order that I put them on, that is, panties on top, then bra, skirt or pants, some kind of casual shirt or sweater, socks and shoes. This system has often saved me when I've hit the snooze button a second time. It only takes a few minutes to throw me off schedule. I also use the limousine driver provided by ABC-TV as an extra measure of safety. He usually backs into the driveway about 4:20 and his first job is to check for a light in the upstairs bathroom. If he doesn't see that light then he is instructed to start knocking on the door, softly at first so as not to wake the whole house, then as loudly as necessary until I answer the door. This system has also been put into use several times over the years. Knowing that the driver is down there as an extra safety valve allows me to go to bed feeling secure. I really can't stand to be late for anything and

I'm terribly compulsive about it. I'd rather be half an hour early for an appointment than five minutes late. It drives other people crazy but it makes me feel good.

By the time I'm dressed it's around 4:15, so I have about ten minutes to take a look at my little girls, Jamie and Lindsay (sometimes tucking one of them into bed with Michael), to leave a note for our nanny, and to tiptoe downstairs as quietly as I can. I'm a fanatic about not disturbing the family in the morning, so I take the extra, rather obsessive, precaution of oiling the door hinges every month or so to prevent any loud squeaks.

Outside the limousine is waiting.

My driver, David, has been awake longer than I have and he is usually full of energy. His pleasant greeting—"Good morning. How are you this morning?"—is a reminder that someone else is awake at that hour and his words are usually the first ones I've heard that morning.

It's hard for me to understand how my drivers can be so cheerful, because they make my 4:00 A.M. wake-up call seem a bit tardy. These men wrote the book on getting up early for work. By the time the driver gets to my house he has already made four stops. He has picked up the car, the morning papers, and the day's script at the studio and has stopped at an all-night diner to get coffee for both of us. This means he starts his day at around 2:00 A.M. Even I call that early.

We live in a very quiet neighborhood in a close-in suburb of New York City; there is absolutely no traffic at that hour except for my car and another limousine that, somewhat ironically, picks up our neighbor, the man who reads the news on *Today* on NBC. It must be a very strange sight to see these big cars rolling down the deserted streets in a small caravan, the reading lights shining through the heavily tinted glass in the rear windows, as we head for the highway. As our car swings onto the main road at 4:30, my work day begins.

The ride to and from Manhattan on the parkway is quite scenic during the day, but in the pitch-darkness of early morning there is nothing to see and the only extraneous sound is the "whoosh" as we pass an occasional car along the nearly deserted highway. But it really wouldn't matter if it were broad daylight because I don't have time for the scenery. I tear a little semicircle in the plastic lid of my coffee cup to keep from spilling it all over myself and I get down to work.

First, I go through the daily papers—*The New York Times* and the *Daily News*—scanning the headlines, reading the stories I know we'll be covering that morning. For example, the morning following a major news event like a natural disaster or hijacking, I'll read the entire article because I know we will be covering the story and I'll want to have the whole picture. I try to avoid those local horror stories that have become such a big part of our everyday life in this country, and everywhere in the world for that matter. Nothing like a headline that reads, "Child Falls to Death from Ninth-Floor Window," to start your day off with a bang, especially when you're supposed to appear full of life and good cheer when you're on the air.

When I've finished the papers I pick up the latest script the driver has brought for me. It is in nearly final form by this time, but it still needs some changes (more will be made even later) so I work on those revisions. Then I review the research that goes with the day's interviews, even though I will have spent anywhere from forty-five minutes to an hour and a half being briefed on the phone the night before.

Some thirty-five minutes or so later, I've usually finished all I can do in the car, and as we enter Manhattan I sit back and relax for a few minutes. It's always a strange sight to look at the empty streets of one of the world's busiest and most crowded cities and know that in another hour the commuter traffic will start pouring into the city and in two hours many of these same streets will be so clogged that traffic may come to a complete standstill. It's a very surrealistic scene, broken only by an occasional delivery truck, a police car or ambulance, or an early riser walking his dog. We come into the city on the west side of Manhattan Island, down the Henry Hudson Parkway, past the remains of rotting piers on the river, and then turn east to the ABC studios near Central Park and the home of *Good Morning America*. ABC has several buildings in the same area but the doorway I use to get into the *GMA* studio is as inconspicuous as it can be. I often think it must look rather strange, even suspicious, to somebody watching this long black limousine pull up at an unmarked door at 5:15 A.M. and discharge this blond woman dressed in a sweatshirt, a pair of slacks, and my treasured Chicago Cubs baseball cap, the souvenir the team gave me when I covered spring training a few years ago.

Once I am inside, there are "Good mornings" all around, and I go directly up the stairs to the second floor. I make a quick stop in my dressing room to drop my coat and purse and then, before changing into the clothes I'll wear on the program, I head straight to the makeup room where Robert, my hairdresser, and Josephine, my makeup artist, are waiting. The makeup area is really a small beauty salon with four swivel chairs (the guests on the program are also made up in this room), brightly lighted mirrors on two walls, and a stock of makeup, eye shadow, nail polish, and whatever—it would do justice to one of the cosmetic counters in Bloomingdale's.

The three of us have gotten to be friends, working so closely together, and we normally are very chatty. But there is an unnatural quiet now, because as Robert works on my hair, I am concentrating on rereading my script and writing out my interview notes. During that time we all keep our comments to a minimum. When he finishes I start with makeup and while Josephine does my eyes we do our socializing—it's very difficult to read with an eyebrow pencil poised directly over your eyes.

At about that time I need a little conversation anyway. It's nearly 6:00 and I've been concentrating totally on the program for about an hour and a half. Our chatter ranges from the state of the world to the latest gossip and the current round of jokes, and I must admit we're not always reverent. The jokes often have a tinge of black humor, and most of the punch lines are acknowledged with a chorus of groans. There is something about the early morning and the fact that we so often deal with bad news that bring out this sort of thing.

When I travel for the show, Robert and Josephine may go with me on one-day or overnight trips, but when I make longer jaunts—to the Olympics in Yugoslavia, for example, or to the Normandy beaches for the fortieth anniversary of D Day—I do my own hair and makeup. Last spring I took a fast four-day trip to Morocco to tape a three-part interview with Michael Douglas, Kathleen Turner, and Danny DeVito, who were on location filming *Jewel of the Nile,* Douglas's sequel to the incredibly successful *Romancing the Stone.*

We rode by car to the location outside of Fez, a rather remote desert area, where we spent the better part of three days underground in the ancient grottoes, catacombs that were built centuries ago as travel routes under the desert. These tunnels were absolutely fascinating and completely primitive. You couldn't move without raising a cloud of brownish dust. Of course, that wreaks havoc with your complexion and your hair. Fortunately we did most of our interviews back at the hotel in Fez, where the movie company's makeup artist and hairdresser were nice enough to help put me back together.

There I was, sitting on the terrace of Michael Douglas's suite overlooking the ancient city of Fez. Kathleen, Danny, and I were chatting, the sun was beating down on us, and Michael Douglas was walking around barechested, looking absolutely gorgeous. Incongruously, in this scene overlayed with romance and history, I was sitting with hot rollers in my hair, having mascara applied so I'd look good for the taped interviews. But that's part of the fantasy world of show business.

But back to reality. It's a little after 6:00 A.M. when I'm handed a newly revised version of the day's script by one of the production assistants. It's now that things begin to get really serious. The changes made from this point on are final. The guest list and the interview schedule probably won't change unless something as serious as an international incident or national crisis occurs, or unless a guest is late, which sometimes happens, so I begin to review my questions and make notes to myself in the margin of the script. These notes always include a little diagram of where people will be sitting during my interviews and a few words to identify each of them. When you're interviewing celebrities it's one thing, but we're not always interviewing well-known people; with three or four interviews a morning, things can get confusing and potentially embarrassing.

In the course of a year we may have a guest on the show more than once. In this type of situation you want everything to be fresh, but you can't remember exactly what you covered the last time. That could be 300 interviews ago. The writers can be a big help here and we have some great ones. For instance, in order to get a sensitive, poignant, or probing interview, one of them will say to me, "Joan, you're going to do Bette Midler tomorrow. I looked back at your last two interviews with her and the last one David did as well. You've covered these three topics before, so let's move on to some new material." That's a skilled TV writer. This interest and enthusiasm is good for me, the guest, and the audience at home. This keeps things lively and new and makes us all care.

When Josephine and Robert finish, I go back to my dressing room, just a few steps down the hall. I call it a dressing room and it is that, but I've also turned it into a giant closet. On one side there are shelves with my shoes, on another wall are hanging racks for my dresses and skirts, and there are drawers for my sweaters, blouses, and underthings. I have an extensive television wardrobe that is provided by Lillie Rubin South and West, a chain of fine women's stores, and I'm free to wear almost anything I want. Sometimes, however, what I wear is predetermined by what I wore during an interview that was taped a few days before the live show. I want to wear the same clothes on the live show that I wore in the taped interview in order to provide visual continuity for the viewer at home. It could be confusing to someone who watches the show in bits and pieces to see me in one outfit at 7:15, another one at 7:40, and then the first one again at 8:10.

Near my dressing table, which has a large mirror surrounded by lights, I've tacked notes to remind me when to match up those same interview outfits. That's where I have a wall calendar that I use to keep track of all the clothes I have worn on the show for the previous thirty days. So, for example, I can refer back three or four weeks and find out the last time I wore the St. John yellow knit dress. If it's been long enough I can wear it again. If not I'll choose something else. This also keeps me from wearing the same style, a knit dress for example (though not the same one), three days in a row or even on a Monday three weeks in a row. I also have to change clothes with the seasons (wearing a heavy sweater in August looks ridiculous, even though the studio is cold enough to merit it), and I have to keep up with the changes in styles. Consequently, I need a large and ever-changing wardrobe.

Not surprisingly, I get a tremendous amount of mail asking about my clothes. I've found over the years that women pay close attention to what I wear (sometimes I think they keep better track of my wardrobe than I do myself). And though I have to please myself I have to think of the taste of the audience at the same time. I try to choose my wardrobe accordingly. Most often women want to know where they can shop for the clothes I wear, but there are other comments like "Why do you wear such high heels?" or "That dark-blue knit skirt you wore last week was smashing" or "You wore that red outfit two weeks ago."

Taped interviews, the frequency of wearing certain styles, and the change of seasons are factors that help determine the way I dress, but what I wear is also partly determined by the type of interview I'm going to be doing. If we're talking about the MX missile, I'll probably wear a suit as opposed to a feminine silk dress. For fun things—a story about bicycling in the park or outdoor cooking—I'll wear fun clothes. On location—in Normandy or in Morocco—I'll usually wear a casual pants outfit because it looks more appropriate in that kind of setting.

It's about 6:40 by the time I finish dressing but the preparations for the day's show aren't over. There are still last-minute script changes, makeup and hair touch-ups, and occasionally those unforeseen problems that can cause some anxiety in the control room—like the live interview with Charlton Heston from London: It had to be delayed three times and was finally aired during the last half hour of the show because Heston got stuck in traffic and couldn't get to the ABC studio in London on time. And sometimes we're told only seconds before airtime which interview is ready at a remote location. These kinds of circumstances cause all sorts of fast reshuffling in the show lineup. But it is the job of the hosts to make sure that these problems aren't communicated to the people at home. And with years of experience I feel that David and I have learned to handle just about any situation in front of the camera with skill and professionalism, even though there may be havoc reigning behind the scenes in the control room.

I don't get nervous before the show but as 7:00 A.M. nears I can feel the adrenaline start to flow. About five minutes before airtime, I go down to the set and get "miked" by the sound person. This entails clipping a tiny microphone to my lapel or collar, running a wire inside my dress, and plugging that wire into a small transmission box that weighs about six ounces and is about the size of a pack of cigarettes. That box is clipped to the back of the waistband of whatever I'm wearing. This creates a rather unsightly lump in the small of my back that can't be seen on camera but usually elicits a ritual comment from the crew. Someone will invariably say, "Ah, Joan, you look great this morning but you really ought to see about having that lump removed."

I'm now ready to go on the air. But even during these last couple of minutes, I'm still making minor changes in the script, and there will often be a phone call to the set from the producer in the control booth about something or other, even as late as fifteen seconds before we go on.

The crew is busy putting the flowers on the coffee table that sits in front of David and me, moving cameras, adjusting the lighting, and shifting furniture from place to place. David comes in, usually with a flourish, about one minute before airtime. As the seconds tick down we get comfortable in our chairs.

Then: "Quiet on the set please, everybody. Now in ten . . . five, four, three . . ."

"Good morning. I'm David Hartman."

"And I'm Joan Lunden."

What you're about to read is my story, both on and off camera.

CHAPTER
TWO

~~~·~>I<~·~~~

Close, but No Cigar

The day I received the call from Bob Shanks, the ABC network vice-president in charge of *Good Morning America,* I was sitting at my typewriter in the newsroom of the local ABC station in New York City. I was trying to finish the copy on one of those "three-handkerchief" stories, so much a staple of the local television news these days, about a Columbia University honor student who had been beaten to death with a baseball bat by a gang of teenagers because they wanted his portable radio.

I had just written, "His friends describe Harvey Marston as a well-rounded young man who was not only a brilliant mathematician but also a fine athelete, a young man who . . ." I was trying to figure out what came after the "who" when the phone on my desk rang. "Eyewitness News, Joan Lunden," I answered.

"Miss Lunden, please hold for Mr. Shanks." It was the very businesslike voice of an efficient secretary. It took me a second or two to connect the name with ABC corporate headquarters.

A moment later Bob Shanks was on the line. I had been doing some work for *GMA* for about a year so I knew who Shanks was and I think I may have talked to him once on the set of *GMA,* but we weren't exactly old friends. Still, he opened the conversation as if we were. "Hi, Joanie," he said, "how's everything in the news business?"

"Fine," I answered, and I felt a little ridiculous as I said, "And how are you doing?" I was on deadline and tense and had the urge to say, "Hurry up and tell me what this call is all about," but I managed to restrain myself.

"Joan," he said in a confidential tone, "we're considering making a change in the host of the show and we're considering you. Would you be interested?" He didn't say which show and he didn't say which host but he didn't have to.

"Of course I'm interested, Bob," I said, trying to put the timbre of national television into my voice while attempting to keep myself from flying out of the chair and hitting the ceiling.

"Good," he said, "I'll be back to you to set up a lunch." It was all short, sweet, and absolutely thrilling, though far from what could be considered a job offer. I tried to temper my excitement so I could finish my story but at the same time I wanted to yell to everyone in the newsroom that little Joanie Lunden from Sacramento, California, was going to be the new face on *GMA*. Instead I sat there with a silly grin on my face and finished the sad story I was going to do on the news that night. I completed it by writing, ". . . who was a Rhodes Scholar and planned to work in international finance after graduation next June." Normally I would have been depressed about this story, and I was near tears, but not because of the tragedy I was writing about. I guess you can't help but be excited when you're struck by a bolt from the blue.

It's hard to keep a secret in the television business. In the fall of 1976 most people connected with ABC in New York had heard the rumor that *Good Morning America* was looking for a woman to replace Nancy Dussault as David Hartman's cohost on the show. So Bob Shanks's call, though certainly news as it pertained to me, was not really news at all, only an official confirmation of the rumor about big changes, a rumor that we all wondered if Nancy had also heard.

At that time I was a street reporter with *Eyewitness News,* WABC-TV's top-rated local news program on Channel 7 in New York City, and I was also doing what were called "new-product spots" on *GMA* from time to time.

A street reporter is the person you see on the nightly news shows, covering murders, strikes, and assorted disasters and interviewing the interesting, semi-interesting, and downright dull personalities who show up in every town from time to time. The new-product pieces, which amounted to a couple of minutes a week on *GMA,* consisted of solid, hard-hitting reporting in which I talked about the merits of the latest design in spare tires, jogger's wastebaskets, and radios that float. The spots weren't always hard news but they were interesting, informative, and often entertaining. Still, with the combination of my news stories on Channel 7 and those national spots on *GMA,* I was beginning to make some headway in both jobs and my name and face were both recognized in public, at least in New York City. But public recognition or not, my television career was still young, and if I had considered it at all, I had given only the most fleeting of thoughts to the *GMA* job. I admit that I did have my sights set on a major anchor job someday but that seemed pretty far off.

About a week after my initial conversation with Shanks, he called again to make lunch plans. We set a date and he suggested the dining room at the Dorset Hotel, one of those lovely old-world places that hasn't yet been replaced by a sleek skyscraper. That was fine with me. God knows, McDonald's would have been fine with me under the circumstances. But later he called back and said, "I've been thinking about it, Joanie. An awful lot of ABC people go to the Dorset, so let's make it the Warwick." That was fine with me too, but it was becoming clear that he didn't want anybody to see us talking and come to the conclusion, real or illusory, that it was Nancy Dussault's job that was under discussion.

A couple of days later, a very nervous Joan Lunden met Bob Shanks for lunch at the Warwick Hotel and, sure enough, there wasn't another ABC person in the dining room. It was a pleasant enough lunch and our conversation covered virtually everything but *GMA* until dessert; by that time my nervousness had disappeared and I was beginning to wonder what was going on.

Then, between bites of raspberry sherbet, Shanks said, "Joan, we'd like to consider you for Nancy's job." It was a pretty low-key approach and a little offhand, I thought, but there it was, nevertheless, at least half a job offer.

"I'd love to be considered," I answered, and that was essentially all there was to it. All cordial and light as the raspberry sherbet. I left that lunch full of hope but with no idea of what to expect next, if anything. Still, you get a warm feeling all over when you're being considered for a big job, and that feeling wouldn't go away.

That lunch was on a Monday and on the following Thursday, after the six-o'clock news, I was handed a message which said simply, "Call David Hartman," with his office phone number. I called the next morning and was told by David's secretary that he wanted to set up a breakfast meeting with me as soon as possible. "What mornings are you available, Miss Lunden?" she asked.

Since I worked afternoons and evenings, any morning was good for me, but in my short time in New York I had learned to play it a little cool, not to be too anxious, so I said, "Either Monday or Thursday of next week looks fine on my calendar."

"One moment," she said, as she checked with David. She came back on the line and said, "Make it Monday, then, at ten at Wolf's Delicatessen. Do you know where that is?"

"That's fine," I said. "Yes, I know Wolf's."

When Monday morning rolled around I was mentally ready to talk to the man himself. At exactly 10:00 David arrived at Wolf's and I was there waiting. Wolf's is mostly a tourist place, but David liked it and as a regular he was given special treatment. The hostess quickly ushered us to a corner booth. When the waitress came to take our order David said, "The usual." I didn't have a usual so I ordered my favorite breakfast (so fattening I should never touch it) of French toast with powdered sugar, well-done bacon, orange juice, and coffee. We made small talk until his "usual"—a toasted English muffin with butter, a glass of juice, and a cup of coffee—arrived, along with my platter of French toast.

The conversation then turned serious. "Have you ever considered the possibility of working with me on *GMA*?" he asked. I may not have thought much about it before, but I'd thought about it a thousand times since the first call from Shanks. "Sure, I've thought of it," I answered. "It would be a wonderful opportunity for me and a great experience working with you. What woman in television wouldn't want the job?"

He seemed to be taking me seriously but in my limited experience with him he was always so friendly, so full of curiosity and energy, that it was hard to get a clear reading. After all, I'd seen him respond with a genuine sense of wonder to some of the least interesting people in the world. I had heard, however, though I had no personal experience, that he expected perfection. So the pressure was on me. Would I be able to measure up, to be whatever it is that makes a perfect cohost?

We chatted for a few more minutes and then he said, "We'll be making a decision very soon. I'm glad we got a chance to talk."

That's how it was left at the time and it seemed to me that things had gone very well indeed. I was a little concerned, though, because I had heard some discussion about the way Nancy appeared to be treated on the show. It was said that she didn't get the proper respect, that she didn't get enough time on the air, and the time she did get was devoted to "women's stories" and interviewing minor celebrities, animals, and so forth. But these things didn't bother me because the job was so big, so desirable, so unique, that I knew things would be different with me. I think one always has that feeling of difference, that self-confidence that says, "Despite the fact that everyone who has tried to climb that mountain has failed, I'm going to make it."

My breakfast with David was the last I heard officially about the *GMA* job, though it certainly was uppermost in my mind, until I got a call from Ed Vain about three weeks later, asking me if I'd be willing to meet with Felix Shagin, David Hartman's agent, to talk further about the job. At that time Vain was Bob Shanks's boss and one step closer to the job.

I immediately called my own agent, Richard Leibner. He said, "This isn't exactly a normal request," and he was ready to tell them to forget it. But I've since found that agents are sometimes all too willing to tell their clients to forget things their clients really want to do. They never want to forget the ten-percent commission they get from the job you take against their recommendation, however.

He would have gone on but he had to pause for breath, and when he did I said, "It's a very big job, Richard. What can it hurt? I want to go ahead and do it. Besides, my breakfast with David was lovely and I think successful. As far as I'm concerned, this should be pursued."

He was still sputtering on the other end of the line. "I know it's a big job," he said. "If you're set on going ahead then I'm coming with you. I don't think you should go to another agent's office without me being there."

"Fine, then you'll come with me," I said. In fact, I was actually glad Richard insisted because I didn't really want to face this unknown person alone, a person who could determine what happened to me in the immediate future.

The morning of the day of the meeting Richard met me at WABC-TV. We grabbed a cab and as it crept down Broadway from Lincoln Center, Richard looked me in the eyes and asked, "Nervous?"

"Silly question," I said. "I'd rather be doing a live remote from a snake pit."

"Let me give you a little advice," he said. "First, don't volunteer too much information. Try just to respond to the questions you're asked. Be a little like your idea of a bad interview. In other words, try to be interested but noncommittal, bright but careful, pretty but not gorgeous."

We had given ourselves plenty of time, but because of the traffic we were just going to make it and my palms were sweating—as I said, I hate to be late for anything. Finally the driver stopped in front of one of those big, old, nondescript office buildings that line Broadway in the theater district. Richard paid him and we hurried inside. As we rode up in the elevator, I couldn't help but think that my whole future in television was going to be decided in the next few minutes. I was either on my way to the top or on my way back to Sacramento.

As we stepped out of the elevator I looked at Richard and said,

"Here goes nothin'." As it turned out it *was* nothing, though I didn't know that at the time.

The hallway leading to Shagin's office was poorly lighted and dingy, not at all the kind of place one would expect to find an agent who handles the likes of David Hartman. As in many of those vintage buildings, the floor was made of those small black and white tiles that were the standard for bathrooms in the 1920s, and my high heels clicked like tiny gunshots on the hard surface. The doors on either side of the hallway were mostly un-marked and made of that opaque glass that shows only shadows and rattles when the door slams. I thought I recognized the pro-files of both Philip Marlowe and Sam Spade as we walked toward my future. The door to Shagin's office was like all the rest, ex-cept that his opaque glass said FELIX SHAGIN in gold letters out-lined in black.

I opened the door and there was Shagin. There was no secre-tary, no staff, only a small unassuming office with a desk, side chairs, and a lot of memorabilia. Shagin shook hands and said, "Hello, Joan, it's nice to meet you." He was very cordial, though he seemed somewhat surprised by the presence of another per-son. I introduced Richard and Shagin offered us chairs.

Shagin sat down behind his desk and started twirling a pencil in his fingers. He was looking at his pencil as he said, "I wanted to talk to you because when we choose someone to work with David we want to make sure that it's someone who can work well and closely with him and look right with him." Then he said, "I'd like to ask you a few questions, if you don't mind."

I said, "Fine, that's why I'm here."

His first question was "Would you be willing to change your hair?" I didn't know what to expect but I sure wasn't expecting that for openers. That's like starting a televison interview with "I notice you wear false teeth" or "Don't you think you should go on a diet?" It's just a curve out of left field.

I did a classic double-take on Shagin, then I looked at Richard, who was looking at me. I was nonplussed for a few seconds. In a quizzical voice I said, "What do you mean by 'change my hair'?" I thought he might have meant radically change the color or cut it all off or wear a wig or something. It wasn't clear and I was nervous and defensive anyway.

He said, "You know, change your hair."

I thought for a moment and finally said, "If the producers of the show felt my hairstyle was not appealing to America and thought it would be better a little darker or shorter or longer and I thought what they were saying was valid, I would be willing to make changes. Sure."

As I sat there I was trying to figure out if I had said the right thing. I kept trying to catch a glimpse of Richard's face to see if he approved or disapproved.

"I've always been willing to make changes that I think are for the better," I went on, "because I know it's necessary to be appealing to a mass audience. But frankly I'm a little surprised by the question. Why did you ask?"

"To find out how much you're willing to bend," he said, "but mostly because the one potential problem we see is that you may look too young."

Still, my answer seemed to satisfy Shagin and we moved on to other questions. He asked me what my aspirations were and what I thought my role on the show might be. He also asked where I wanted to take that role.

I said, "I realize David has been with the show since its inception and that this is not a job that gets equal billing but it is a *very* good position for a woman and I'll be happy with it the way it is." I added, perhaps a little strongly, "Depending on how women's roles grow in the industry and in society as a whole, I expect to grow in the role proportionately."

Richard was trying to be as quiet as possible but he chimed in here. "What Joan is saying," he said, "is that we realize this is quite an opportunity for her, and she is willing to make necessary changes. But I want you to know that she is also a good student and learns quickly, that she likes David and the way he works and they already get along very well together. I think it would be a good relationship and good for the ratings of the show to team them up."

If this all sounds a little wishy-washy on my part, it was. After all, we were there to say the right things and to sell me. There were a couple of other questions that I don't recall now and that was it. The whole thing took less than thirty minutes.

As Richard and I got up to leave everyone shook hands but I didn't know what to think. As we walked toward Eighth Avenue to catch a cab back uptown, Richard said, "You did very well in there. There is no way that Shagin could have been put off by your answers."

In retrospect I felt that my separate meetings with Shanks, Hartman, and Felix Shagin had all gone well, and although I had no concrete reason to think that I would get the job, I was feeling somewhat confident about the prospects. Later, in my apartment, I sat down to reflect on what had happened. I thought to myself, "Oh my God, it is so great to be offered this job. This is a network job. The chance to be part of a team with a star like David Hartman, whom I remember from *The Bold Ones, Lucas Tanner,* and other shows. There aren't many jobs like this available in the world." Then, almost immediately, I got nauseous at the thought of actually having to do it. The prospect of taking a job that would require me to do live interviews every day was a scary one. I knew how nervous I got when I did my live two-minute product pieces. At that point I told myself, "Oh God, I hope I don't get it because if I do I don't know that I can pull it off." You can get a sense of the way I felt if you stop and think for a minute about sitting there and calmly chatting with heads of state, movie stars, musicians, artists, doctors, and leaders from all walks of life. This was responsibility on a grand scale. The ego side of me wanted to hear them say, "It's yours," and the other half of me was hoping and praying that I wouldn't get the job. I also knew that there had to be other people under consideration, probably people with more experience than I had at the time, and that realistically my chances were not very good. Still, I couldn't help starting to think about how I was going to spend my big raise in salary.

One night less than a week later, I was in the bathroom just before leaving the WABC-TV studios after doing the evening news. The men's and women's bathrooms happen to share a wall and as I was washing my hands I couldn't help but overhear a loud conversation in the men's room.

That conversation went like this:

Man's exuberant voice: "Hey, you ought to see this new girl named Sandy Hill they hired to do *GMA*. Wait till you see the legs on this broad." Some mumbling in the background.

Man's voice: "I heard she's going to be doing some stuff for *Eyewitness News* too." More mumbling.

In one stroke this gorgeous girl with long legs had gotten "my" job on *GMA*, not to mention the fact that she was going to cut me out on *Eyewitness News* as well. It was one of those instances in your life when time stands still. I was glazed. I wasn't supposed to hear what I heard and I didn't want to hear it, but nevertheless there it was and there was no taking it back. I knew it had to be true but didn't want to believe it.

That night I had dinner with Michael Krauss, the man who was later to become my husband. Michael and I had met when he was the producer of WABC's *A.M. New York* show. Later he took over as one of the founding producers of *GMA*, and it was when I began doing new-product spots on *GMA* that we started to date. We had already had a few dates and he asked me out that particular night because he had heard directly that I had not gotten the job and he wanted to break the news to me as gently as possible. He was worried about my feelings being hurt, which was very thoughtful.

As we sipped some wine he said, "Joanie, I have news for you and it isn't good. I think you should know that Sandy Hill got the job at *GMA*. I wanted to tell you before you found out some other way. I know how much you wanted that job, but there will be other chances, believe me."

"I already know," I said. "I overheard one of the guys at work telling everyone about 'that new *GMA* broad's great legs.' But don't worry, Michael," I said. "I did my best and I'm just fine."

Even as I said, "I'm just fine," I made up my mind that next time around things were going to be different.

CHAPTER THREE

Who Would Have Dreamed?

I'm sure you remember those books we all read in the first grade, those with pictures of the perfect mother and father, the two perfect children named Dick and Jane, the perfect little dog named Spot, and the perfect little cottage in the perfect little town. I used to love to read those books but I didn't realize until much later that those primers offered a pretty accurate picture of my life as a child. I had "perfect" parents, a brother, and a dog (and even a horse at one time) and we did nice, happy, all-American things, just like Dick and Jane.

In many ways my childhood insulated me from the vagaries of life and it wasn't until I reached high school that I realized that there were actually people who lived a life radically different from my own and those people weren't even from foreign countries, they were from my own. I don't think I'm unusual in this way, though my case of social isolation may have been a bit more severe than most. After all, this was the 1950s and the world was a lot different in those days.

I suppose you could classify my family as upper middle-class—a bit more affluent than the average household in Fair Oaks, a small, semirural suburb northeast of Sacramento, California. That was, even in retrospect, the perfect place for a child to grow up.

My father, Dr. Erle Murray Blunden, was born in Australia and grew up in China where his parents were missionaries. He came to this country to go to college and he stayed on to go to medical school. During the Second World War he was a surgeon with the Army Air Corps and when I was born he was what they called a country doctor in those days. He would travel for fifty miles in any direction to make a house call on one of his patients. My mother used to say, "He's a real missionary at heart," and I guess he was. My mother, the former Gladyce Lorraine Somervill, was a housewife and mother, like nearly all women her age in that period in America, but she was charged with energy and enthusiasm and was involved in nearly every organization in town.

My parents had been married several years when my older brother Jeffrey was born, and I was born about a year later on September 19, 1950. I was named Joan Elise Blunden. (Obviously I later changed my name, but more on that later.)

My first memories of my father are colored by the way I remember the house calls he made on sick neighbors. The phone would ring and he'd be out the door, often in the middle of the night. I used to hate hearing the sound of his car starting up and backing out of the driveway when I was in bed. I was always concerned that he might not come back. I also remember that those calls were very important to him because he genuinely liked to help people and was proud of the service he was able to render. Except for my childish anxiety about him being out at night, it made me very proud to be the daughter of such a great and helpful man.

Later my father decided to practice surgery and we moved from Fair Oaks to an area farther from Sacramento, a move that had a great deal to do with the fact that my father was an avid flier. I was about six when we moved to a new house, one very different from our hillside house that had overlooked my father's office in Fair Oaks.

The new house was right on the edge of a small dirt airstrip that Dad and about ten flying friends built to make it easier for them to fly and maintain their planes. It fulfilled one of my dad's fantasies, to be a pilot with his own airport. Our new house was surrounded by five acres of open land; there was a stable for horses, a swimming pool, and a hangar for his plane. In fact, as far back as I can remember, we always had a hangar for an airplane but never had a garage for the car. In this case the hangar was actually part of the house and there was a taxi strip that came right up to our dining room door. Friends used to pull up to the door and park their planes just as other people parked cars in their driveways. It was unique, to say the least.

I remember that some of his patients helped build the house and put blacktop on the runway in lieu of paying bills, but what I remember most about that place was that we had freedom to leave at any time and were just as likely to hop in the plane as we were to get into the car. We got to see scores of places that most kids didn't have the chance to visit in those days before jet travel became commonplace. That plane was so much a part of our life, like a car to most people, that on a nice day we'd all pile in and fly to some other town for lunch or dinner, for a Sunday outing, or to visit friends or colleagues of my father. In the summer, when school was out, we used to take longer trips, and in the winter, during school holidays and on most weekends, we usually went to Lake Tahoe to ski. It was a good life for anyone, and for a child it was wonderful.

My mother has always said, "Your father was born with Gypsy blood," and I think I surely must have inherited a gallon or two of that blood from him because I love to travel and I always have, perhaps because of my early exposure to the wonders of the world.

At about the time we moved, my dad also became involved in the construction of a hospital designed to serve an area around Sacramento that had never had such facilities. He had persuaded a group of doctors to join him in the project, and since it was another of his dreams he spent a lot of time overseeing its development. At the same time he maintained his practice, so he was always on the go.

In early January 1964 my father bought his first twin-engine plane, the fulfillment of another of his dreams. He had a Johnson

Rocket, a Piper Comanche, and several others before he bought the Cessna 310 and for him the Cessna was a real step up. I remember that my mother was not particularly happy about the new plane. "You've always flown small planes," she told him before he made the purchase, "and they're plenty big enough. This is more dangerous and I don't want you to have it." But he prevailed; he studied for and obtained his twin-engine pilot's rating so he was ready to fly it when it was delivered.

Dad was scheduled to attend a medical convention in Los Angeles several days after the new plane arrived and he wanted us all to go along for our first ride in the new plane. But Jeff and I were in school, and since we were all going to Tahoe to ski that weekend anyway, Dad relented and made plans to meet us there after his meeting.

But the day he was leaving for LA my mother changed her mind. She picked us up at school, told us that we were all going with Dad "to share that new toy," that we could go to Tahoe from LA, and that we had to hurry because she hadn't had time to tell him about her change of heart and he would be leaving in a few minutes. We rushed home and she drove right out onto the edge of the runway. But we were a couple of minutes late. Dad and his new plane were already roaring down the runway and we all got out and waved like mad for him to stop. He thought we were just waving good-bye. He just smiled and waved and was off. I suppose we could have radioed him to come back and pick us up but Mom decided that wasn't necessary and we'd stick to the original plan. Dad was in LA for three days and Mom, Jeff, and I drove to Lake Tahoe.

We skied all day Friday, January 17, and when it started to snow hard in the late afternoon, we went back to our condominium. That night, a group of us went out to dinner at an Italian restaurant. When we ordered, we all remarked that we were starved. Yet when the food arrived, my mother suddenly lost her appetite and didn't eat a bite. None of us thought anything about it at the time, but it wasn't like my mother at all.

When we went to bed the storm had gotten worse, and we heard that all the roads were being closed to car traffic. It was the middle of the night when my brother came into my bedroom, gently shook me awake, and said, "Mom wants to talk to you, she needs you." I went downstairs and saw two policemen. My mother was sitting on the couch, crying. I didn't have the slightest idea what was happening.

The police had told her that my father, who was supposed to make a stop in San Francisco to drop off another doctor, was late and had not been heard from. His plane was presumed down somewhere between Los Angeles and San Francisco. I just stood there, letting the news sink in, but the implications were too unbearable to accept. The police said that there had been heavy rain and a lightning storm in LA when he left and that it was still so bad they had been unable to send out search planes. Meanwhile, the snowstorm continued to rage outside our windows and we all started packing so we could leave at daybreak and make our way back to Sacramento.

The next morning the police returned and escorted us behind a snowplow until we got to clear roads. It was slow going and we all sat in the car in an unnatural, uncomfortable silence. And we were so anxious that it seemed slower still. By the time we got to Sacramento the wreckage of Dad's plane had been found in Malibu Canyon less than half an hour's drive from the LA airport. There was no sign of life. Wreckage covered both sides of the canyon. We learned later that witnesses said the plane had crashed at full speed after going down into the canyon, back up again, and then down again, this time disappearing into the mountains. The authorities speculated that the plane might have had electrical problems (Dad had work done on the radio while he was in Los Angeles) or that Dad might have had a heart attack. True, he was only fifty-one, but he was a hard-driving man and a heart attack wasn't out of the question.

Even after the funeral I found it hard to believe that my dad was dead and that here I was, not even fourteen years old and without a father. For weeks I dreamed that they had actually found the body of Dad's passenger and that Dad had walked out of that canyon, that he had amnesia and was alive and that we'd all get together again someday. Of course, that was only a young girl's wishful fantasy. Since the accident I've often wondered why fate had prevented us all from being on that plane, and we could easily have been, and another thought crosses my mind— that if we had been with Dad, things might have turned out differently.

My father's sudden death changed our lives dramatically, and my mother took over as both mother and father for Jeff and me. She was made of "strong stuff," as they used to say. She formed us into a threesome that would, in her words, "have to fight the world together."

My mother has always been a pusher and I'm sure part of her drive comes from her midwestern background. I remember when I was in grade school, friends would say, "Boy, Joanie, you're sure lucky to live in that house by the airport," and my mother would tell me to answer, "Yes, and the harder my father works the luckier I get." She has always valued the "seekers" and the "achievers" and those who dream of a better life. I know she has said to me a thousand times, "Hitch your wagon to a star, baby doll." As far back as I can remember she has tried to instill high aspirations, to get me to dream, to expand my horizons, and especially to go to college and be a success.

Through a combination of her urging and my own ability, I always did extremely well in school. During high school I started taking correspondence courses from the University of California at Berkeley and took some night-school courses in Sacramento as well. I also seemed to have time to do other things, like enter beauty contests, play in piano recitals, take dancing lessons, or lead a parade, and I credit my mother for my aggressiveness and my desire for independence. I eventually skipped a year in high school and graduated when I was just sixteen.

The summer following my high school graduation I got a job in the X-ray lab of the hospital my father helped build. I wanted that job for two reasons. First, being an independent little soul, I wanted to nurture that independence by earning my own money. Second, I had been thinking seriously about following in my father's footsteps and wanted to get a taste of medicine on my own. Then I'd go to medical school and become a surgeon, just as he had been. Those three months in the X-ray lab put me in close contact with blood and pain and convinced me that I didn't really want to be a doctor, after all. At the same time the long hours and hard work made me appreciate the idea of going to college all the more.

In the meantime, at my mother's urging, I had applied and been accepted by a school called World Campus Afloat, a division of Chapman College in California. This, I'm sure she felt, would accomplish her twin goals of broadening my horizons and getting me out into the wide world.

And broadening it was. I flew off to New York by myself to meet the ship, the SS *Ryndam,* and off I went to study and see the world at the same time. There were 500 students, 100 staff and faculty, and 300 crew members on board and I was the youngest. During the next three and a half months we traveled from country to country, stopping in Spain, Portugal, Morocco, Senegal, South Africa, Kenya, Uganda, Tanzania, India, Malaysia, Thailand, Taiwan, Hong Kong, Japan, and Hawaii and then back to California. There was a great deal of academic work on board (I was majoring in psychology at the time) and courses were well taught, but the real learning experiences were those we had in the countries we visited. It was all very far removed from Fair Oaks and the airstrip.

Until that time I had never been confronted with many of the harsh realities of life. I clearly remember the acrid smells and teeming streets of Bombay, the vast desert of Senegal, and the beauty of the huge waterfall at the top of Mount Kilimanjaro in Tanzania. These sights were sobering, majestic, and enlightening for me. And I'll never forget the sights and sounds of the zebras and giraffes on the plains of eastern Africa, the children with their noses pressed against the windows of our van in Morocco, the soldiers with machine guns who checked us as we crossed the Kenyan border, the snow falling on a tiny bridge in Kyoto, or the fun of watching a John Wayne movie in Japanese. The contrasts of wealth and poverty, sickness and health, black and white and brown skins had a tremendous impact on my thinking from that point on.

My mother had succeeded beyond her wildest dreams. There was no going back to a life at home or to Sacramento State College. My horizons were definitely broadened and I could see that the world offered all sorts of exciting possibilities. What I didn't know was that this experience would later help me get my first job in television.

It was now 1968. I had my exposure to the world and loved to travel and I wanted to continue in school, but I had no real plan. So I tried to achieve two things at once by enrolling in the University of the Americas, then in Mexico City, where travel would be built-in and I could get an education at the same time. After seeing so many of the peoples and cultures of the world, I decided that I wanted to study anthropology. What better place to learn than in the midst of a rich culture and the magnificent ruins of Mexico. I originally planned on staying in Mexico one semester, or two at the most, but I ended up staying in the country for three and a half years.

The concept was good but my noble intentions came unraveled. Not all of those three and a half years was spent just studying and what I now call my "flaky period" set in. Anthropology fell by the wayside as psychology had before it. Art and the dramatic arts were the next to receive my attention, and since they didn't seem to require my complete concentration, I found some other things to do.

It costs money to do most of the extracurricular things we like to do, so I again struck an independent chord. Through a friend I got a part-time job as a fashion model to earn extra money while I went to school. The type of modeling I did consisted of fashion shows in restaurants in the Zona Rosa, the posh shopping area in Mexico City. The other models and I wore the clothes of a specialty shop as we walked among the diners at lunchtime. This required that I speak Spanish and though I had not mastered the language I didn't let that little detail slow me down. I learned the words necessary for each presentation, and as my accent was quite good, the patrons actually thought I was fluent in the language. Sure, there were some embarrassing moments but in general I was able to pull it off. Modeling has a way of attracting other glamorous job offers and as they came in I realized I really did need to speak Spanish. This need served as a catalyst for the next step in the ever-widening circle of my academic career.

In order to continue modeling, to take advantage of other opportunities, and to learn Spanish, I maneuvered my way into one of the most exclusive private girls' schools in Mexico, a school that catered only to the daughters of wealthy and prominent Mexicans—and to Joan Blunden. I took all sorts of esoteric subjects, all taught in Spanish of course, and I learned the language rather quickly because no one, but no one, spoke English in the school. I learned quickly because I had no choice, and my new-found language skills led to some small parts in Mexican television commercials and to my short-lived movie career, which began and ended with a bit part in an American movie being shot in Mexico.

I was returning to Mexico City from visiting my mother in Sacramento and happened to be sitting next to a man who was doing public relations work for a movie, starring Lee J. Cobb, Jean Seberg, and David Janssen, being filmed on location outside Mexico City. We chatted and he told me that they needed some American extras and that I looked enough like Jean Seberg (this is a man with a vivid imagination) so it was possible I could stand in for her in some of the scenes.

"Do you have any acting experience?" he asked.

"Well, at age five I sat on Captain Sacto's lap"—this was a local TV personality in Sacramento—"on his Christmas program," I said with tongue in cheek. "At seven I tap-danced on Bill Race's *Amateur Hour* and as a teenager I was on *Dance Party,* a Dick Clark–like dance program."

"That should be enough experience," he said with a laugh.

I didn't tell him that my appearance on the dance program had made my mother very angry. She was mad, not because I was dancing on TV, but because she thought the blue jeans that I wore on the show were too tight. In those days before stretch jeans, we used to turn new jeans inside out, sew them as tight as possible down the seams (what we called "pegging"), then put them on and sit in a hot bathtub so they would shrink to fit exactly. She was right. They were too tight and they were supposed to be.

I told him I'd also done some modeling and some TV commercials since I'd been in Mexico, and this combination of experience seemed to do the trick. A few days after I got back to Mexico City he called me and told me to report to the set of a film called *Macho Callahan*.

I played a saloon girl and got to wear a costume with one of those corsetlike tops, spike heels, and fishnet stockings. I could be seen hanging around the card tables and the bar and walking down the street. I was probably on the screen a total of a minute and a half and didn't say a word, but it was a lot of fun and my first real bite of show business. It was all over in four or five days and I went back to school.

I didn't see the movie until a few years later. My mother and I were driving through Reno, Nevada, and we saw a movie marquee advertising *Macho Callahan*. We stopped and went in the theater. You had to be quick to catch me but of course my mother was able to spot her little girl. Afterward, ever loyal, she said, "I think you should have had a bigger part and your name should have been on the marquee." The next time I heard about the movie was more recently, when a cousin of mine asked me if I'd ever been in a movie. "Well, kind of," I said.

"I thought so. I saw you in one of those 2 A.M. movies the other night on television," he said.

Macho Callahan, however, did not die. One night when I was still working for *Eyewitness News*, Michael called me at the station. I was in the makeup room, where I was getting ready to do the Sunday-night news. I picked up the phone and Michael said, "You know, you're going to be on against yourself tonight."

I had no idea what he was talking about. "What do you mean against myself?" I asked.

"*Macho Callahan* is on at the same time as the news," he said.

That's the last I've heard of *Macho*, but it brings up an interesting point. I didn't do anything risqué in the film, but as I said, I was young, only about twenty at the time, and impressionable, and that film could easily have been less legitimate. I could have done something I would later have been sorry for, and as we've seen so often, such things can come back to haunt you.

I have two other experiences that could have led to later problems and that illustrate the same point, that is, that young girls while growing up can get into troublesome situations through no fault of their own. The first occurred when I was about twelve or thirteen. My mother wanted to have some pictures taken of me so she made an appointment with a photographer in Sacramento who had come highly recommended. I remember that I was quite modestly dressed, wearing a skirt and sweater for the occasion. My mother went to run some errands while I was having my picture taken. After a few minutes of shooting the photographer asked me to pose nude. I was very offended and a little afraid. I said no, but it wasn't all that easy since this was an adult talking, a professional man, an authority figure.

Thank God I had the good sense it took to say no in that situation. This sort of experience, viewed from an adult perspective, makes it easy to see how teenagers and even younger children can be coerced to pose nude without the question of sex ever coming up. This man was a professional photographer. My mother, by virtue of choosing him, had put her stamp of approval on him and he had been referred to her by several friends. Those are powerful influences on a child and I probably felt more guilt at the time about not doing it than if I'd actually done it. In a way I was going against all this adult authority.

One other time I was put into a position that could have compromised my entire professional life. A childhood friend, Barbara Klein (later to become known as Barbie Benton, Hugh Hefner's girlfriend for many years) was living at the time in the new Playboy mansion in Los Angeles. She called me in Mexico to ask me if I could get away for a few days and fly to Hawaii with her. A few arrangements were made (I smooth-talked my mom into this one) and a week or so later I was in Los Angeles. Barbie was overseeing the renovation of Hefner's house there and I stayed with her in one of the finished areas. Two days later we left for the islands.

As we sat on the plane Barbie said, "Actually, I'm not alone. There's a *Playboy* photographer and a model going to the same resort with us." It turned out that the man, one of the magazine's top photographers at the time, was escorting a girl he was going to photograph on the beach in Hawaii. We landed in Honolulu and then took a small plane to Maui, where Barbie had made reservations for us at a very private resort. We spent most of our time sunning ourselves on the beach and talking. One morning, as we sunned, we could see the photographer taking pictures of this naked girl rolling around in the surf.

I dozed off and was awakened by a tap on my shoulder from the photographer. He said, "While we're here, why don't I shoot you too? It pays good money if we use them on the cover or the centerfold, or both. It's two thousand dollars just for posing for the pictures, five thousand if they're used in the magazine, and ten thousand more if they use them on the cover."

I had never even fantasized about such a thing and I said, "That's very flattering but I don't think so." He tried to persuade me but I held firm. I was about nineteen, living alone in Mexico, wanting to be totally independent, and not making enough money to make that happen. I had thought of doing some modeling in LA and here I was sunbathing on the beach in a bikini, not far from being nude anyway. It could have been a tempting combination at that moment, but once again I said no.

I guess you could say that those were both close calls and that if I had responded to either suggestion, the first out of innocence and the second out of the desire to get ahead, I would not be where I am today. That is an absolute certainty. Not long after I went back to Mexico I realized that these side trips into television commercials and movies, flying back to California for visits, and all the rest, though they provided me with a lot of good times, weren't very productive and my college education was certainly not progressing.

I had now been out of the U.S. for the better part of five years, from 1967 to 1971, and I missed out on some tremendously important events that were shaping the lives of American youth and the course of the world. While I was busy "finding myself," young Americans were being sent to Vietnam and thousands were dying there, students were protesting on college campuses around the country and many of them were going to jail, bras and draft cards were being burned, the sexual revolution was in full swing, street demonstrations were an everyday event in many cities, and drugs were as much a part of daily life, perhaps more so, than cornflakes.

In Mexico, the war in Vietnam and its attendant domestic problems in the U.S. received only perfunctory attention in the press and on television, the women's rights movement was ignored, drugs were strictly banned, and the sexual revolution was virtually unknown. My Mexican boyfriends, not concerned about a war on the other side of the world, *were* concerned with social propriety and they put me, and any other woman they dated, on the proverbial pedestal. They would no more think of sleeping with their *novia* than of cursing their father or mother. In contrast, in the States, four-letter words were becoming staples in the vocabulary and no young man would think of "going steady" with someone he couldn't make love to in short order.

I completely missed that period in America and though I had no way of knowing it quite yet, when I returned to the States, the demon achiever was going to suffer from a bad case of retarded social development.

But I was out of my holding pattern and at age twenty-two I enrolled in American River Junior College, my first time in a typical U.S. college. I worked hard and got my associate of arts degree there and then went on to California State University at Sacramento, where I majored in liberal arts. In fact, I was so anxious to see what normal college life was like that I joined Delta Gamma sorority. It had taken literally a world of education (and a long time) to get to that point.

Looking back now, I realize that my privileged childhood presented me with opportunities to learn, travel, dream, and grow that most children don't ever have. Still, if my father hadn't died when I was so young, the course of my life might have been drastically different. I think he would have insisted that I go straight to college (on land, that is) and concentrate on nothing but school. I also have a feeling he would have influenced me strongly in the direction of medicine, as much by example as by suggestion. I might even have learned to handle the sight of blood.

But a person's direction in life, though at least partially determined by his or her parents, is still open to other influences. So far, I had bounced around and flourished in my own way and though I had no real direction to follow I did know that the world of real work still lay ahead and that for me part of that world had to include the romance of travel.

My first stop in the real world was flavored with the residue of my old one. I decided to go to modeling school. I felt that would surely lead to those coveted opportunities for travel for which I yearned and I was able to visualize myself wearing the clothes of famous designers in fascinating locations all over the world. Perhaps a white linen sundress aboard a sleek yacht in the Mediterranean, or a silk caftan in the Colosseum in Rome. No Sears catalogs for me. I enrolled and was an avid student, and I learned enough in sixty days—at least I thought I did—to go out on my own and open a competing school. I used part of my given name—Joan Elise—and called it rather grandly "The Joni Lisa Charm and Modeling School of Sacramento."

I was doing quite well with thirteen- and fourteen-year-olds who wanted to be cover girls and with thirty-five-year-old women who thought they might make enough extra money as lunchtime fashion models to get them out of their unhappy marriages. But I soon found myself doing as much personal counseling and career planning as runway and makeup training. I became wrapped up in my students' problems and ambitions, in trying to make them over in their image or mine, and I was making less progress with the business than I should have been. My mother saw this happening and one day over lunch she said, "Joanie, if you spent half the time on yourself that you spend on those perfect strangers, you'd be a star in no time." Mothers sometimes know exactly what they're talking about. Then fate, or tenacity, or a combination of the two, took control of my life.

In 1973, at the age of twenty-three, about as close as I'd come to thinking about a career in television was my secret desire to be the next Marlin Perkins, who at that time had a weekly television show about the wild animal kingdom. I was a real animal lover and I thought it would be wonderful to travel around the world and take pictures of animals and get paid for it as well. But the idea of a real job in television was as remote from my mind as training to become an astronaut.

In fact, neither television nor space was a very realistic career choice for females in the early 1970s. There were no American women astronauts in those days and it took some hard looking to find the few women television correspondents around who could serve as role models. Pauline Frederick was at the United Nations and Barbara Walters was on *Today,* but television was by and large a man's field dominated by Chet Huntley and David Brinkley and Walter Cronkite and a few others who had that special fatherly image that we depended on when it came to telling us the truth about what was happening in the world and how worried we all should be. The network executives weren't convinced yet that the public was ready to trust a woman when it came to the hard news.

I was still running my modeling business on a part-time basis while looking for something else when Bill DeBlonk, a salesman for KCRA-TV, the NBC affiliate station in Sacramento, came to the school, looking for a woman to do some hand modeling for some commercials for a ski manufacturer that he had sold on the station. I took the assignment myself and afterward DeBlonk said, "Why don't you talk to Paul Thompson, the news director here, about the possibilities of going on the air at KCRA?"

My surprise was genuine as I said, "Doing what? What's a woman going to do on the air?" I had no frame of reference.

"Well, for one thing there is the news," he said. "Things are starting to change and they are looking for women to put on the air. You have a good education, the looks, a lot of travel experience, and if you want I'll set up an appointment."

"Why not," I said. "Nothing ventured, nothing gained." I left that conversation thinking this was some harebrained scheme, but in those days I was open to any idea that seemed to have potential for the future.

I met with Paul Thompson and we had a nice talk, during which he told me that he had been skeptical when Bill DeBlonk suggested me but that I seemed to have a "good presence" even though I'd never been on TV. "Let's go into the studio and see how you do," he said. Without any preparation (and without any time for me to get nervous) he took me to the studio and had me sit on the actual KCRA news set, which I'd seen so many times on the TV set in my living room, and read some news copy.

It was the first time I'd ever done anything like that but apparently I made an impression. When we went back to his office he asked me if I'd be interested in doing consumer reports once or twice a week during a new early news program that would go on the air in three or four months.

My response was immediate though uninformed; I didn't know what was going to comprise these consumer reports. "Of course, I'd love to give it a try," I said with confidence. The area of consumer reporting was as new and untested as I was at that time, so we decided to start with me finding out what, if anything, there was to report to consumers and how to go about reporting it, and then we'd talk about specifics. There was no talk of hours or salaries or benefits or any of those things that are so important to discuss in job interviews today.

I left his office with the unmistakable feeling that a great opportunity had just been dropped in my lap. Here was a chance to work for a big television station, to report on a field that was just opening, and to mold my own job to fit that field. I also was wondering if I had done the right thing and how I would go about this business of consumer reporting.

As I was leaving the station I became aware that I was being followed. When I turned to see who it was, I immediately recognized Harry Geise, the weatherman on KCRA, who had been an institution in Sacramento for as long as I could remember. There was even a running joke that he had been the weatherman since there had been weather.

He introduced himself and said, "You may think this is a little strange, but I saw you auditioning just now and I know you were talking to Paul about a job. I've been wanting to start a woman in the weather department for a long time and I'd like you to come to work for me."

I was completely taken aback by two job offers in fifteen minutes, but I said, "It's all right with me, if Mr. Thompson agrees." The chance to work with an institution was appealing to me, though I knew no more about the weather than I did about consumers.

"Good. Be here tomorrow morning at five"—my first taste of the early morning life—"and we'll get started." He warned me that this was not what you would call a well-paying job and he was right. It turned out that I was classified as a trainee and trainees made $30 a week in those days. I was still living at home with my mother so the salary wasn't a real issue at this point.

The next morning I was at the station at 4:55 to begin my apprenticeship. Harry worked closely with me and was a good and patient teacher. In turn, I worked hard for Harry and I enjoyed it. In a short time I was doing his weather summaries for him, I learned to identify the high- and low-pressure systems and locate them on the map, and how to select weather slides that illustrated cloud formations and weather systems. I also did his weather maps for him. If you remember, in those days the maps were like plastic bulletin boards; you wrote on them with a black marker, putting in temperatures and storm systems, and then erased them for the next forecast. I remember that I used to be up to my elbows in black marker by the time the day was over but I was learning.

One morning, after I'd been on the job only two months, Harry called me at the office a little after 5:00 A.M. "I'm sick this morning," he said, "and there's nobody to sub for me. Therefore, Joan, you're going to have to do the weather on the air today."

"You've got to be kidding," I said.

"No, I'm not," he said emphatically.

And with that I went to work.

To this day, I don't know if Harry was really sick (I tend to doubt it) or if it was his way of getting me on the air, whether the station was ready for a female weather person or not.

I'll never forget that day with its mixture of panic and exhilaration. I ripped copy off the wire-service machines and the weather machine, I selected the slides, summarized the current weather, and wrote the forecasts. I had to prepare not only for the noon TV spot but also for the morning and afternoon radio spots.

At 9:05 that morning in December 1973, I made my radio debut, and at 12:20 that afternoon I made my live television debut on the noon news.

The radio spot went very well, I thought. The TV spot was a different matter. I had not exactly dressed for the occasion—white leather pants, a little white leather jacket with white rabbit fur on the sleeves, and a long blond fall. I must have looked like an aspiring Mouseketeer and the white must have given the cameramen fits. Nevertheless, there I was getting black marker on my white pants and talking a mile a minute. When you're nervous you tend to talk faster and higher and I was doing both. I must have sounded like a tape recorder at the wrong speed. In the 1970s there were no TelePrompTers (those marvelous inventions that roll the script right in front of the television camera) so you would just go to your maps and tell the viewers that there were thundershowers in Montana (or was it Wyoming) and hail in Florida (or was it Georgia). My knowledge of basic geography eluded me in the heat of the moment.

At any rate, I had finished everything I had to say in about a minute and a half and I still had three and a half minutes to go. The only thing I could do was go back and repeat what I'd already said. And worst of all, I must have said four times that we weren't going to have a white Christmas in Sacramento. We certainly weren't. Up to that time it hadn't snowed more than four times in the history of the city.

When the longest five minutes of my life ended, I couldn't go back upstairs to the newsroom because I knew they would be rolling in the aisles. I just wiped off my weather board, packed up my markers and went home. But that was my initiation, my baptism by fire on live television, and I can still feel the anxiety build up when I think about it.

The next day I found out that apparently I hadn't been as bad as I thought; Harry asked me to do the noon weather a couple of times a week. Bob Whitten had been an anchor on that news show for years, and after my second appearance he took me aside and said, "Let me give you four words of advice, Joan. Think s-l-o-w and low. You're like a little toy that's been wound too tightly and you end up screeching. Remember, slow and low." It was one of those little pieces of advice that still comes to mind from time to time and it was certainly very helpful to me in the beginning.

I don't really know why Harry Geise took a liking to a total stranger; it was one of those serendipitous things. He wanted to pioneer a woman weather person and I happened to be there at the time.

But I'm also a quick study. I worked hard and I worked long hours. Harry admired tenacity and devotion and he would do anything for people who showed these qualities. He nurtured those qualities and he nurtured me and I owe a great deal to him.

But I must have also had something of my own, perhaps the presence that Paul Thompson first saw, because I had been on the air only a few times when he approached me again about those consumer report spots we had discussed initially. Now, he felt, was the time to get me started on them.

"What about the weather?" I asked.

"I want you to continue the weather spots too," he said. So now I had two jobs.

Research has always come naturally to me and I started to dig into the subject of consumerism like a miner looking for gold. I went to the library and dragged out all the books I could find related to consumerism, I trekked to government agencies and collected all their documents, I went to the colleges in the area and talked with their economics teachers, and then I went to the state legislature in Sacramento to check on pending consumer legislation. I got tremendous cooperation from everyone and a mountain of information because all the people I talked to had been laboring for years, trying to get the public interested in their subject; they recognized that my consumer reports would offer them that opportunity.

A few weeks later, I started with a single two-minute consumer spot each week. Then it grew to two, and eventually I was on every day. And of course, I still did the weather.

I was getting great experience and was growing more confident every day despite the jibes of local television critics, notably a man named Chris Wise. He used to make mincemeat out of me at least once a month. Admittedly there was plenty to criticize. I used to say "pitcher" for "picture" and "nuculur" for "nuclear," among other mistakes. His criticism was justified, if a little vicious, and I still have his columns if I ever need to remind myself of those early days. I was beginning to learn not to take that kind of criticism personally but rather to use it constructively. I never met Chris so I don't know how I might have reacted to him in person; my mother did meet him, though, and she said it was all she could do to keep herself from punching him in the nose.

I was also stumbling onto some of the more technical aspects of television, and one common production technique resulted in some jokes at my expense. There is a process known as Chroma Key which allows one picture to be superimposed over another. So, for example, you can see a weather map or even film of a stormy day behind the weatherman as he gives his report in the studio. In reality he's standing in front of a solid blue wall. The TV camera that is on him does not register the color blue and you see only him. Then the control room superimposes his image (minus the blue parts, of course) over the map or the film. This is a very basic technique, but since I did not yet know any such procedures I was not aware of what was happening.

I didn't know that using blue eye shadow made my eyelids invisible when I looked down at the script. When I was doing my first consumer spots, the control room was superimposing my image over a film of fruits and vegetables; and since the camera could not see blue, when I lowered my eyes to read from the script the blue eye shadow made my eyes disappear. The viewers could see bananas, apples, and lettuce coming out of my eye sockets. Someone finally told me about it and my friends kidded me for weeks about having fruits and vegetables coming out of my head.

At the same time I was coming in for my share of criticism from some of the other members of the KCRA news department. They were wondering why this blonde who seemed to have just walked in the door was getting all this time on the air. There was a lot of snickering behind my back from those men at the station who had been in the business for years and felt that they deserved the opportunities for advancement that were coming my way. They didn't say things to me directly because I was protected by the persona of Harry Geise, but it wasn't hard to detect their hostility. This made it a little harder for me to work but I refused to let it get me down.

After about six months of my consumer reports and weather spots, Paul Thompson called me into his office. "How would you like to take a shot as anchor on the noon news?" he asked.

Eager to move up, I jumped at the chance.

Paul's belief in me and my ability to learn quickly was certainly encouraging but I was still worried. "You'll make mistakes," he warned me, "but I know you can handle the job and I think you have the kind of image that will increase our audience for that program."

There was no way I was going to refuse that kind of positive approach, and a few days later I became a news reader. I didn't have to write my own script, it was handed to me and I was expected to read it. That first day, I had gone over the script a dozen times but I was still very nervous. At about 11:55 I was putting on fresh lipstick (we didn't have makeup people at KCRA) when I noticed small, red blotches on my neck and I could see that they were growing larger even as I looked. When I looked at my arms, I saw the blotches were spreading there as well. I had no idea what it was but I didn't have time to worry about it—I had to go on the air in a couple of minutes. All I could do was dab some powder on my neck in an attempt to cover up the mess. I got through that show all right and later that day the red disappeared.

The next day the blotches were back and this time they spread to my chest and were creeping up my neck. I used massive doses of powder and told myself to calm down. My co-anchor, noticing I was agitated, assured me everything would be all right and told me to let him know if I needed any help while we were on the air. Again I made it through, but clearly this couldn't go on every day or I'd be a nervous wreck. That afternoon I went to a dermatologist who said it was just a nervous reaction to stress and there was absolutely nothing to worry about. Frankly, I would have preferred a real skin rash because then the dermatologist could have given me something to treat the problem.

To make a long story short, for nearly two weeks I continued to break out; I must have used up ten pounds of powder. Then one day the blotches didn't return. It was obviously my body's reaction to the tension of the new assignment, and when I adjusted mentally my body did too.

The only other time in my career that I had come close to missing a show (I never missed a day during my pregnancies) was also at KCRA. I was scheduled to do the 6:00 P.M. news that evening—a first for a woman in Sacramento—so, instead of going to dinner to celebrate the occasion, my mother took me out to lunch. We went to one of our favorite restaurants and we had a lovely time eating and chatting. This place was famous for its seafood and I had clams, among other things. After lunch I went to the station and as I walked in the door I got so sick to my stomach I could hardly stand up. I went directly to the bathroom where I put cold compresses on the back of my neck but I still felt sick. I looked in the mirror and told myself, "You can't possibly be this nervous. Get it together." But my face had absolutely no color at all and my hair had gone limp.

As newstime approached I did as much as I could to look presentable and then walked unsteadily to the studio. That newscast was an ordeal. Try to imagine working under hot lights with the worst case of the flu you've ever had. That's what it was like and it was just about the longest sixty minutes of my life. At every commercial break I ran to the bathroom. Again I made it through the show, but you can be sure that I haven't eaten anything that comes in a shell, except eggs, since that day.

After those first uneasy days as a noon news anchor I did quite well but the bad part of not writing my own material is that I was not really involved in the news and I could make stupid mistakes—like calling the Russian newspaper "Pravada" instead of *Pravda*—that only added fuel to the fire for my detractors.

But I wasn't worried about my detractors. I could see that things had started to happen. I could see also that television was a fertile field for a woman and that if I could learn quickly enough, I could move up more quickly than a man. So I threw myself into the new job (while still doing consumer spots) and jumped at every opportunity to learn a new skill. My job as anchor led to the chance to write and produce the noon news program. This was the best thing that could have happened to me at that time and it's one of the good things about starting in a small, local station. I learned how to use the news wires, how to write and edit copy, how to put an entire program together in a way that was interesting enough to keep an audience tuned to our show.

A couple of months of production experience, added to my on-air time, put me on a new plateau. I was learning and mastering new skills every day and I was beginning to think that there was a future for me in the field. The television business is funny in that when a person gets just barely enough experience to handle a particular job, he or she starts thinking about the job that is one step farther up the ladder. I've found this to be true for me in every job I've held in television. So after being on the noon news for only a short while, and then producing it for a while longer, I started thinking about anchoring the nightly news, and once I'd done that I'm sure I would have wanted to produce that show as well. Then I would have started to look for a job in a larger city than Sacramento. That's the nature of the beast.

As it turned out, the noon news program, in a totally unforeseen way, was what brought me to the attention of other stations around the country and eventually to New York. Interestingly, the next step was totally out of my hands. I couldn't have dreamed that things could happen as they did.

CHAPTER
FOUR

New York, New York

It didn't seem quite real. It was September 1975, and I was going to New York to be interviewed for a job in big-time televison. It didn't seem real while I was packing, or when I drove to the airport in Sacramento, or when I got on the plane. In fact, it didn't seem real until my flight from California turned into the last leg of its approach to La Guardia Airport. The flight path was bringing the plane in over the Verrazano Narrows Bridge at the mouth of New York Harbor. The descent was taking us past Staten Island and the Statue of Liberty and then, heading due north, the plane passed directly over the twin towers of the World Trade Center and up over the very heart of Manhattan Island. It's a breathtaking sight that brings to mind all you've ever read and heard about New York, all the movies and television shows you've seen, and all the glamour that you've always associated with the city.

The only other time I had been in New York was when I was sixteen, on my way to join World Campus Afloat, and I was so excited then that all I remember is that there seemed to be a million people on the street and the traffic was bumper-to-bumper. On this flight I was much more aware of everything and as I looked down on the city, I tried to imagine myself actually moving here, walking through those streets, going to work and coming home.

It was truly hard to believe that in less than two years, Dr. Erle Blunden's little girl, Joan, the kid from Sacramento, was heading for a job interview as a street reporter with WABC-TV in New York, ABC's flagship station. And it was all happening because of a series of events with which I personally had very little to do.

I had been doing my consumer reporting and anchoring the noon news at KCRA for only about ten months. I was pleased with my progress and so was Paul Thompson, because at that time we were the highest-rated news program in town. In fact, the other two stations weren't even close and at least one of them reacted the way the competition in television always reacts. They hired a consulting firm to help them improve their program. It is a truism in all of television that when one station achieves dominance in a market, whether it's children's programming or hard news or entertainment or sports, the other stations try to figure out why their competition is ahead and then to emulate those features that seem to have made the other station's programs a success. This happens in New York, Chicago, and Los Angeles, but it also happens in Des Moines and Boise and Sacramento.

To find out what the competition is doing right, a station sometimes hires a consulting firm that specializes in communications (and in charging huge consulting fees) and these consultants do audience polls. They actually go out into the community, knock on doors and stop people on the street. Primarily they ask people what programs and personalities they like and don't like and why. And they use other methods of rating people and programs. One of them is called the Q Score.

The Q Score is a rating which television personalities live and often die by. The Q Score is a polling method developed by TVQ, Inc., of Port Washington, New York, and it's used to measure the familiarity and likability of a television personality or a TV program.

It works like this: A questionnaire is mailed to several thousand people who represent a random sample of the population. The questionnaire contains a list of about 300 people from every area of television—news, sports, entertainment. Next to each personality's name is a brief identification (there are no pictures), and the person receiving the letter is asked to answer two questions about each person in the questionnaire. The first is "Do you recognize this person?" The second asks the recipient to rate the personalities they recognize as follows: (1) That person is one of my favorites; (2) Very good; (3) Good; (4) Fair; (5) Poor. So for example, a person can be well-known and a favorite or little-known and rated as poor, or can fall anywhere in between. The rating, or Q Score, is a ratio between familiarity and likability, and it is computed based on 2,000 replies to each mailing. An excellent score is 50%, and not many personalities reach that level.

Two things happened next that I learned about after the fact. One of them was legitimate, the other something that might be called a dirty trick, or worse, in any other industry. As the trailing stations in a television market get reports from their consultants, they start to look for something, usually a personality, to help them catch and pass the other station. They may try to hire someone away from another local station, but more often than not they will go outside the city to look for fresh talent. But even before they do that, they sometimes take other steps. There is an axiom in the television business that covers that step when it comes to a news show. It goes like this: "If a show is going bad you can do two things. You can change the set or fire the girl and it doesn't matter in which order you do them." Now you know why a lot of sets get changed and a lot of girls get fired. At least these remedies are pretty straightforward.

At the same time, however, the trailing stations send out completely unsolicited tapes of certain personalities on the competing station to their colleagues in other areas of the country who just might be looking for someone new or know someone who is looking. In other words, they try to get the competition out of town.

In this case I was the one to benefit. After determining that I was one of the reasons for KCRA's good ratings, the consultants started passing my tapes around to places like Detroit, Atlanta, and Minneapolis, in the hope that I would get a job offer from some other city, which would effectively remove me from Sacramento.

Since I didn't have any idea this was happening, I was very surprised when I got my first call and potential job offer. The phone rang and I heard a voice say, "Hi, I'm the news director at WWJ, the NBC affiliate in Detroit. We have your tape here and we'd like to talk to you about an opening in our news department. We're interested in hiring a female anchor." I honestly didn't know what he was talking about. I hadn't sent out any tapes and here was some stranger calling me about a job. This had never happened to me before and I was a bit mystified.

When I got that first call I reacted by playing a role. I said, "I'm glad you like it"—not even knowing what was on it—"and I'd love to talk to you but I'm on deadline right now. We go on the air in thirteen minutes. I'll have to get back to you."

To try to unravel the mystery I went straight to Bill DeBlonk, who got me into KCRA in the first place. "Bill, something strange just happened," I said. "I just got a call from a station in Detroit. They say they have my tape and are interested in talking to me about a job with them. The problem is, I didn't send out any tapes and I haven't been looking for another job. What's going on?"

It was then that DeBlonk explained to me how and why this sort of thing happens. He advised me to think seriously about making a change, even if I thought I was ready, because, he said, "In this business, like any other, the grass isn't always greener in the next town."

Bill was right and I knew it. On top of that, I was perfectly happy in Sacramento. I had just bought a little house and some furniture for it and I was quite comfortable. I was also pleased with my progress on the job, I was dating a really nice guy, and my family and friends were all there, in and around Sacramento. I was content and the last thing I was thinking about was leaving

good-old comfortable Sacramento, where I was becoming something of a big fish in a small pond.

And needless to say, I had learned enough about the competi-
tiveness of the television business to have my own doubts about
my ability to handle jobs in another, bigger city. I knew deep
down that after less than two years I was not the most experienced newscaster or consumer reporter in the world. Still, when
you get calls from stations in places like *Detroit,* saying they want
you to anchor their news program, you start to think things like
"This place isn't really so great" and "Maybe I am a lot bigger
than Sacramento."

My tapes were obviously traveling fast because in the next few
days I got two more calls, from stations in Minneapolis and Atlanta, similar to the one from the Detroit station. I thanked both
of the callers and told them I'd give them a call in a few days. My
ego was beginning to grow.

I went back to DeBlonk. He said, "Joanie, if you're getting all
these offers, maybe you should think about them seriously. I
know someone who can give you some advice."

Bill gave me the name and number of Phil Boyer at WABC-
TV in New York. I called Boyer, vice-president of programming
for ABC-owned stations, who listened to my story and then said,
"You must be pretty good to be getting these calls. There aren't
that many good women in the business, so send me a tape and
maybe we'd be interested in you for one of our ABC-owned stations."

"I don't have a tape of my own, Phil," I said. "I'll have to put
one together and that will take a few days."

"Fine," he said, "but make it as soon as possible because I
know there is an opening in New York right now."

With the help of one of the tape editors at KCRA, I pieced
together a five-minute demonstration tape and sent it off to Phil
Boyer the next day.

Less than a week later I got a call from Phil Nye, the news
director at WABC-TV in New York. Boyer had seen my tape,
liked it, and had given it to Nye. Now Nye wanted me to fly
there for an interview and an audition right away. This time I

went to Paul Thompson. "Paul," I said, "there is a chance here to go to New York and I'm tempted to grab it."

"I know that it's flattering, Joanie," Paul told me, "but the fact is, you have had very little experience. You're learning and learning fast and Sacramento is a good place to train. I won't tell you not to move on, but I have to tell you I don't think you're quite ready. Besides, I'd hate to lose you."

"I still would like to try," I said.

"If that's the way you feel," he answered, "go ahead. You'll never forgive yourself if you don't try it. And remember, if things don't work out, you still have a job here as far as I'm concerned."

That was all I needed. I called Phil Nye and told him yes. The next day he called back to set up a meeting. In the course of just a few days I had quickly gone from not even knowing a job was available, to not particularly caring about the job, to wanting it very badly. Besides, I've always felt that certain things are preordained and that when they come along you have to recognize them and then grab them. This opportunity to me seemed preordained. I had lunch with my mom that day and I clearly remember saying to her, "Something big is going to happen. I can feel it inside." And I did feel it strongly.

The people in the newsroom at KCRA had been needling me about being dumb enough to think that I could get a job in New York, and they had given me Sally Quinn's *We're Going to Make You a Star* as a sort of negative going-away present. Sally Quinn was a newspaper reporter who, a few years earlier, was plucked from her job and, without any previous TV experience, put on the CBS early-morning news show. She was quickly thrust into stardom and had almost as quickly failed. At one point in her book she relates a conversation she had with her agent, Richard Leibner, one which I completely understood. When she asked him about her chances at CBS, he said, "Sweetheart, before I say anything, I want you to know something. If you're twice as good as they say you are . . . if they use all the potential they have to make this a great show, if they spend the amount of money they'll have to spend to make it any good . . . if they get the best producer and staff in the business . . . your chances are one in ten you'll last out the year." These words struck home.

When I read the book on my way to New York, it reminded me that I wanted to get this job. I was mad because I was sure that to at least some of the staff the book was a way of saying "Dream on." They saw what they thought was this inexperienced twenty-four-year-old heading for New York and a possible job in the big leagues while they continued to labor in Sacramento. I wanted to show them that I could do it.

My appointment in New York also precipitated a confrontation with Jon Kelly, the owner of KCRA, a confrontation that gave me another reason for wanting to get the job. I had told Paul Thompson that I was going for the interview and he had told Kelly. On that same day, my mother had come to the station to meet me for lunch and as we were headed out the door we ran into Jon Kelly. He half blocked the way and said, "Hear you're going to New York."

"That's right," I said. "I'm leaving in the morning but it's only an interview."

He didn't care. He had a message to deliver. "You'll never make it, you know," he said, "because you don't have the talent." I had no idea that he felt that way about me until that moment, and my mother, of course, was as shocked as I was. It was a cruel thing to say to me, but in front of my mother it was a compound felony.

"And even if you do get the job," he went on, "you'll be back here in six months on your knees, begging for your old job back."

All I could manage was "Thanks for the good wishes, Jon," and my mother and I went on out the door. When we got outside we both let our rage out. It was a stupid thing for Kelly to do and about five years later I had my sweet revenge on him.

I had been on *GMA* with David for several years and I happened to be back in Sacramento to visit my mother and to tape some public-service spots for the California Highway Patrol on the importance of using auto seat restraints for children. I called my good friend Paul Thompson and asked him to join my mother, my husband, Michael, and me for lunch at the Firehouse Restaurant. As luck would have it, who should be there but Jon Kelly, who was entertaining a table full of advertisers and some of his salesmen. His back was to me as we walked in, so he didn't see me or our group.

Paul said, "Well, look who's here. It's your good friend Jon Kelly. You ought to go over and ask him to give you your old job back."

"That's a great idea," I said, thinking that it was a perfect setup since my mother, who had witnessed my humiliation at Kelly's hands, would now be there to witness my redemption. "Just watch this," I said.

I got within six feet of his table and then got down on my hands and knees and crawled up behind him. He couldn't see me, but the people with him did and they must have wondered what in the world was going on. Why was Joan Lunden crawling toward their table? As I got right behind him, he turned to see what the commotion was about, and I said, "Oh, Mr. Kelly, you told me when I left Sacramento that in six months I'd be back on my knees begging for my old job. Here I am. Can I please have it back, please?" The people at his table were in hysterics and he started to turn beet red.

Sometimes it takes years to settle an old score and most of the time you never get to do it, but this was one of those rare moments of opportunity. I have to add that I'm not naturally a vindictive person, I don't usually bear long-term grudges, but in this case I felt my action was justified and so did my mother.

To return to Quinn's book, there was another interesting thing about it, aside from its tell-all narrative. Before I left Sacramento, I wanted to find out what the weather was like in New York and I asked Harry Geise, my mentor in television, and one of the country's foremost weathermen, what kind of weather to expect there in the early fall. He gave me his forecast and then suggested I call a friend of his, Gordon Barnes, who did the weather for WCBS-TV in New York at that time, and get the weather directly from the source.

I called Barnes and he gave me a complete rundown on the

New York weather, and in the course of the conversation I told him the reason for my visit.

"It sounds like a great opportunity," he said. "Who is your agent in New York?"

"My what?" I said.

"You mean you're going to talk to WABC-TV about a job and you don't have an agent?" he said.

"We don't have agents in Sacramento," I said. "I only make two hundred forty dollars a week."

"Well, when you start talking about sixty thousand a year, you're going to need an agent, Joan," he said. "Why don't you call my guy, Richard Leibner?"

I took Gordon's advice and called Richard Leibner but the conversation was so short and direct that there was hardly time for his name to register. He said he would represent me (and why not, since I already had a good shot at a job and he would only have to do the paperwork), and we'd be in touch when I got to New York. That was it.

As I read Quinn's book on the flight across the country I kept seeing the name Richard Leibner. It was Richard Leibner this and Richard Leibner that. Still, it didn't penetrate my consciousness. It took me until Missouri to realize that the same Richard Leibner who was going to represent me in New York had plunked an inexperienced Sally Quinn into a hot seat, a job too big for her to handle. It was the same Richard Leibner who was going to try to plunk me into a new job that could also be a hot seat. Was there a parallel here? I surely hoped not.

Now, along with the crowd, I made my way through the jetway and into the lobby of the airport, where I picked up my bag and headed for the sidewalk to catch a cab to the city. As the taxi made its way slowly through the afternoon rush-hour traffic on the Grand Central Parkway, the driver said, "Visiting?"

"Yes, I am," I answered. "I'm here for a job interview."

"Been here before?" he asked.

"Years ago," I said, and then added, "but not really because I was just passing through."

He then began to point out some of the landmarks. It just

happened to be one of those clear late-summer days and the Manhattan skyline loomed up ahead like a giant ship with masts of all sizes. "If you look straight ahead," he said, "you can see the Empire State Building and then way to your left the World Trade Center. We'll be going across the Triborough Bridge and the East River and then across town to the hotel." As I said, I remembered virtually nothing from my first trip to New York so everything was enthralling. The driver continued to describe this and that sight but I was fading with the wonderment of it all and finally wasn't paying much attention anymore.

The cab pulled up in front of the Park Lane Hotel, facing Central Park in midtown Manhattan, where WABC-TV had made reservations for me. A top-hatted doorman was there to open the door and I went into the lobby while the bellboy handled my two small bags. I was duly impressed by the surroundings and after I signed the register the bellboy led me to the fortieth floor, settled me in, and opened the drapes to reveal a panoramic view of the park and upper Manhattan.

The bellboy closed the door and I realized that less than eight hours after leaving the familiar surroundings of Sacramento I was looking down at the very unfamiliar surroundings of Central Park and the luxury apartment buildings lining the park along Fifth Avenue on one side and Central Park West on the other. The view from the fortieth floor was amazing, but my first thought, after all those years of listening to Johnny Carson's tales about muggers in Central Park, was that the green trees and the lakes made it look like the most beautiful, peaceful spot in the world. So far everything was perfect.

After those few minutes of sightseeing, I called Richard Leibner and told him where I was staying. "I'll be by to pick you up at nine-thirty in the morning," he said. "Your appointment isn't until ten-thirty, but we can walk from the hotel over to WABC at Sixty-sixth and Columbus and that will give us enough time to talk."

"Thanks for everything," I said. "See you in the morning."

I was still on California time so though it was not quite three in the afternoon in New York, for me it was only noon. I was ready to see some of the sights and I decided to do a little window-shopping at the same time since I knew there were stores in New York that we didn't have in Sacramento. The Park Lane is only a few blocks from some of the fanciest Fifth Avenue shops, and after being pointed in the right direction by the same top-hatted doorman, I was off. When I got to the corner of Central Park South and Fifth Avenue, I could hear the sounds of live jazz, and I followed my ears until I got to the far side of the fountain in front of the Plaza Hotel. There, arranged in big-band style, was a group of about twenty musicians playing something from the 1930s, a song that I recognized, called "In the Mood." They were so good and the crowd surrounding them was so pleasant that I just stood and listened in amazement. In California one doesn't stumble on a jazz band on the corner very often. I soon discovered that this type of street entertainment is commonplace in New York when the weather is nice. I decided to move on and as I left I dropped a dollar in the collection box, an old fedora, and crossed the street to Bergdorf-Goodman to begin some serious looking. Winter fashions were already being shown in the store windows and it occurred to me that if things worked out in New York, I'd have to buy a whole new wardrobe because heavy wool isn't the fabric of choice in Sacramento. From Bergdorf's I made my way to Henri Bendel's off the corner of Fifth Avenue and Fifty-seventh Street, and then went down Fifth to Tiffany's, Gucci and other chic Italian shops, past St. Patrick's Cathedral and Rockefeller Center, and finally to Saks Fifth Avenue. When I looked at my watch it was nearly six o'clock and the sky was beginning to cloud up, so I walked slowly back to the hotel.

When I got into my room, I kicked off my shoes, plopped down on the bed, turned on the television set to see what the local news shows looked like, and promptly fell asleep. When I woke up it was after nine and rather than go out to one of the restaurants on my list (friends had given me enough suggestions to last a month), I ordered up from room service. I must admit that I thought $14.00 was a little steep for a chef's salad, but then this was New York and, besides, WABC-TV was picking up the tab so I sat back and enjoyed it.

I ate in front of the TV set while watching *The Towering Inferno,* which was a bit ironic, since I had never stayed this high up in a hotel and here was this story about a fire in a skyscraper. After the movie, I again picked up Sally Quinn's book, thinking I'd finish it. I caught myself dozing off after a couple of pages and decided the best thing to do was watch the eleven-o'clock news to see how they did it in New York and then get some sleep. The next day was looming large in my life.

At exactly 9:30 A.M. the phone rang.

"Joan, it's Richard. I'm in the lobby. Are you ready?"

"I'll be right down, Richard," I said.

I had actually been up for hours and had been dressed since 7:30. In fact I'd awakened several times during the night, wondering what in heaven's name I was doing here and worrying that I was going to make a fool of myself the next morning. I had slept only fitfully at best and was glad to see the light coming through the window at about six because that meant I could get up instead of lying there with my eyes wide open, thinking disastrous thoughts. During those hours of half-sleep I tried to tell myself that nothing could really go wrong, that I was perfectly capable of reading the news, and that the worst thing that could happen is that they wouldn't like me. Of course, that *was* the worst thing that could happen.

I think what bothered me most was that I didn't know the people I'd be talking to, I didn't know if they were going to ask me to perform in front of the camera, to do a song and dance, or what. It was all a little frightening and, as they say, it's the fear of the unknown that is the worst.

Richard was waiting for me in the lobby and as we left the hotel, he took my arm and steered us toward the *Eyewitness News* station on Columbus Avenue. I had put Quinn's book in my purse and Richard noticed it. He said, "Uh oh, Joan. Don't believe everything you read in that book. I'm innocent." That, coupled with the fact that he seemed like a nice guy, reassured me.

As we walked the few blocks Richard told me what to do and what not to do. "Basically be yourself," he said. "They won't ask you anything technical so don't worry about that, but try not to say, 'We didn't do it that way at KCRA,' because they don't give a damn what you did or how you did it there. They're only interested in the way they do it here and in your talent."

I felt that I should say something but I couldn't think of anything to say except, "At KCRA we didn't call it talent."

He went on: "If they start to talk about salary or contracts or anything negotiable just say that they have to speak to your agent about that. Don't get drawn into a money conversation. If they say the starting salary would be around fifty thousand dollars, don't say, 'Great, I'll take it.' "

I wanted to say, "Fifty thousand dollars, you must be kidding? I'm making only two hundred forty a week in Sacramento. If they offer me anything like that I'll say, 'Where do I sign?' "

But I kept my mouth shut and Richard added, "Again, try and be yourself. Only you can do that. They don't know that much about you but they're obviously looking for someone with your image, so sell your image and not that of someone else." When we got to the corner of Sixty-sixth and Columbus, Richard said, "Good luck, and give me a call this afternoon."

I walked toward the door with my heart in my mouth and as I opened it I got cold all over, not from the air conditioning but from my own nervousness. The receptionist in the lobby called to check on my appointment and then sent me to the news director's office. "Mr. Nye is expecting me. My name is Joan Blunden," I told the secretary.

I was ushered into Phil Nye's office where he and several other WABC executives were waiting. He introduced me to everyone and we sat down to talk. Nye was very pleasant and I liked him immediately. After a few minutes of casual talk and the exchange of a few generalities, Nye and Don Dunphy, Jr., the assistant news director, took me into a huge studio where the local news show was produced. I was wide-eyed. It was so huge and so much more professional-looking than our news set in Sacramento that it was intimidating. I had never seen so many lights, cameras, and props on a set before, nor such an elaborate set for the news. Nye then suggested that I go upstairs and get ready for my audition. I was too embarrassed to ask him why I was going upstairs. As it turned out, they were sending me to makeup so that I could get ready for an on-camera appearance. This was also a first for me. In Sacramento we put on our own makeup and did our own hair in the bathroom. Here, a nice, reassuring lady named Sylvia did both of those things for me. She was very complimentary about my skin and hair and that was a boost because I was plenty worried about going in front of the camera.

But I did it. I went downstairs to the studio, someone handed me some news copy, the red light on the camera went on, and I read for five minutes. Just before I started to read I couldn't help but remember what Sally Quinn had written about her debut on network television. She said they put her in a chair, gave her the script and that was it. When they said, "You're on the air," she didn't even know that the camera with the light was the one she was supposed to face when she talked. I was way ahead of her on that score at least.

When I finished I had no idea of how well or how poorly I might have done, but afterward Nye and Dunphy took me to lunch at La Scala, an expensive and quite wonderful Italian restaurant that wasn't on my list, and they both praised my performance. I wanted to ask them some questions about the work at WABC-TV but I was reticent because I didn't want them to think I was too pushy or too uninformed. And though I thought that I'd need some training if I got the job, it would have been hard for me to say, "You people will have to give me some help," without admitting, "You see, I really don't know what I'm doing." So I played it quiet and answered their questions instead of asking my own.

What they were offering was a reporting job with the promise of anchoring the weekend news at some unspecified time in the future. It wasn't exactly what I had expected and it was a little frightening because I had no real experience in street reporting. I voiced my concerns but Nye and Dunphy didn't seem to be worried. Looking back on it now, I can't imagine why they thought being a reporter in New York was such a piece of cake, because it certainly isn't.

After lunch we shook hands on the sidewalk in front of the restaurant and went our separate directions. That was it. I called Richard from a telephone on the street and told him what had gone on, that we had not talked about money at all, and that I had given them his name as my agent.

I was a little numb. I walked slowly back to the hotel, changed clothes, and spent the rest of the afternoon wandering in and out of little shops on Madison Avenue. That night I went out to dinner with Jed Johnson, an old friend from Sacramento. He invited his boss, Andy Warhol, and they took me to an elegant French restaurant, where we had a delicious meal. I thought to myself that I could get used to that kind of thing quite easily.

The next morning I flew back to Sacramento with a variety of fascinating dreams dancing in my head. The exposure to the people and shops of New York, to the WABC-TV studio, and to the people there had started me thinking that of course I was right for that job. How could anyone be more right than I? I was too big for Sacramento. They didn't understand my "talent" (remember, this was a new word for me) and my ability and I was being wasted there. Soon I'd be shaking the dust of California from my shoes and moving into the exciting world of a major television station—and Manhattan.

That kind of thinking can get you in trouble because it can get you too far from reality. Back home I analyzed the situation and I realized that my experience couldn't match up with that of other job applicants; though I felt I was good in the interview and the taped audition, realistically my chances of getting the job were slim at best. With that bit of rationalization in place, I could go back to work the following morning and face up to the questions which I knew would boil down to two. My friends would ask, "How did it go?" and the rest of the people would say, "Didn't get the job, eh?"

I was to be spared the second set of comments for that same night the phone rang. The secretary said, "Please hold for Mr.

Nye." My heart was in my throat. I hadn't expected to hear anything this quickly so I wasn't prepared.

"Hello, Joan, it's Phil Nye calling," he said.

"Hello," I answered, searching for some special inflection in his voice, but I couldn't read anything.

"I'm happy to tell you that you've got the job," he said, "and we're looking forward to seeing you in New York as soon as possible."

I managed to thank him, to utter something appropriate, and to say good-bye, and then I almost fainted. It was the most exciting thing that had ever happened to me. About five minutes later, Richard called with the details.

"You start in two weeks and they're going to thirty-six thousand a year to start, with extra for on-air fees," he said, "and that means you can easily make fifty to sixty thousand a year. That's not bad for a start."

"Are you kidding, Richard?" I said. "That's not bad, that's great." I nearly shouted, "It's damned incredible. That's more money than I ever dreamed they'd offer."

"That's what a good agent is for," he said. This is a line I've heard many times since, interspersed with terms of seeming endearment like "Baby" and "Sweetheart."

"What's the next step?" I asked.

"I'll have the contracts in a few days and when you get here you can sign them," he said.

"That sounds fine," I said. "In the meantime I have a friend in New York who has volunteered to help me find an apartment."

"Good luck on that one," he said. "You'll need it. If you've got any questions just call."

"Richard, thanks very much for all your help," I said. "I hope this is the beginning of a long and successful partnership."

"I do too, Joan," he said.

I could hardly wait to hang up the phone so I could call my mom and my friends and tell them the good news. It was a great day, a great feeling. I picked up the phone and dialed my mother's number so she would be the first to know.

Almost immediately, I realized I had two hurdles to face—my mother and Paul Thompson.

First Paul. The next morning, Monday, I went into Paul's office, told him I had accepted an offer in New York, and gave two weeks' notice. He recognized the opportunity, promised to smooth the way out the door for me, and wished me the best. I gave him a kiss on the cheek and hugged him. "I hope that someday I can return some of what you've given me," I said.

I told the rest of the people at KCRA that I was going to be a field reporter (something I had never done before) and a weekend anchor. My friends were excited and pleased and my detractors nearly choked. Here they were trying to get jobs in San Francisco or LA or Denver, and I was going to New York to work for the flagship station.

The reaction of my coworkers was predictable. One said, "Are you nuts, Blunden? You've never been a reporter. How are you going to know what to do?"

I said, "I've been producing the news and anchoring and consumer reporting and that's how I'm going to do it."

He went on: "You've never covered a fire, a murder, a demonstration or even worked with a camera crew."

He was absolutely right. He knew my credentials but he didn't know my determination. I said to myself that he was just jealous, and to him I said, "When opportunity knocks, you might as well answer the door and have at it."

Next came my mother. Despite her determination to see me get ahead, I realized she also had a strong protective instinct that would most certainly go into gear. She would worry that I was leaving my success in Sacramento behind, tempting fate and possible failure. We would have to discuss not only the terrific career possibilities, but all the ramifications of my move across the country, including the fact that I wouldn't be able to visit very often. I knew that on the surface she would be excited for me, but I knew her well enough to sense that deep down she was going to be worried about her little girl leaving for the big city.

When my mother and I had our talk it wasn't as hard as I had thought it would be. She said, "Of course you're taking the job.

It's an incredible opportunity and you'll be wonderful and I'll come to New York to visit as often as I can." She was proud of me but I could tell that she wasn't delighted at the prospect of me moving so far away, not to mention at losing the celebrity that my being on television gave her in Sacramento. She really got a kick out of seeing me on TV each day, and with me working in New York she would lose that. Still, I could always count on my mother to say the right thing.

Two weeks is not much time to change from one life to another. I put my house up for sale, I began packing what I thought I'd need in New York, and I had those traditional farewell lunches. The exhilaration of the move kept me from worrying too much about what was in store for me, and before I knew it I was headed for the airport and another flight to New York.

I kissed my mother good-bye at the airport gate and boarded my plane. I knew that I was beginning an exciting and different phase of my life and that what I did from that point on was going to dramatically affect my entire future. But at that moment I didn't have the slightest idea that it would be as different and challenging as it turned out to be.

CHAPTER
FIVE

~~~~

The Making of a Newswoman

I was a little more subdued on this second flight to New York, and though I had plenty of time to read the magazines I'd brought along, I spent most of that time just staring out the window, trying to block out any thoughts that I might have made a huge mistake. I'd been so wrapped up in getting things in order before leaving Sacramento that I'd given almost no thought to the task of getting settled when I got to New York or to the realities of the job I'd be starting the next day.

Beyond the job itself, the first task I had was to make a new home for myself. People had been quick to tell me horror stories about looking for an apartment and that I'd be fortunate to find a nice place at any price. As it turned out, however, my friend had done the impossible. He found a furnished apartment for me in less than two weeks and it was going to cost only $750 a month. I must admit that $750 a month seemed a bit expensive, but everyone had told me New York was going to be expensive and, believe it or not, an apartment in that location at that price was considered a bargain.

Besides the apartment there were other things to think about. Since the only clothes I owned were the typical cottons and light-weight wools that were fine year-round in California, but not so great for the New York winter ahead, a new wardrobe was one of them.

I decided not to worry too much because I figured one of my new friends at the station would help guide me over the first hurdles of life in the big city. I couldn't have been more wrong on that score.

This time my plane landed at La Guardia in a rainstorm so the wonderful view of Manhattan that I'd had on my last trip was completely obscured. If I were a person who believed in omens I might have thought those clouds foretold a stormy period in my life. Fortunately, I don't tend to think that way, though in this case that line of thinking might have prepared me better for what was coming.

The taxi took me from the airport to my new home, an apartment in a beautiful Park Avenue building with polished brass frames around the doors and a doorman who shot out to open the taxi door even before the car came to a complete stop. When I got my bags upstairs and opened the door I immediately understood what people meant when they talked about "small" New York apartments. My first thought was that there had to be some mistake. This was in the East Sixties, one of the finest neighborhoods a person could choose, and it was a wonderful old building. But my apartment was the size of one room in my old house in Sacramento and the kitchen was no bigger than a large postage stamp. There was a tiny refrigerator under the kitchen counter and a hot plate on the counter. Those two items constituted the kitchen appliances—no oven, no dishwasher, no garbage disposal, and practically no cupboards! The bathroom had fixtures from the last century but of course in New York–apartment talk that is referred to as "charm." I now know this is fairly typical of city apartments but I didn't know that then. At any rate my new place clearly wasn't the Park Lane Hotel overlooking Central Park, and I began to wonder if this move was really a step up or not.

But I needed to get settled in so I hung up the few clothes I'd brought with me, wiped out the refrigerator, and set out to get some food to fill it. I asked the doorman of my building where to go and he pointed me in the direction of what he called the "supermarket," which he said would be open on Sunday. I walked the three blocks to the store and what I found was not a supermarket as most of us know supermarkets, with giant shopping carts and wide aisles. This was a tiny little grocery with carts about a foot wide and aisles so narrow and so stacked with merchandise that it was impossible for two carts to pass in the same aisle. It looked to me as if it had been designed by and for midgets.

I managed to get my necessities, although I was surprised by the limited selection, and when I got to the checkout counter the clerk said, "What's your name and address?"

A little suspicious, I said, "What do you want it for?"

"So we can deliver your groceries," he said, a bit testily. This was a first for me. In California we drove to the grocery store and there was no such thing as delivery.

At any rate I didn't have that much and I wanted to get settled in, so I carried my two grocery bags back to the apartment and put things away. Later on I went out again because I wanted to get the feel of the Manhattan streets on a Sunday and because being all alone in this new apartment was a bit depressing. The rain, which had been heavy when I arrived, had stopped by then and there were people out, but the streets were much less crowded than I had seen them when I came for my job interview. It gave me time to do some people-watching and some time to try to orient myself to the geography of Manhattan, where the numbered streets ran across town from east to west and the named and numbered avenues (Madison, Park, Lexington, and the others) run north/south. It sounds easy and it is, until you get turned around, which I managed to do. But a helpful hotdog vendor pointed me in the right direction and I found my way back to my building. When I got upstairs I fixed a tuna sandwich and plopped down on the couch and there I stayed, through the Sunday-night movie and the late news. I went to bed around 11:30. I had to be at work at 8:00 the next morning and I wanted to be fresh and alert my first day on the job at *Eyewitness News*.

Let me take a minute here to tell you a little bit about the news department at WABC-TV, Channel 7, in New York. When I went to work there, *Eyewitness News* prided itself on local reporting. The station had consciously gathered a staff of reporters with diverse backgrounds and then developed those people into television personalities. They thereby changed the nightly news from a program with a group of interchangeable and faceless people into something of a soap-opera ensemble company that viewers could get to know and rely on. Back in 1975, the stars of *Eyewitness News* were Rose Ann Scamardella, Gloria Rojas, Melba Tolliver, Anna Bond, Roger Grimsby, Bill Beutel, John Johnson, Roger Sharp, Doug Johnson, Milton Lewis, and Bob Lape. They were a wonderful family of black and white and Hispanic, Catholic and Protestant and Jewish people who delivered the news to the people in a more personal way. The audience tuned in as much to see their favorite personalities as to hear the news. They wanted to know what Rose Ann had done that day and if Milton's cold was better. This combination of local reporting and personalities had been getting high ratings from the public, but I was later to learn that it also got a good deal of bad-mouthing from colleagues in the news field and from the critics.

It was a wonderful advertisement for New York and a format that worked exceptionally well. It worked so well that it was copied all over the country and labeled "happy-talk news" because the anchor people and the reporters bantered back and forth like members of the family at the dinner table.

The "Eyewitness News Team," as they called themselves, was a close-knit group. They thrived on their closeness and their ethnic identification. You can imagine, then, how they felt that Monday morning when this young blond woman from California, dressed in her light-peach polyester outfit, walked into the newsroom. Mouths didn't exactly drop open, but all eyes were on me.

When I interviewed for the job I had been told that they were missing the blond, WASP category in their ethnic mix and that I would fill that category very nicely. I knew that one of the reasons I was hired was to fill this gap on the nightly news shows, to provide a look that the station management thought would appeal to a suburban audience and thus raise the station's ratings in the bedroom communities surrounding the city, where the ratings were not as strong. That seemed perfectly all right to me and I didn't give it a second thought because ethnicity and religion, or lack of either of them, had never bothered me anyway.

I'll never forget that first morning. I was shown to my desk and sat down without any introduction, formal or otherwise, and I was left to figure out what to do next. The "warm welcome" of the people in the newsroom, which ran the gamut from active disinterest to icy coldness, made me feel like a pussycat who had accidentally strolled into a pack of lions.

To compound the situation, that same day Peter Bannon, a reporter hired from Atlanta, also joined the news staff. Peter, a mild-mannered and soft-spoken young man who also happened to be blond, and without identifying ethnic marks, was as shocked by the atmosphere as I was. He had more news experience than I did but that didn't cut any ice with the other reporters. The very first day, someone dubbed us "Ken and Barbie" (cute if it isn't you they're talking about), and Peter and I became the butts of a lot of jokes.

Of course, I was also the new kid on the block and new kids are always outsiders for a while. Plus I didn't have nearly as much experience as the rest of the people there—the understatement of the year—and I knew it. My inexperience didn't worry me too much, however, because I had been assured during my job interview at WABC-TV that I would get some orientation before I hit the streets. Unfortunately that word never quite filtered down to the newsroom, or they decided to ignore the fact that I wasn't really a seasoned reporter and let me learn the hard way.

By now I'm sure I don't have to tell you that it wasn't at all like the movies in which the curmudgeonly news editor with the warm spot for beginners puts his arm around the young reporter and introduces her to the staff who, realizing the new recruit is a little insecure, show her the ropes, take her out to lunch, and become her friends. No, I walked in, was briefly shown around, and was told within a half hour that I was to go with Doug Johnson to an event honoring a famous retired prizefighter. The next day I was to meet another reporter, Bob Lape, and go with him to a local prison to film part of a series on the treatment of prisoners. I have to say thanks to both Doug (who did become a good friend) and Bob for paying some attention to me and my questions those first days. I now know there isn't much spare time in the news business so for them it must have been like having a kid sister tag along when they and their friends went to the movies. In other words, a real pain. It was an intimidating way to start.

I had prepared and read the news at KCRA but I had covered an actual story in the field only once. I happened to be the only one in the newsroom when the call came in that day, so Pete Langlois, the assignment editor, sent me with a cameraman to report on the discovery of a woman's body in a river in the older section of Sacramento. We got to the scene and I saw a group of policemen hovering over a sheet that covered something on the river bank. They saw us coming and were very cooperative. Not knowing exactly how to go about this business of field reporting, I asked the police sergeant, "Who found the body?"

"A couple of kids walking along the river," he answered.

"When did they find it?" was my next thoughtful question.

"About nine-fifteen this morning," he said.

"Is there any identification?"

"Not yet. She wasn't carrying anything with a name on it."

"How old was she?"

"We don't know for sure, but somewhere in her seventies, I'd say."

I reached back into my repertoire of police movies and asked, "Are there any signs of foul play?"

"Yes," he said, "it looks like she was strangled and then thrown in the river."

I thought that just about covered the story. Fortunately, the cameraman took the necessary film without any direction from me. I thanked the police sergeant, remembering to get his name, and the cameraman and I went back to the station. As we walked in the door, the news director asked if we'd gotten enough film and then asked, "Was she raped?"

"Was she what?" I asked incredulously. "I don't know, I didn't ask. After all, she was an old woman."

"That's great, Blunden, you're really terrific," he said. "That's always a question you have to ask. Don't you realize that people want to know those things?" This is a typical television-news mentality but I didn't know it at the time. The piece ran that night with some additional copy written by another reporter that said, in fact, that the woman had not been raped and the police had no clues to the crime. That was the sum total of my experience and my training as a field reporter.

I had not made an auspicious beginning as a reporter in Sacramento, though it had been a learning experience, and suddenly here I was about to go out to cover a story in New York City. I was organizing myself at my desk when Doug Johnson came up and said, "Let's go, Joan."

We went down to the street, where a car with three men inside was waiting to pick us up. The three in the car were the camera crew. I had no idea what their jobs were since we didn't have crews in Sacramento, only a cameraman who did everything. We stuffed ourselves into the car with all the camera and sound equipment and started driving through the streets of Manhattan. When we got out to cover the retired prizefighter story, one man took the camera, another took the sound equipment, and the third handled the lights. Since this was clearly on-the-job training I made mental notes; I really couldn't say, "Pardon me, fellas, but what do you guys actually do with all that stuff?"

I watched as they set up for the shoot (that's the word used to describe the filming of a TV story) and listened carefully as Doug did his interviewing and his on-camera open and close. The activity of the event itself, the sea of totally strange faces, and the perpetual motion of Doug and the crew left me with a blurred image of what was happening, but I got a sense of the overall picture, which I filed away in my mental notebook.

Fortunately I didn't have any real responsibility that first day, or the second, when I went with Bob Lape to talk with the warden of a local prison. I had never seen the inside of a jail before, so the prison itself—the guards, bars, clanging doors, the smell, the gray paint and gray faces—represented another brand-new experience in this rapidly changing kaleidoscope of new experiences. I paid close attention to the type of questions Lape asked, to the way he presented himself on camera, and to the way he directed the camera crew. I was sure these observations would be helpful.

When we got back to the station, Phil Nye called me over. "I've got a story for you tomorrow, but before you go out we'd like to talk to you about changing your name."

"Change my name?" I said, surprised. No one had ever suggested that Joan Blunden was a bad or difficult name for television.

"Yes, we think it has problems," he said. "When written quickly the *n* can look like an *r* and we wouldn't want a reporter to be a 'Blunder.' The critics would have a heyday." As it turned out they had one anyway, but I didn't have to give them a written invitation.

"I used my real name the whole time in Sacramento, and there were never any problems," I said. I learned then that I should never use my previous experience as a guide, since there is a certain disdain in New York—and not just in the news business—for the way anything is done elsewhere.

"That may be the way you did it in Sacramento but this is not Sacramento," Nye said, "so start thinking of a name that you can live with."

When Nye said "Blunder" it did stir up some old memories. When I was young our family used to go out to eat from time to time in Sacramento. If the restaurant was crowded my dad would leave his name with the hostess while we sat down to wait. Occasionally we'd hear, "Dr. Blunder, table for Dr. Blunder." He used to get very upset: If Blunder was not a good name for a newswoman, it was an even worse name for a surgeon.

That night I called my mother to tell her what I'd done so far and to break the news about my name to her. I didn't think she was going to like the idea so I introduced the subject by saying, "Mom, remember how Dad used to get so upset when they said his name wrong? Well . . ." I gave some thought to a new name, but where do you start when every name in the world is available? Do you look for something common like Smith or Jones or something ethnic like Schwartz or Kazinski? I went to sleep without coming to any decision.

The word that I was in search of a name had gotten around the newsroom by the time I came in the next morning, and Gloria Rojas, one of the reporters, stopped me as I passed her desk.

"I hear you're looking for a new name," she said.

"That's right. Phil Nye thinks I need another last name," I said.

"Why don't you call yourself 'Joan Cartwright'?" she suggested. I guess somehow I reminded her of the Ponderosa Ranch from the old *Bonanza* show. I have a feeling there were some other names suggested that I didn't hear—I'm sure one of them was "Barbie."

Later that morning I got my assignment. As I was passing the news director's office I stuck my head in and said, "I'm going out on my story now and there's this one small detail that hasn't been resolved, Mr. Nye, uh, . . . my name. I think I should sign off with the name I'm going to be using."

Doug Johnson and Don Dunphy, Jr., were sitting there along with Nye. Gloria Rojas's suggestion of "Joan Cartwright" was tossed around and then Doug said, "Why don't you just drop the *B* and call yourself 'Lunden'? It will remind people of the city and Julie London, and it's easier than changing your whole name." They all looked at each other and at me. In half a minute there was a consensus that "Lunden" sounded good. That day I became Joan Lunden. It was no big deal, this name change. It just happened. It was over and done with and matter-of-fact.

Twenty minutes later Joan Lunden was on her way to her first assignment in New York City, a trial that was taking place in the New York State Supreme Court in lower Manhattan. Again I was in a car with three men. We introduced ourselves and we were off. At that time I didn't yet know upper from lower (or East Side from West Side), and as the car made turn after turn through the narrow streets I became disoriented. You have to realize that the streets of New York are always crowded during the day, the traffic is a constant horror, and the noise level can be deafening. I have to admit that I was a little giddy, with a tinge of panic and exhilaration, as we drove through town. It seemed to be taking forever to get where we were going when we suddenly stopped in front of an impressive Greek-revival building with columns and a long, wide staircase leading up to its doors.

Herb Todd, the cameraman on this assignment and a real professional who was always helpful and friendly to me, said, "This is it. Let's do it."

We all got out and Herb said matter-of-factly, "Joan, how many mags"—the canisters used to hold the film for a TV camera before the advent of tape—"do you think you want? Do you want a six hundred or what?"

It was a very good question, I suppose, but I didn't have the slightest idea what a mag was at that time and I didn't want to appear stupid in front of this group, so I said, "Oh, I don't know. What do you think, Herb?"

What Herb thought was that I didn't have the slightest idea what a mag was and that most likely I didn't have the slightest idea what I was doing in general. He gave me a quick look and a little smile, "We may need a four hundred and a six hundred," he said, then he grabbed his entire bag and we headed toward the steps of the court building.

As we walked, I got close to him and whispered, "Herb, what's a mag?" He now knew he was dealing with a real greenhorn, if he hadn't known it already, but instead of screaming with laughter, he explained that "mag" is short for *magazine,* that the mag contains the film, and that mags come in various sizes which indicate the length of time they run.

"Most stories take at least one mag," he said, "which gives us enough film for you to edit it down to anywhere from one to three minutes for air." Lesson 1 for Lunden.

Lesson 2 came right on the heels of lesson 1. Herb said, "In New York they don't allow cameras in the courtroom so, though we can go in the building, we can't go in the room with you. You go in, take notes, and when you come out we'll find you somewhere near the courtroom door."

"Where will you be, exactly?" I asked anxiously, since we had walked up two flights of stairs and turned three corners by then.

"Don't worry, we'll find you," he said.

I didn't know how that would work but I didn't have time to worry about it because I was too busy listening to the rest of his instructions. He said, "When it's all over, if the woman is found not guilty you stick with her like glue. Stay right next to her and don't move away for any reason. If she's found guilty she won't be able to come out of the courtroom and in that case you stick to her attorney like glue. Find him in the courtroom and stick with him. And remember, we'll find you." I checked my watch. It was 10:30 A.M.

I walked toward the courtroom door and looked back to see which direction Herb and the crew had gone. I opened the door to that room with some trepidation and found the place packed. I had never been to a formal court proceeding so I didn't know the protocol. I didn't know where to go or where you were allowed to go. As I scanned the room I saw a row of people taking notes, surmised that they belonged to the press, and walked in that direction. I "excused" my way through a crowded aisle and sat next to a man who turned out to be from the local CBS affiliate. Before I was settled in my seat he leaned over and said, "Here's what's happened so far." As I later found out, many of the reporters from competing stations and newspapers are helpful and quite nice, and it's actually possible to become friendlier with the competition, in a personal sense, than with your own colleagues because you spend more time with the competition. It's a rare thing when two reporters from the same station go out to cover the same story. At any rate, he brought me up to date and I made notes on the rest of the trial.

The wheels of justice turn very slowly. I was in that room all day and I had plenty of time to identify the defendant, the defense attorney (if I needed to find him), and all the other characters in the drama. Yet despite having to sit for more than five hours on a hard chair, I found the whole process fascinating.

In the end the defendant was found guilty so, as Herb had told me, I got right next to the woman's attorney, walking with him out of the building. There were several television crews there vying for position along with WABC but I was in close and had my microphone right in front of his face. I was able to get in a couple of questions and then it was all over. I had spent a whole day for a couple of minutes of film.

With the interview, such as it was, in the can (TV talk for "finished"), I did my first New York sign off. We had to shoot it three times. The first time I said, "Joan Blunden, KCRA-TV." The second time I said, "Joan Blunden, Eyewitness News." The third time I got it right: "This is Joan Lunden, Eyewitness News." My baptism by fire was over for the moment. I had met my first big challenge and survived.

That night I went back to my apartment, absolutely exhausted, not from the hours I had spent working but from the tension. I went over the details in my mind and decided that I had not done too badly for someone who, only a few hours before, didn't know what a mag was. The next day I learned more.

I started to work in New York at the height of the worldwide oil crisis, and the following evening I was sent to cover a meeting between Henry Kissinger, then Secretary of State, and the leaders of the OPEC nations at the United States Mission to the United Nations. Before I left the office the assignment editor told me, "You're going to be out in front of the mission and I want you to get the OPEC people, Kissinger, and the demonstration across the street. We obviously want something from him but you probably won't be able to get it."

When our car pulled up in front of the mission there were several hundred people being held behind police barricades directly across the street from the mission. Many of them were carrying placards and banners protesting the Arab oil policy and they were chanting protest slogans. We set up our camera and got some shots of the demonstration and talked to some of the demonstrators. My instructions were to stay out in front but I could see reporters from every newspaper, radio station, and TV station going through the Secret Service clearance at the door and then into the building to cover the actual meeting. Before then I had never seen anyone who worked for the Secret Service and certainly not the kind of physical search to which the newspeople were being subjected. At one point I even called the office to see if there was some mistake.

"Are you sure you don't want me inside?" I asked. "I'm the only one left out here."

"Stay put" was the answer and so I did.

Then a line of limousines began to pull up in front of the building. Each one of them deposited one or two of the OPEC leaders who then walked quickly up the steps and went into the mission to the accompaniment of jeers from the demonstrators. I said to Ronnie, the cameraman that night, "How do you tell which one of these guys is from which country? They all look the same in those turbans and beards."

"You don't," he said. "We'll shoot them all and when we get back to the station they can figure it out if they want to. Just call them 'OPEC leaders' for now."

As one limousine after another pulled up I began to get nervous. "How will I know when Kissinger arrives?" I asked.

"You'll know," was all Ronnie said.

About five minutes later four unmarked cars with flashing red lights pulled up at the same time. They were followed by a limousine with Secret Service agents on the front and back and that car was followed by four more unmarked cars with flashing lights. The sound man handed me the mike and said, "Guess who?"

From my vantage point on the steps I could see a man get out of the limo, but he was immediately surrounded by a cordon of Secret Servicemen five deep. "How do I get to him?" I asked Ronnie in a panic. It didn't look to me as if there was any way to break through that wall of bodies.

But Ronnie said, "Don't worry, when the lights go on you'll see why they call it the magic of TV."

He was right. When the TV lights flashed on in the darkness I was amazed. It was like Moses parting the Red Sea. The beam of the light seemed to force its way to the core of the action, opening a path that I instinctively followed with my microphone. Suddenly I was very close, in fact face-to-face with Henry Kissinger. The first thing that came to my mind was that he looked just as he did on the evening news. "Excuse me, Mr. Secretary," I said. Quickly three Secret Servicemen shielded him and one of them said, as he pushed me, "You can't talk to the secretary out here." But Kissinger saw me too; in fact, he gave me a real once-over from head to toe. Then he came toward me and said with a boyish grin, "It's perfectly all right. I'll talk to the young lady."

My heart nearly stopped because now that I had him, I didn't know what to ask. I was a little like the dog that chased the car and finally caught it. With the adrenaline pumping, I quickly looked down at my notes and said, "Mr. Secretary, the Syrian foreign minister has charged that negotiations are dividing the Arab nations. Could you respond to that?"

He replied, "Well, I'm seeing the Syrian minister tomorrow morning and I'll have to have a talk with him. That's not our intention."

It was all over in a few seconds. It was short but it was on film. Then he rode the wave of Secret Service into the mission and it was all over. The lights were turned off and the sea of people rolled back together. I did my closing, getting it right in only one try this time, and we packed up and went back to the newsroom.

I rushed in very excited but nobody else in the crowded newsroom was the least bit concerned with my coup. I was a little let down. I began to write my script and realized that in fact Kissinger was the first major political figure I'd ever seen up to that point. I had had one other opportunity but that had fizzled. I was anchoring the news in Sacramento when then President Gerald Ford came to town. There were so many places to be covered that I was actually sent out to cover one of them. But as you may recall, there was an attempt on Ford's life by Squeaky Fromme, one of Charles Manson's gang, and it all happened before Ford got to where I was, so I never did get to see him. Kissinger, then, was a first for me and a pretty good one, I thought.

It turned out that my short interview was the only piece of film anyone from any of the stations had gotten with a quote directly from Kissinger. It was used that night on *Eyewitness News* and the next day on *GMA*'s predecessor, *A.M. America*. I had made the local news and national television on my first real assignment. I was pretty impressed with myself but apparently I was the only one who was impressed; no one around the office said a word to me about it.

Two days later I was sent to the world-famous Waldorf-Astoria Hotel to cover a news conference in which Bob Hope was to be announced as the spokesman for Texaco. The Waldorf is one of those classic, opulent, and generally spectacular old hotels and Texaco had rented the main ballroom for the presentation. The room's huge, ornate chandeliers, thick draperies, and Oriental carpets made a very elegant setting. Bob Hope was introduced by the president of Texaco; he told a few jokes and then answered some questions from the press. After the formal presentation I decided to see if we could get a little more from him and I told Herb Todd to bring his camera up front. No one else, it seemed, had the same idea and we were the only news-people at the table when I asked Hope if he'd like to say a few more words for Channel 7. He graciously gave me a short interview spiced with a couple of jokes and I proudly took that back to the station. Again, I made the evening news. It looked good to me as I watched that night and I was proud of myself for the second day in a row. The next afternoon I expected a little official praise for my work but there was not so much as a "Nice going" from Nye or any of my colleagues.

Nonetheless, here I was, four days on the job, and I'd covered a major trial at the New York State Supreme Court, Secretary of State Henry Kissinger at the United Nations, and Bob Hope, one of the world's best-known entertainment figures, at the Waldorf-Astoria. It was an auspicious start and I was beginning to think there was going to be a lot of glamour in the TV business. Unfortunately, from that point on, things took a definite turn away from glamour and most of my assignments were of the more mundane variety, though they were definitely learning experiences.

Since I was a naive rookie on *Eyewitness News,* I was sent out on assignments that only a rookie would be willing to touch. It was a case of not knowing where to fear to tread and there were a number of times that I had my eyes opened but good.

On one assignment I was sent to the Forty-second Street area, a neighborhood well-known for its sleaziness, to do a story on prostitution. I went out with a crew and we shot a rather interesting interview with a prostitute. When we finished we packed up and drove away. We'd gone only about half a block when we had to stop for a red light. I was sitting in the back seat with the cameraman and the other two members of the crew were in the front. As we waited for the light to change, a face appeared at the half-opened window on the cameraman's side of the car. The cameraman rolled the window down to see what was going on and he rolled it a little too far. The man outside quickly stuck a knife through the window and put it right up to the cameraman's throat. The man with the knife said he was the prostitute's pimp. He made a few choice threats and then said, "I want the film out of that camera. Give it to me."

The cameraman said quickly, "You don't have to worry about it. We won't run it."

All the time this conversation was going on, I was telling the driver in a loud stage whisper to get going. He was so scared, however, that he didn't react very quickly. When he finally zipped away from the light, we went straight back to the station, where we all collapsed with relief. Did we run the film? We did.

Another Forty-second Street story came my way not long after that. It was during one of those periodic "Clean Up Times

Square" campaigns and I was sent with the crew to a peep show
to get an interview with the owner. The proprietor wasn't exactly thrilled with the idea, and he chased us out of his shop with
a baseball bat.

For the next several weeks I saw a lot of exciting stories on the
evening news, but none of them was mine; the memory of the
elegance of the Waldorf ballroom began to fade. I was, however,
getting to know the inside of most of the police precinct houses
and fire stations in New York. No chandeliers or drapes in sight.
In fact, I became something of a specialist in fires. It seemed as
though every time there was a fire story they turned to me. I was
becoming as much a fixture at major fires as the firemen.

I remember my first fire very well. For me it was like being
thrown into the deep end of the swimming pool without knowing
how to swim. This was a massive blaze in an abandoned ware-
house somewhere along the Hudson River. As we pulled up,
there were flames shooting out of the windows of the massive
building and the smoke was everywhere. There were at least
twenty fire trucks on the scene and scores of firemen were running all over the place. It was chaotic and I didn't know whom to
talk to in order to get the details I needed for my story. As the
film crew took their shots I began stopping firemen and asking
them questions about the fire and was genuinely surprised when
they didn't respond. I learned a few minutes later (I did a lot of
learning later, it seems) that you're supposed to get reports only
from the man in the white fire hat—the chief—and not from the
guys in the black hats who are too busy fighting the fire to answer anyway.

I knew I was learning but it was a trying period. After four
weeks I had made some headway but I was becoming more afraid
of failure and was still embarrassed by my inexperience. I didn't
know anything about the people of New York City or its streets
and neighborhoods and I didn't know much about the terminol-
ogy of the news business in the city. One day the assignment
editor sent me to interview a borough president and it was only
then that I learned New York is divided into five boroughs, each

of which has its own governmental units. New York is a huge, chaotic place, and when you go out to cover the news in the street you're in the heart of that chaos—and sometimes, because of the camera, also the focal point of that chaos.

My first assignment in the Bedford-Stuyvesant section of Brooklyn is a case in point. The area has had its ups and downs through the years and it isn't considered one of the city's better neighborhoods. On this day a group of students had taken over one of the high schools and the police were trying to get them out. I was sent to cover it. We drove within a block of the school and it didn't seem that things were too bad, but when we pulled up in front of the building it was pure havoc. I was a little uneasy getting out of the car and walking into a group of hundreds of screaming teenagers but I was a reporter and I was ready to do it. As the crew and I sat there, Bob Alis, the cameraman, turned to me and said, "Okay, kid, do you want this to be an A story, a B story, or a C story?"

To me A meant good, B meant pretty good, and C meant average, so I said, "A, of course."

With that Bob was out the door, running right into the middle of the kids with his camera going. I was following him and we were being jostled on all sides. Things were being thrown in our direction and we were being called names that were relatively new to me at the time. We passed the police barricades and then, all of a sudden, people started scattering in every direction and Alis and the rest of the crew dived to the ground. I was standing there looking around when I heard a policeman with a bullhorn say, "Hey, news lady, you think you're invisible? There's a sniper up there." I dived in beside Alis and then we all got up and ran into a nearby building. As we stood there breathing hard, Alis said, "Boy, when you want an A story you mean it, don't you."

I decided this was as good a time as any to find out what those three letters meant. "Bob," I said, "what the hell is the difference between A, B, and C stories?"

Alis gave me his definition. "An A story," he explained, "is kind of like shooting up from under the wheels of a runaway truck. The B would be like sitting in the truck and aiming the camera down at the wheels, and a C is going across the street and shooting out the window while being served tea and sugar cookies." From that point on, I realized that not only did the camera and my press badge offer me access to the action and a degree of protection from it, they could also be the cause of some of that action.

If I wasn't an expert field reporter yet, neither had I learned to handle the constant time pressure of daily assignments very well. I would get back to the newsroom and sit in front of the typewriter to prepare my script and instead of typing I'd just stare at the paper. I wasn't sure what to say or how to say it, and there is very little room for hesitation in a business in which you're always up against the clock and sometimes have as few as thirty minutes to put a story together. I was working twelve and fourteen hours a day, which didn't bother me, but I was getting no help or encouragement of any kind, except from the camera crews.

And something that bothered me just as much was the fact that I had not been able to make any personal friends at the station. This was another new experience for me. I had never had any problems finding friends, even in Mexico, where I didn't speak the language. I think I'm personable and outgoing but here I was, on the outside looking in, never asked to be part of what the others were doing. For whatever reasons, my coworkers had not taken me to their collective bosoms except in one case.

I had been working only a few days when Anna Bond asked me where I was living and what I was paying for rent. This may seem like a strange question in most parts of the country, but it's a basic question in New York, where half the population is always on the prowl for a place to live. When I told her I was paying $750 a month she wasn't sure if I was a rich kid, if I was making more money than she was (in which case there would have been a mutiny among the reporters), or if I was merely a typical newcomer. Assuming that I was your basic patsy, she told me the facts of apartment living in the city. "You can get a much bigger and better apartment for much less money if you move out of that part of town," Anna said. "Where you are is probably the most expensive area in the city. Why don't you look for a place around here?"

That was good advice. I started to look for a place in the neighborhood around the WABC-TV studio and was lucky again because in less than a month I found a decent and afford-able apartment right across the street from the newsroom door and directly across the street from Lincoln Center, the city's cul-tural mecca. It was a one-bedroom apartment on the twenty-eighth floor of a high-rise building. I had a view of the uptown skyline and of the street scene below. When I put some furniture in and hung some curtains it took on a homey feeling. My new place saved me not only rent but round-trip cab fares across town as well.

I had been taking cabs to and from work for convenience but also because I had had a funny and embarrassing experience on my first bus ride in New York City. I had been told that the bus, which stopped at my corner on Park Avenue, was the cheapest and best way to get from one side of town to the other. So one morning not long after I started work I gave it a try.

In California almost everyone travels by car and I had never had to use any form of public transportation. My only previous experience, in fact, was on a cable car in San Francisco and there you get on the car wherever you can and the conductor comes around and takes your fare. I thought that was the way it was done everywhere. When the bus pulled up that morning, it stopped with the back door right in front of where I was stand-ing. Some people got off, and I got on through the rear door and sat down as I had done on the cable car. I could see that people were staring at me but I was vain enough to think it was because they recognized me, even though I'd only been on TV a few days. I saw a couple of women across from me whispering to each other and shaking their heads but it didn't register, and I wasn't paying attention to what the people who were getting on at the front of the bus were doing. No one ever came to take my fare and I was so busy looking out the window that it never even crossed my mind that I hadn't paid. I just got off at my stop when we reached the other side of town.

Well, several weeks later I was assigned to do a story on public transportation and for part of it my camera crew and I rode a bus. They got on before me (and of course they got on through the front door) and dropped their fares in the box. When I saw what they were doing I must have turned red from head to toe. After I paid my fare and sat down all I could do was laugh. Now I knew why those people had stared at me. There I sat, a young, well-dressed woman who had sneaked in at the back of the bus without paying and who didn't seem to care. They just couldn't believe their eyes. My crew couldn't figure out what was causing me to go into hysterics until I was able to stop laughing for a minute and tell them. Then I broke up all over again.

At any rate, getting out of that expensive apartment and moving within easy walking distance of the studio was definitely a positive event in what seemed to me to be an ocean of negativism. Here I was, a small-town girl living in a tiny apartment in a new city, I had no friends, and I was insecure and tense at work. A wonderful combination. To say that I was miserable would be an understatement. I'm not sure if it was the fact that I was considered an intruder by my colleagues, the lack of direction from anyone on the job, the long hours, or the loneliness, but I was kicking myself for having pulled up stakes and made the change.

I was now beginning to realize that I had left a cushy job in Sacramento. I used to come in at ten in the morning and leave after the six-o'clock news, I knew everyone at the station, I had a nice house to live in, I had girlfriends and boyfriends and my mother for solace when I needed it. Now I was at the station by 6:00 A.M. and sometimes out on the street until midnight or 1:00 A.M. in all kinds of weather, surrounded by police, dead bodies, devastation, fire and smoke, prostitutes, and demonstrators. And since I was still learning the ropes, I had to work twice as hard to try to close the gap. I was beginning to think that Jon Kelly may have been right after all. In a few months I might be back in Sacramento begging for my old job back.

When you're all alone on your day off, looking out the window of your apartment at all the couples walking arm in arm down the street, you can get pretty depressed. You begin to feel as if you're the only one in the world suffering this kind of isolation. I wasn't able to look at the situation objectively and say to myself, "I'm going to change all this and meet some of those people," but not being the "woe is me" type, I found other ways to fill my spare time and one of them was shopping. I got very familiar with the merchandise in a number of the city's best stores. After all, I was making good money so why not spend it? I also covered every floor of the Metropolitan Museum of Art, the Guggenheim, and the Museum of Modern Art, all very educational—but more fun with a friend.

I needed a social life, but since my hours were generally irregular and I often worked at night (the new kid always gets the night shift) it was even harder to find time to socialize. And before long I learned another interesting fact. When you're on television you become something of an untouchable. You get asked out by nuts, jerks, and wimps, but the nice guys, the ones you might like to meet, are scared off. They don't call, because a TV personality obviously has a line of rich and famous men beating down her door. Michael Krauss (who was to become my husband) didn't ask me out for a year, even though we knew each other, for that very reason. He figured I must have been dating someone. I've found that this is true for many women in this business. It's plain hard to get a date with a nice man. Little do those nice men know that when we're not working we aren't having cocktails at "21" and dinner at The Four Seasons, or dancing until dawn at the newest disco. More than likely we're sitting in front of the TV set, eating a tunafish sandwich and wishing the phone would ring.

The result of this curious phenomenon was that I had so few dates I can actually remember them all, especially my first New York date. I had gone to cover a party at one of the embassies in the city. In the course of the evening I met a nice-looking suave young Italian diplomat who asked me out to dinner that weekend. I said yes and on the appointed night he picked me up in his

Ferrari. We went to a very fancy restaurant. We had drinks at the bar before dinner and the conversation was quite pleasant. I was thinking to myself, "This isn't a bad way to spend an evening." Later, we were chatting over dinner and things were still going well, when he said, "I'm taking you back to my place tonight and then tomorrow we're going to Bermuda."

I didn't think I'd said anything that could lead to that announcement and I said, "What did you say?"

"Tomorrow we're going to Bermuda," he repeated. "Come on now, did you really expect just to have dinner?" Then he added, "And don't worry about picking up clothes, we can buy you some new things when we get there."

"I thought that's what you said," I answered coolly, and then I did something I'd never done before. I got up from the table, threw my napkin down on my plate, and stalked out leaving him sitting there with his wine glass in his hand. I don't suppose it actually bothered him but it made me feel just great. I walked home from the restaurant feeling like one tough cookie.

My second date (I told you I could remember them all) was less distressing and a lot more interesting. I had been sent to The Atrium, a new high-rise apartment building, to do a story on a penthouse apartment with a huge garden that was being built by Stewart Mott, the heir to the General Motors fortune and I don't know what other financial empires. I met Stewart as we were touring the apartment and the garden, where workmen were using a bulldozer to move his garden dirt around. As we chatted I told him that I had recently moved from California and was so busy working that I hadn't had time to replace two things I missed, my cat and my houseplants. I filed my story, went out to eat, and by the time I got home that night my apartment was filled with plants and there was a beautiful white Persian cat lounging on my couch. There was also a card that said, "Welcome to New York. Best, Stewart." I told myself, "Now here's a guy with class, a very interesting kind of guy."

A few days later he called and asked me out to dinner. We had a pleasant evening, and it was a big improvement over the diplomat. A few days later my mother came to visit—it was around

Christmas—and when Stewart learned she was in town he asked us both out for the evening. Another touch of class, it seemed to me. My mother was excited. She just knew I was going to marry this fabulously wealthy heir and she'd never have to pay for another Cadillac.

As I said, this was December and the weather was cold and damp. When Stewart arrived at my apartment I opened the door to find him standing there with his bicycle, the basket of which was filled with fresh asparagus and strawberries, somewhat rare commodities in New York at that time of year. My mother was a bit shocked that one of the richest men in the world was riding a bike in December in the rain and this was my first indication that I was dealing with a bit of an eccentric. But it reinforced my image of him as different. Stewart, a philanthropist who spends most of his time giving money to good causes, was active in the Democratic party at the time and as we sat and ate strawberries he told us our evening was to be spent attending two fund-raising events for Democratic candidates. An "interesting" way to spend the evening. I should explain that my mother is a staunch Republican (a member of "Redheads for Reagan" when he campaigned for governor of California) who has very little to do with, and nothing pleasant to say to or about, Democrats. But she was a good sport and she jumped at the chance to rub elbows with the opposition.

We caught a cab and went to the first party, a gathering in a Park Avenue apartment for Senator Frank Church, who was running in the presidential primary. As I circulated around the room I happened to pass behind my mother and I could hear her warming up for a fight with an Adlai Stevenson type. Just as voices were beginning to rise, I moved in to prevent a main event. I then took my mother by the hand and led her into the bathroom for a little mother-daughter chat.

"Mom, if you get into any arguments tonight I'm going to be very upset," I said. "You're going to have to promise me that you'll listen, smile, and not argue, okay?" She agreed, I think because she didn't want to upset my future with Stewart Mott.

The next party of the evening, in a Central Park West apartment that the hostess called her "flat," was for Morris Udall, another primary candidate. This flat was one of those duplex affairs with a panoramic view of the skyline and a wraparound terrace that was bigger than most apartments. After we'd been there for a few minutes I looked over and saw my mother sitting on a sofa between Mo Udall and Gloria Steinem, a juxtaposition that I never thought I'd see. It would have made a great picture. I caught her eye and she just smiled to let me know that she was behaving herself. Later I saw her in the corner pointing an accusing finger at Bella Abzug but I didn't hear any explosion so I knew she was keeping her politics to herself, an incredible feat for her.

As for my future with Stewart Mott, well, that night proved he was a little bit out in left field for me. His idea of an enjoyable evening—asparagus, strawberries, and fund-raisers—was different from mine, and several similar evenings put an end to Mom's dream of her daughter marrying an heir.

Believe it or not, I have just related the sum total of my social life during my first six months in New York City, considered by many the social capital of the world. It was quite an unimpressive record, and with each passing day I was becoming more depressed about it and Sacramento was looking more and more like a viable option. One day I went into the bathroom at the *Eyewitness News* station to freshen my face and Rose Ann Scamardella walked in right behind me.

"How's it going, Joan," she said in a friendly voice.

I turned and looked at her and burst into tears.

"I think I get the picture," she said. "Let's have some dinner together after the program tonight and we can talk."

It was the first time anyone at work had offered a helping hand and I grabbed at it. That night we went to a Chinese restaurant near Lincoln Center and we had a conversation that went a long way toward keeping me in New York.

I went through the whole litany of my fears and insecurities about doing the job and then launched into my feelings about being an outsider.

"You have to stick it out," Rose Ann said. "I'm sure you're

going to make it, but you have to accept the fact that New York is a tough place for a newswoman. Frankly, some of the people at the station are resentful. They know you came in without any real street experience. They see you as an outsider. And the truth is, even without that experience that we all think is so necessary, you're doing very well."

"I know how that works," I replied, "because the people at KCRA felt the same way. All they could see, and I don't really blame them, was me moving up quickly at the station and then getting a chance to go to New York after only a year, while they had been working a much longer time to get that chance. I understand but that doesn't make it any easier to be the odd man out. You guys have treated Peter Bannon and me like Martians or worse and it's hard to take."

Finally she suggested that one of the things that might make New York a little more pleasant for me would be at least to find a guy to date.

And she added, "My husband is a New York State legislator and he has a friend who is a Republican state senator. He's running for Congress right now. I think the two of you might just hit it off. His name is Bruce Caputo. Would you let me fix it up?"

As we left the restaurant I gave her a big hug and said, "Thanks, you've been great."

Sure enough, a few days later Bruce Caputo called me for a date. But since he was running for Congress his itinerary resembled Stewart Mott's. Only instead of attending Democratic fund-raising parties he had to glad-hand Republican fund-raisers.

Bruce and I dated for several months. He was a terrific guy, very bright and very nice, but he was in the capital, Albany, most of the week and in the city on the weekends. I worked many weekends, so though we were dating we didn't see a whole lot of each other.

Then, out of the blue, Michael Krauss came into my life. I had seen him quite often since as producer of *A.M. New York* he had an office upstairs from mine at ABC. We had never had much more than a casual conversation before but we had both exchanged those telling looks that say you're interested in each other. Our first date was really to discuss a story I was doing, but nevertheless it got us together. He later told me that a few months before he had asked one of his friends if I was dating anyone and had been told that I was involved with a politician who was going to be a congressman so he had backed off.

We had that first date (so to speak), a hamburger dinner at a place right across the street from the *Eyewitness News* studio, to discuss a spot on *GMA,* and we enjoyed each other's company. Michael was different from my other New York dates, different, in fact, from anyone I had ever dated. He was not only an extremely bright guy, but also the supercreative type. He had a great sense of humor, he worked in television, and he didn't go to political dinners. I started dating Michael regularly about three weeks before Bruce Caputo won his congressional race and I knew right away that Michael and I were going to be together for a long time.

Michael's entrance into my personal life dramatically improved my overall outlook but I was still struggling some on the professional side. I was able to put stories together with a new assurance and I could now put a fire story together on my way to the fire. It had taken me a few months to see that it was a fairly simple matter once you established the pattern. So as our crew car wound through the streets toward the smoke I'd make notes: "Fire broke out this morning at about _____ A.M. on the _____ floor of the wood-frame house on _____ Street. _____ residents have been taken to _____ Hospital and _____ firemen were treated at the scene for smoke inhalation. Fire officials said the cause of the blaze, which apparently started in the _____, is still unknown." The whole story could then essentially be finished by filling in the blanks and when we got back to the station I had only a few minutes' work to do.

I was growing, and during this maturation period I was sent out to cover the story of an apparent murder. The police had found the body of a dead woman in a vacant lot on Manhattan's Lower East Side, an area of tenements and burned-out buildings. When we got there the body was covered with a tarpaulin. I talked to the officer in charge. "Have you determined the cause of death?" I asked.

He pulled back the tarp to reveal the body and pointed, saying, "She had her throat cut."

I was shaken, but I covered up by saying, "Any identification yet?"

At that the officer pulled up the woman's sweater. "She's not wearing a bra," he said. "She must have been a prostitute." The insensitivity of his actions and that remark floored me. I couldn't understand how not wearing a bra equaled being a prostitute, but it certainly did in the mind of that policeman. I realize that people who work in certain fields—doctors, nurses, policemen, firemen—become inured to death, and they have to, but there has to be a level of insensitivity beyond which as human beings we do not go.

Still, I found that eventually I was able to cover murders and bodies much more easily than some other types of stories. The "three-hanky stories," as Rose Ann Scamardella called them, were getting easy to handle professionally, though they were more difficult to handle emotionally. One day Rose Ann burst into the newsroom and yelled, "I won't go out on one more story this week that's going to make me cry. It's only Wednesday and I've cried twice a day for the last three days."

I could sympathize with her because I felt the same way. You're supposed to be objective but you can't help but be moved by the plight of an old woman who has just been kicked out of the house she's lived in for fifty years or by the anguish of the young mother whose child has just been hit and killed by a car, and you can't go up to the door and ask for the photo of a young man who has committed suicide without having it tear you up. I felt so bad that I gave money to old women, sent gifts to people who had lost a family member, and bought clothes for people who had been burned out of their homes. I would get very depressed and often went home at night feeling the weight of society on my shoulders. It was difficult to separate the work from my feelings and I never got hardened to the human tragedies I was covering.

It became obvious after a while that there is a fine line between covering a story and getting the information to the public, and the invasion of privacy. During the much-publicized "Son of Sam" murders I was sent to the homes of the victims to get interviews and film only a few hours after the bodies had been identified. The victims were all young girls and their families were totally devastated, often unable to respond to us. Yet the news demands that we cover these types of stories. I have to admit that several times during this siege of killings, the film crew and I would drive to the neighborhood of the victim and then sit in a coffee shop and debate whether we should go to the house or just phone in an excuse, something creative like "The family wouldn't let us talk to anyone." The moral question of a person's right to privacy is one that needs more investigation.

Suddenly things started to fall into place for me. Press conferences, interviews with public figures, coverage of city and federal government actions became routine. I was moving around the city from story to story in a "let's get down to business" fashion. When I went out to cover a story I didn't worry if there were twenty other reporters there because I knew how to handle myself and the camera crews. Though at times I felt very un–New York, very inexperienced, and not very hip to what was going on in the streets or at City Hall or Bellevue Hospital, those times were becoming fewer and farther between. And now when I got back to the studio and sat in front of the typewriter I rarely asked myself, "How do I put this together?" I just did it. And most important of all, I never missed a deadline.

The station's confidence in me seemed to be rising as well because I was assigned to cover one of the candidates in the mayoral campaign, a relatively unknown politician named Ed Koch. I followed the Koch campaign through the primaries and was at his headquarters on election night when he won the nomination of the Democratic party. It was exciting to be in on an upset victory like that and I fully expected to continue to follow his campaign until the election in November. I was wrong in that assumption. I later realized that no one had expected Koch to win and that's why they had assigned the new kid to his cam-

The Blunden family—my mom, Gladyce; my dad, Erle; my brother, Jeff; and me at eight.

My brother Jeff and me modeling when I was five and he was six.

A favorite photo of my husband, Michael Krauss, and me, taken in 1986.
Jacques Silberstein.

Up at bat at spring training with the Chicago Cubs—fulfilling my husband's dream.

On my first day back on the set after Jamie was born, ABC announced that I was David's new cohost. *Steve Fenn/© 1986 American Broadcasting Companies, Inc.*

Sammy Davis, Jr., meeting my infant daughter, Jamie, on the *GMA* set. *Joe McNally/© 1986 American Broadcasting Companies, Inc.*

Every day is Mother's Day. Interviewing my mom *(above)* and my mother-in-law, Joie Krauss *(below)*—on the set of *Mother's Day*, a real family affair. *Michael Krauss Productions.*

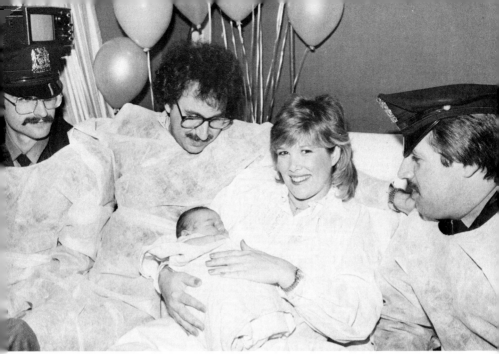

Thanks to two of New York's finest, Lindsay was born in a hospital and not on a highway. *Donna Svennevik/© 1986 American Broadcasting Companies, Inc.*

Michael briefing Jamie for a spot we are about to tape on "Mother's Minutes." *Michael Krauss Productions.*

Our whole family was involved in the taping of *Your Newborn Baby*, a videocassette for new parents. *Michael Krauss Productions.*

The official *Good Morning America* portrait of David Hartman and me.
Eddie Adams/© 1986 American Broadcasting Companies, Inc.

In my *GMA* dressing room, my assistant, Debbie Bergenfeld, helps keep my on-air wardrobe in order.
Fred Watkins/© 1986 American Broadcasting Companies, Inc.

Chatting over the fire with His Royal Highness Prince Charles at United World College in New Mexico. *© 1986 John Bryson.*

With the Grimaldis of Monaco: *(from left to right)* His Royal Highness Prince Rainier, yours truly, Princess Stephanie, and Prince Albert in Los Angeles. *Long Photography, Inc./© 1986 American Broadcasting Companies, Inc.*

paign. As soon as he became a viable candidate I was taken off the case, so to speak.

Then Phil Nye, the man who had hired me for *Eyewitness News,* was replaced by Ron Tindiglia. He brought in an assistant news director who was the first person at Channel 7 who ever sat down and showed me some of the finer points of putting a story together. He explained how to mix pictures and "sound bites" (the words of the people on the scene), how to vary the pattern, and how to change opening and closing shots to avoid repetition. He and I spent a considerable amount of time together, worked hard on stories, and quite naturally went out to lunch from time to time. He then began to try to turn our working relationship into something more personal. It may have been naive of me to think that you can work with a man, have lunch with a man, and not have other thoughts in mind, but to me it was not an impossibility. Besides, I was dating Michael, our relationship was getting serious, and I wasn't interested in anyone else.

But this man was openly upset by my lack of interest, and to get even with me he started killing my stories, that is, he kept them off the air for one reason or another. I knew that these were good stories and all of them were on deadline, but he found ways to keep them off the news—and he had the power to do it.

Not only was this bad for my ego and my reputation with the other reporters but it also cost me money. A television reporter is paid a base salary and an additional fee for each piece that appears on the air. If you don't get on the air you earn less money. But it wasn't the money as much as it was his attitude and what that attitude said to me as a woman and to other women who only want to work as equals. That attitude was that women are not equal to men, that he could treat me as a sex object, and that when I didn't respond to that treatment, he was free to seek revenge. If a man asks another man to lunch and he refuses it isn't taken as a sexual rebuff, but that's not true for a woman. Lunch is sometimes more than lunch in male-female relationships, dinner is more than dinner, and bed is more than a place to sleep.

At any rate this man had gone on this way for a couple of

months when I decided to take matters into my own hands. I took him into my office, shut the door behind us, and said, "You're about to get it. I'm not putting up with this any longer."

He played dumb but he knew what I was talking about.

"You've been keeping my stories off the air for no valid reason," I said. "I know it and you know it and everyone else in the newsroom knows it. I talked to my lawyer and he advised me to file a suit against you and WABC-TV for sexual harassment and sexual discrimination and he says we'll win." Before he could say anything I told him, "You have a chance to rectify the situation right now but if I see another hint of what you've been doing I'm filing suit."

He knew he was in trouble and he began to get red in the face. He just stood there for a minute with his hands on his hips and then, to his credit, he said, "I'm sorry. You're right. It's unprofessional of me and it won't happen again."

He walked out and we both went back to work. It didn't happen again but after that he spoke to me only in the line of duty, and if looks could kill he fired enough shots at me to kill me many times over. But the important thing is that he didn't drop any more of my stories after our confrontation, and I felt vindicated for myself and for other women in the same position.

I must admit, however, that his help had put my reporting on a higher plane and I continued to improve from that point on. I was becoming more confident in every aspect of my work.

Not only was I doing my regular reporting but, to the dismay of many, I began anchoring the local Sunday-evening news and in a few more months there was talk of my anchoring the local news sometime in the not too distant future.

But my immediate and distant future would have been greatly in doubt if my friend Doug Johnson had not been co-anchoring the six-o'clock news with me one night in December. At the very least he saved me from great embarrassment and at the most he saved my on-air career.

As I've said, New York is full of different ethnic groups and the Jewish population is one of the most prominent of them. Even non-Jews spice their everyday speech with Yiddish expressions and the Jewish holidays are important aspects of life for all New Yorkers—where else outside of Jerusalem do they close the public schools on Rosh Hashanah and Yom Kippur, the most sacred of Jewish holidays?

That night, I was about to go on the air to tell the story of Chanukah, the Festival of Lights, which is often correlated with the Christian holiday of Christmas. Being from Sacramento, where the Jewish population is not highly visible, I had not been exposed to the names of the Jewish holidays. I looked at the word "Chanukah" as it was written in the script, I pronounced it to myself as "Cha-*new*-kah," and it sounded all right to me. Just before we went on the air, Doug said, "Joan, you're doing the Chanukah story, right?" He pronounced it "*Ha*-na-kah."

"Right, I've got that one," I said, not really catching his pronunciation.

"Don't forget to say "*Ha*-na-kah," he repeated slowly and distinctly. It was a subtle and thoughtful way of telling me how to say the word, a word he realized I probably wouldn't know.

I said, "Oh God, you just saved my life, Doug, thanks."

When I got back to the newsroom, the writer, a nice Jewish boy from Brooklyn, said, with a smile on his face, "You did okay on that 'Cha-*new*-kah' story, Joan." To this day I don't know if that was a setup or not.

I could have made that mistake in Sacramento with no serious repercussions but in New York I might have been out on my ear the next morning. Today, I ask about any word I'm not a hundred percent sure about and I'll ask more than once if necessary. Another lesson learned.

Then, for no accountable reason, my career started moving, and moving quickly. I got a call from Woody Fraser, who was then the executive producer of *Good Morning America.* "I'd like to talk to you about doing some spots on *GMA,*" he said. "Could you come over and meet with me?"

Could I come over? "Of course. When do you want to get together?" I answered.

We made an appointment for the next morning and after I hung up I remembered that just before I came to New York for my interview with WABC-TV I had turned on the ABC station in Sacramento just to see what their programming was like. One of the shows I watched was called *A.M. America,* the forerunner of *GMA,* with Bill Buetel and Stephanie Edwards. As I sat there watching, I thought to myself that if I went to work for ABC in New York I could end up doing something like that. It was a wild fantasy but the idea appealed to me. I'm sure it was the first time I'd thought about the potential of a career in television at a higher level than anchoring the news in Sacramento. In retrospect, that kind of thinking was a little premature. I'd been working in TV for less than a year and until my invitation to interview in New York my sights had been set no higher than that local anchor job. In fact, when Woody Fraser called, I had only started to think seriously about the possibilities of anchoring the evening news at Channel 7.

Woody explained that they were trying to put together a "family" of people who would be seen semiregularly on the relatively new program, *Good Morning America,* and they were thinking about me to do occasional pieces on new products and changes in the American life-style. He wasn't any more specific than that because he didn't actually know himself exactly what these spots would look like.

David Hartman and Nancy Dussault had been the hosts of *GMA* since its inception in November 1975. The rest of the "family" that had been put together initially included Rona Barrett, Erma Bombeck, former New York mayor John Lindsay, Jack Anderson, Geraldo Rivera, Howard Cosell, Dr. Lee Salk, Helen Gurley Brown, and financial advisor Sylvia Porter.

After Woody reviewed the rather nebulous guidelines of the job, he said, "Would you be interested in joining that group?"

"Absolutely," I said, "but how did you happen to find me?"

"You work in television in New York," he answered, "and most of the people who make decisions about television live in New York. We watch the local programs. That means you are seen by television executives from all the networks, by producers, directors, and all the rest. When they see something they like they go after it, and it's a whole lot easier because the people they see are already here, not out in the sticks someplace."

Woody went on: "We're also considering adding Cheryl Tiegs to the staff to do fashion pieces. It's all part of an effort to get some fresh young faces on the air to attract a younger audience and give the *Today* show a run in the ratings."

I reiterated my interest and said, "I'm not sure you know it, but I was a consumer reporter before I came to work for *Eyewitness News* so I'm more qualified for this kind of work than you may have realized."

"Great, you'll be terrific. I'll call Channel 7 and set everything up," he said.

Fraser called and told Ron Tindiglia, my boss at the time, that he'd like to have me do some work for *GMA* and that since all the pieces would be done live, I'd be through by 9 A.M., and therefore the assignments wouldn't interfere at all with my work at the station.

This may appear to be a simple act of corporate communication but there seems to be a built-in animosity between the local stations and the network. The local stations listen to what the network has to say but they resent it greatly when someone takes their talent. If you think about it, it's understandable. After all, the people at *Eyewitness News* plucked me out of California, they took a real chance, they invested a lot of time, energy, and money in me, they made me known, and now the network comes along and "borrows" me part-time. To make matters worse, *GMA* had just done the same thing with Geraldo Rivera, who had been a Channel 7 reporter. But in Geraldo's case, the part-time became full-time after a very short while.

Channel 7 was justifiably mad and I was in the middle. I made my bread and butter there and I did owe them a good deal, but the opportunity to work, even part-time, in national television was too good to turn down. It became my job to keep both parties happy and that meant being available when *GMA* wanted me and always being available for my regular assignments on *Eyewitness News.* Many days, that meant beginning at *GMA* at

5:00 A.M. and working at Channel 7 until after the late news at 11:30 P.M. I did both for more than three years; it was hectic but worth it. More important, it was those little new-product spots that finally landed me the job as cohost at *GMA*.

Things were really churning in my cosmos. One morning I got a call from Dustin Hoffman. I was sitting at my typewriter when the phone rang on the next desk. One of the other reporters picked up the phone, listened for a second, then just shook her head and said, "For you, Joan. Dustin Hoffman."

I took the receiver and said, "This is Joan Lunden."

"This is Dustin Hoffman," a man said. I wasn't sure if this was a crank call or not, but it certainly sounded like *the* Dustin Hoffman. "Joan," he went on, "I'm in the process of casting for a movie and I'm looking for a woman with a combination of softness and authority. I saw you on the air the other night and I'd like to meet with you to discuss a part I have in mind. Could we meet soon and talk about it?"

I calmly answered, "Yes, we certainly could," and though my voice was calm my mind was racing. We arranged a breakfast meeting for the following morning and strangely, I thought, I was to pick him up at his apartment. Then we'd go to a place in his neighborhood for coffee.

I immediately called my agent, Richard Leibner. "Richard, I just got a call from Dustin Hoffman. He wants to talk over a project with me and I wanted to let you know."

"Come on. Give me a break," he said, "you're not an actress, number one, and number two, his movie *Marathon Man* was a bomb. You try something like this and you'll be giving up a great career to become an out-of-work actress."

"That may be true, Richard," I said, "but I still want to meet with him."

"Fine," he said. "So do I."

I gave him the details and the next morning he met me and we went to Dustin's apartment together. I have the feeling Dustin was surprised to see two of us there, but there was nothing he could do about it. As we all walked up the street I couldn't help picture Ratso Rizzo, the slightly deformed character Dustin played in *Midnight Cowboy,* limping up the street alongside me. I'm a good four inches taller than he is, and I figured if this was a role where I'd be playing opposite him, I'd better think short.

We stopped in a coffee shop and while Richard and I ordered coffee and toasted bagels, Dustin ordered a cup of hot water. He then opened his briefcase and took out some bags of herbal tea. While his tea was brewing he told us about his movie.

He explained some of the plot and the role he was thinking of for me. It was a female attorney representing his character in a child custody battle. During the trial a relationship would develop and that was where the plot thickened. "I must tell you," he said, "the role would require some nudity, not gratuitous nudity, but the kind that advances the script."

I almost burst out laughing at the thought of me naked in a movie, but instead I said, "I don't like the idea of nudity at all, and since I've never acted before I'm not sure I want to try a movie anyway, but it's certainly flattering to be asked. Let me toss the idea around." We shook hands and Richard and I left him with his home-brewed tea.

Richard had gotten a big kick out of the meeting, but as we walked down Madison Avenue we both knew that it was a bit of a laugh. The next day I got a call from Dustin's office, telling me that the director was going to have to talk to me too. It all seemed rather pointless but instead of saying no I left the door open.

Before that meeting could be arranged, however, I got another call from Dustin. It was a Friday night. Michael was at my apartment and we were talking about the future. It was the first time Michael had actually broached the topic of getting married. Right in the middle of that conversation, the phone rang. Since Michael was closer he answered. His eyes caught mine and as he handed me the phone he said, "For you. Dustin Hoffman."

Dustin said he thought it would be a good idea for us to get together on an informal basis. He suggested we go out for a drink. I begged off and after I hung up I felt uncomfortable about the whole situation. I decided I'd better call off what was really just a silly dream anyway.

Later, the movie hit the theaters; it was, of course, *Kramer vs. Kramer*. The movie was a smash hit, but I've never regretted saying no, and I have to credit Michael and Richard for advising me on that one. My movie career was probably on permanent hold, but it had all started and ended so suddenly that I hadn't had time to fantasize much about it.

Not long after my meeting with Dustin, I got a call from a television production company that was developing a new game show to be called *Pass the Buck*. They were interested in a female host for the show, something they felt the industry was ready for. For the fun of it, I went to meet with them and happened to walk in on what is called a "development meeting." It's actually a brainstorming session in which people throw out ideas about how a show might work. One fellow was saying, "Here's the way it goes," and he was talking as fast as he could. "You ask the first person a question and if they don't know the answer they pass the buck to their partner and if the partner can't answer the question they pass the buck to other team and if they can't answer it they pass the buck back to you and you win the game. Got it?" There were half a dozen people sitting around the room and at that point they all seemed to be saying, "We could do that but maybe we could do this," "Or we could do this," and "Maybe we could do this." I had never seen one of these idea sessions before and it was like a crazy house.

As I watched and listened, I only had one thought—it was obvious that the prime prerequisite for the job of host on *Pass the Buck* would be the ability to speak incredibly fast without taking a breath for minutes at a time. While the "development" continued, the producer and I met in a corner. He explained some of the details to me and I listened carefully. I had made my decision before he finished. I thanked him kindly for his interest in me and said, "I really don't think the idea is for me." Still, it was fun to see this slice of television life and I laughed to myself as I walked back to the office.

Then, incredible as it may seem, only a week or so later I got another call, this time from Norman Lear's office. I was told they were preparing a new prime-time situation comedy for NBC and they were interested in talking to me about it. The show would be called *Coast to Coast* and it would be patterned after *The Love Boat,* only it would be the flying version, taking place on an airplane. As on *The Love Boat* there were to be several main characters, in this case two pilots and two female flight attendants, and they were thinking of me as one of the flight attendants. There would also be appearances by big-name guest stars who would round out the cast each week.

I was again excited and flattered. As usual I called Richard Leibner and as usual he was aghast. This time, however, we pursued it a bit, even to the point of discussing the fee for my doing the pilot and the logistics of my doing something for another network. But in the end we again said no. When we had come to our decision, Richard said to me, "I'm going to call and tell them no, but I don't want to hear from you six months from now if this thing turns out to be a big hit. Promise you won't give me any of that 'I told you so' stuff."

I promised. But a few months later I opened up *People* magazine and saw an article that predicted the major female star of the next television season would come from a new show called *Coast to Coast.* I couldn't resist, so I clipped the article and sent it over to Richard anonymously. The very next week *Us* magazine carried an article about Fred Silverman, president of ABC Entertainment, moving to NBC and it went on to say where the axe was going to fall when he arrived in his new job. The first candidate, *Us* predicted, was going to be that new prime-time sitcom *Coast to Coast.* I kept expecting Richard to send me that article but he never did.

After that, things settled down and I went back to the "mundane" world of local news. I had my exciting new job to look forward to and I had the distinct feeling that, fantasies notwithstanding, I was going to be at *Good Morning America* for a long time.

CHAPTER SIX

Good Morning America, *Finally*

The chance for me to do new-product and life-style stories opened the door at *Good Morning America* just a crack, but it was up to me to put my shoulder against that door and force it open all the way. I had to make these two-to-three-minute pieces, and myself, so interesting and so appealing that the program's executives would take notice. Then, if one of the cohosts quit or was fired, they would know who was ready and waiting in the wings. This may sound aggressive but I had learned that a certain amount of aggressiveness was necessary if one was to get ahead in television, and though I wasn't willing to step on people on the way up, I was willing to press any advantage I could get.

The first thing I had to do, however, was figure out what a new-product story was all about. Woody Fraser hadn't explained exactly what the reports would entail because, let's face it, the concept was new. Remember, I had been a consumer reporter so I hadn't misrepresented my credentials. However, now I would be doing something more than consumer reporting; I would be focusing on what was ahead for consumers, and it would be up to me to uncover products before they were offered to the public.

So once again, I had to learn a job from the ground up, something that was becoming a habit and something I was getting very good at. As usual there were no precedents, no models to follow, so I had to cut my own trail. I met with Fraser in his office and we talked over a number of ideas, finally settling on an opening piece called "Spare Tires."

This was in 1976, at a time when, because of a rubber shortage, auto companies were selling cars without spare tires. Then they came up with a substitute, a small-size spare tire that was designed to get you only to the next gas station, where the flat tire could be fixed or a new tire purchased. My spot was supposed to explain the purpose of these new tires and demonstrate how to use them.

Michael Krauss was the senior producer of *GMA* at the time and he helped me put that spot together. We decided to show that these little tires were easy to handle by having me pick one up, roll it around, and bounce it on the floor. This was supposed to prove that they were manageable (even for a woman) and durable enough to make it those few miles to the next garage. It was a lively little segment and everyone seemed to like it.

After the spare tires, however, I was on my own. I would take a bunch of ideas to the producers, we would go over them, and then choose the two or three that sounded best. Then I had to do the research to see if they actually were decent ideas. That part was fairly easy. The hard part was building up a network of contacts who would inform me of new ideas as they came up. This would have been more difficult to do while carrying out my other assignments if I hadn't been lucky. I was able to get an intern (a student who worked for me for credit in journalism school) to do a lot of the leg work. Michael Horowitz researched while I was out covering fires. This was another source of irritation for the *Eyewitness News* staff. They couldn't figure out why I had an intern and they didn't. Little did they know that I had had the good sense not to ask if it was all right. I just did it.

Michael Horowitz and I were able to establish that network of contacts by obtaining directories of American trade associations and writing personal letters to hundreds of product development departments. Then I would call the public relations departments of all the major manufacturers of consumer goods and would ask them to put me on their lists to receive information about products that were coming out in the next six to twelve months. I would tell them that if the product met my needs I'd get it on the air. The response was tremendous. After all, what company would not want their new creation, serious or frivolous, to be shown on television to millions of people at one time?

So I was responsible for digging up the products, evaluating and choosing the best of them, getting the ideas approved by the producer, writing the scripts, getting the items to the studio, and presenting them on the air with either David Hartman or Nancy Dussault. I did two or three of these spots a month and that was plenty because I was still working full-time at Channel 7. I was busy.

And evidently I was doing well because it wasn't long before Woody Fraser asked me to do some of these spots from the field, that is, to go out with a producer and a crew to do stories with more depth and breadth. This caused even more problems for me at WABC because they had to give me time off to do these spots; that meant other reporters had to fill in for me. The first field piece I did was on a new type of television system in Columbus, Ohio. Called Qube, it was an experiment in "talk-back" television. The viewer could sit at home and respond to questions or give opinions by pressing buttons on a special control box. It so happened that Michael was the producer on this one and we traveled to Columbus together. We spent three days there working on the story, and Michael, with his extremely creative mind, put together a terrific spot and at the same time taught me a lot about flair and production techniques.

And he should know about creativity. Michael is one of those rare people who knew what he wanted to be from the time he was a little boy—a producer, a creator. When he was seven his father took him to a live radio show in his hometown of Detroit and he was hooked. By age ten he was studying radio acting with one of the early masters of the medium, John Todd, who was known to listeners as Tonto on the Lone Ranger show.

Within a year, Michael was acting on an NBC radio program called *Storyland*. At the same time he formed a band called "Two

Notes and a Beat" (he was the drummer) and the group played regularly on a local TV show.

Throughout high school and college Michael worked as a musician and studied television communications. He landed his first big TV job as producer at WXYZ-TV, where he was one of the creators of the "A.M. show" concept for the ABC stations. That concept was actually the forerunner of *Good Morning America*.

From Detroit Michael moved on to Chicago with ABC but left that job to fulfill his dream to produce *The Mike Douglas Show*. Eventually he returned to ABC as the producer of the *A.M. New York* program and this led to his move to *GMA*, which he joined at its inception. He played a major role as producer of *GMA* during its formative years.

Later, NBC, aware of Michael's talk-show expertise and his incredible track record for raising the ratings of every show he ever worked on, hired him away. There, he produced *Today* for NBC for several years. Eventually, he left *Today,* formed his own production company, and is now creating and producing all types of radio and television programs.

Anyway, after the spot on Qube TV ran, the program received a lot of positive mail about me and the spot itself. If it's possible to pinpoint a time when your career really starts to flower, then this was it for me. I have a feeling that it was that report from Columbus that started the producers at *GMA* thinking about asking me to come to the program on a full-time basis.

It was also at that time that Nancy Dussault was on her way out at *GMA* and I was interviewed for her job. And of course, that's when they hired Sandy Hill, also known as "that gal with the long legs." I don't want to make it sound as if I didn't like Sandy, because I did. It wasn't her fault that she took "my job." She didn't know me at all at that time so I could hold nothing personal against her. In fact, after she came to the show we became friends. Besides, my star was still in ascendance and I couldn't be too unhappy about the way things were going, even though I had lighted the candle at both ends—Channel 7 and *GMA*.

In the next few months I became a full-fledged, part-time member of the *GMA* family. When Sandy was sick, on vacation, or on location, I was often asked to do "People in the News" segments as well as the commercials she would normally do. The commercials were done right in the studio, before the show. For example, at about 6:00 A.M. a troop of dogs might be led in and we'd tape an Alpo commercial that would run that same day. Still, I had not done any cohosting and that is what I was hoping to get a chance to do.

While I was hoping, fate was taking me by the hand. As I said, my apartment was near the ABC studios and for the most part that had been a mixed blessing. The good part was that it was easy to get to work and to get home. The bad part was that when something blew up in New York City (a frequent occurrence) and *Eyewitness News* needed someone in a hurry they always called me since I could get to the station in five minutes flat. Sometimes the calls were important and sometimes not, but my proximity put me first on the call list.

One Saturday night Michael and I were just about to sit down to dinner when the phone rang. It was almost eleven and we were eating late because we had gone to a movie. The roast I had prepared was ready to come out of the oven and the candles were lit. Michael answered the phone. I heard him say, "Okay, right away." He hung up and said, "Joan, you're anchoring the news in seven minutes. Don't ask questions, just put on a blouse and get down to the station." I threw on a clean blouse, snatched up my purse, jumped into the elevator, and ran to the studio. I was wearing tennis shoes, blue jeans, and a silk blouse.

On the studio sets the anchors couldn't be seen below the desk anyway, so they rarely wore anything formal below the waist. It was jeans in the winter and shorts in the summer, with sneakers all the time. I know that it's hard to imagine Peter Jennings sitting there that way but he could easily do it; a woman could be eight months pregnant and you'd never have known because the desks covered everything.

At any rate, I arrived breathless and it was just like the movies. As I got to the studio door the producer was saying,

"One minute to air." I quickly pulled my hair into a ponytail, turned my purse upside down on the desk, grabbed a lipstick, and shoved everything else onto the floor. Things were rolling all over the place and it made a terrible racket. Then we were on. I just sat there, cool and calm as you please, and read whatever came on the prompter. During the first commercial I read the copy for the next stories and put on some mascara. In the next commercial I read over more stories and put on some eye shadow. By the end of the program, the people watching at home, if they were watching closely, must have wondered what in the world was going on—I was transforming myself in front of their eyes.

We whipped through the news, weather, and sports without a hitch and at 11:32 I was on my way back to the apartment. The roast was still warm in the oven and Michael and I sat down to eat. When I'd had a minute or two to relax, I said, "Michael, do you realize what I just did?" "Yeah," he said with a laugh, "you just made four hundred dollars." I had also performed with a minimum of preparation and, to say the least, my outfit and makeup were minimal as well. But it was one of those experiences you don't forget.

But living close to the station really paid off in a big way one morning as well. That morning I was sound asleep when the phone rang. I reached over, picked up the receiver, and said "Hello," as I stared bleary-eyed at my clock radio to see if I'd accidently overslept. It was 7:31. On the other end of the line was the frantic voice of one of the *GMA* producers who asked, "Are you watching the show?"

"No, I was actually sleeping," I answered.

"Sorry to wake you," he said.

"That's okay," I said. "I had to get up anyway because the phone was ringing. Why should I be watching the show?" I asked as I reached over and switched on the set to see what he was talking about. Looking at the picture, I couldn't see anything wrong.

"Because both David and Sandy have laryngitis so bad they can hardly talk," he said.

"No kidding," I said, trying to figure out why he had called to tell me about two cases of laryngitis.

He quickly gave me the answer. "The problem is that it's so annoying people are going to be turning us off. We're going to lose audience. We need you to sit in for the rest of the program. How fast can you get here?" I was suddenly wide awake. I said, "How about ten minutes?"

"You're a lifesaver," he said. "Make it as soon as you can."

I flew out of bed, washed my face, and brushed my teeth in what seemed like one minute, put on a suit and blouse, heels and hose, ran a comb through my hair, and dashed out the door. I got to the studio a little after 8:00, and as I walked in, a mob of people surrounded me. The show was in the five-minute-news segment at the time and that would be followed by the weather, so we had about ten minutes to put everything together. While a hairstylist did a quick job on my hair, the makeup women put some color on my face and lips. Meanwhile, the producer ran through the next few minutes of script.

"There's a commercial following the weather," he said, "and coming out of the commercial, you'll be interviewing that woman over there with all the teenagers around her. She just opened a show on Broadway called *Runaways*. The kids are in the show. She seems a little quiet so you may have to pump her. Here are the questions. Take a look at them."

This wasn't much preparation for my debut as cohost on *Good Morning America* but that was all we had time for. I walked onto the set and sat down opposite the guest, took a look at the questions, got the cue from the floor director, and said, "Elizabeth Swados is here with us this morning to talk about her new show, *Runaways*. Good morning, Elizabeth."

It turned out that Elizabeth Swados was not the best person with whom to begin my career. She probably wasn't happy that her first big television exposure was with this substitute who had just run in off the street. Afterward I wasn't the least bit happy that this substitute had to face a person who seemed unfriendly at best, and curt at worst, for her first interview.

After that, during each commercial break the producer went

over the next item I'd be doing, and by 8:30, much to my surprise, I was feeling confident in my ability to do the job. I made it through the show with no major problems and everyone, including David and Sandy, congratulated me profusely after the sign off. It was one of those occasions where the understudy had come out of the wings and done a good job.

From that day on, I was called whenever they needed a substitute for Sandy, and I'm convinced that the way I handled myself in that emergency really sealed my future at *GMA.*

As proof, not long after that little stint, I was asked to come to *GMA* full-time to do commercials, to report from the field, and to be a substitute cohost. Suddenly things were going smoothly.

Unfortunately, the waters were not calm for long. Michael Krauss and I had been dating steadily for some time and we had announced we were getting married. Then he took another job, which was not bad in and of itself, except that it was as the producer of *Today, GMA*'s prime competition in the morning. Since I was subbing more and more often for Sandy, this "mixed marriage" was apparently a cause for concern at ABC—so much concern, in fact, that I got a call from one of the top brass asking me to stop by and see him. His office was at 1330 Avenue of the Americas. The numbers 1330 are like magic at ABC. All the executive offices are there and when you get a call from 1330 it's like a call from the White House. Your heartbeat rises and your palms start to sweat.

So I went to 1330 with some trepidation. When I walked into this huge executive office I saw the *Daily News* on the desk and could see that it was opened to the entertainment page, where I knew there was an article telling of Michael's new job at *Today* and how he "was planning to whip the pants off *GMA.*" The man was very direct. "We can't ask you this officially," he said, "but now that Michael is going to be at *Today* and you two are getting married, can we be certain that you won't reveal *GMA* secrets when the lights are out? When two people are under the covers they say things they might not say otherwise."

I was truly shocked that he would say something like that to me, but at the same time I thought it was one of the funniest comments I'd ever heard and I started to laugh. He added, "If you don't want to answer that, you can tell me to go to hell."

I said, "If all Michael and I will have to talk about under the covers is the morning shows then we're going to be in serious trouble." That broke the tension in the room so I went on. After all, I was only a sub cohost, I explained, I didn't go to production meetings, and I didn't even have an office at *GMA*. They let the matter drop, but that kind of thing does give you an idea of the extent of the paranoia that exists in the television business.

Believe it or not, there never was even the hint of a conflict of interest, but when David Hartman announced our marriage plans on the air one morning it did cause another kind of problem. David told our audience about us and then said, "And Michael, if you're listening in your control room downtown at the *Today* show right now, and of course you shouldn't be, congratulations." The problem was that ABC management was certain that people all over the country were changing channels to see if anything was happening on NBC and we'd lose audience. Eventually Michael left *Today* and formed his own company, which made him happy—and ABC happy as well. I'm not sure I would ever have been asked to take the job as cohost permanently if Michael had still been at the other network.

Our wedding, in September 1978, was a major event. Since neither of us had ever been married before, we wanted to make it one of those events that we and our families would remember. Michael's father was unable to travel at the time, so we decided to have our formal ceremony in Detroit, where Michael grew up, and then to have another party in Sacramento for all those people who couldn't make it to Detroit.

This meant arranging two major social events 2,000 miles apart while I was working a full schedule for *Eyewitness News* in New York. Nearly everything, therefore, was done over the telephone and I had to squeeze those calls in between assignments. I hardly had time to shop for a wedding dress. Michael and I talked long-distance to Detroit and Sacramento four and five times a day for nearly a month. We found the caterers, the florists, the bands, the rooms for the receptions, and did it all by phone. Michael's mother and my mother were able to take care of some of the details in Detroit and Sacramento, but the bulk of the planning was done by us from New York. *Hectic* is a word that comes close to describing the situation but it was more like a continual fire drill.

Well, it was all worth it. A whole group of us flew from New York to Detroit, and some of Michael's friends and mine flew in from other parts of the country. My brother Jeff won the prize for long-distance travel, however. He flew 12,000 miles from his job in Saudi Arabia to give me away. Michael's brother, Perry, was best man and Diane Chandler, my roommate in Mexico, was my maid of honor. The ceremony was absolutely beautiful and the reception was happy and sentimental and fun.

Then, two days later, with barely a moment to reflect, Michael, my family, and I, along with several friends, flew to Sacramento. The following night we had what amounted to a repeat performance. There was dinner, dancing, champagne, and more fun and sentiment, and it all went like clockwork. Considering the dual arrangements and the fact that it had all been done on the phone, I was amazed and pleased that everything had gone so well.

When Michael and I returned to New York I was right back in the middle of things. In preparation for my taking the job at *GMA*, Squire Rushnell, ABC vice-president in charge of *GMA* at that time, took me to a private production studio to tape some sample commercials for Alpo, Cotton Incorporated, and American Express. He wanted to see how I would appeal to the advertisers. The tapes turned out well and he told me that the clients all thought I was terrific. Squire, therefore, was pleased and all the groundwork was laid.

As it turned out, when the official offer was made, I had to say no. How could I say no to that kind of opportunity, you might ask? How could I say no to something so big? How could I say no to a job I'd wanted for so long? How could I say no after I'd already taken so many less promising chances? Believe me, it wasn't easy. It took a lot of soul-searching, and hours of discussion with Michael and my agent. But the way I saw it, it was a question of (a) economics and (b) the long-term future. Through my agent, *GMA* made me an offer to do primarily commercials and field reporting. There would be some subbing for Sandy from time to time. That was *not* a good financial deal for me because, working on *Eyewitness News* and part-time on *GMA,* I was already making twice what they offered. Imagine how it would affect you if, suddenly, your income was cut by fifty percent. But it was the future that bothered me even more than the cut in pay. What would happen if after six months or so *GMA* decided that I wasn't really what they were looking for after all? Once you've started selling dog food and Polish sausage it pretty well spells the end of any news career.

I knew Squire Rushnell would be none too happy with me because he would have to go back and tell his happy advertisers that the woman they had liked so much had other plans.

When I told Squire, it was a little scary. After all, he was my boss and I had to explain. We met in one of the executive dining rooms on the fortieth floor of 1330. "I'm glad they liked it," I said, "but I just can't take the chance with my career right now, not to mention a cut in pay that is close to one half what I'm making." He listened but he was still angry, and I couldn't really blame him.

If my performance as an emergency substitute had put me in solid at *GMA,* this little move on my part nearly shut me out of any future consideration. The program still needed to hire someone to do the job I'd been asked to perform. They found Jeanne Wolf for the job and my appearances on *GMA* were immediately reduced by 90 percent. If you remember what happened to Jeanne Wolf, you'll see that my fears had been well placed. After only a short stint she was replaced by another woman, Candace Hasey.

I actually heard that Candace was being considered for the job from Richard Leibner. He called one day and said, "There is a woman from Texas who wants me to represent her for the job you turned down at *GMA.* Would you mind?"

I didn't scream but I should have. I said, "Richard, that's a direct conflict. You know I've lost ground at *GMA* and I want to regain it. Would I mind? You bet I'd mind."

He went on: "If you really look at this objectively I don't think your chances of gaining ground are very good. Squire Rushnell"—who had recommended that Hasey call Leibner for representation—"is really mad at you for not taking it when he offered it before."

"I know he's mad," I said, "but that's what agents are for, isn't it, to smooth things over and get what their clients want."

In that convoluted logic that agents often use, Leibner said, "I think if I get this other girl in there, it will get my foot in the door and then I'll eventually be able to do more for you at *GMA*."

"Great thinking, Richard," I said, "but if you represent her it certainly won't cause any conflict between us since you will no longer represent me as my agent."

As it turned out, by trying to play both ends against the middle, Leibner ended up with neither client. Candace Hasey went with someone else and I hired a lawyer instead of an agent to represent my interests.

The morning after talking to Leibner I ran into Sandy Hill in the hallway at *GMA*. She took a good look at me and said, "All right, you look depressed. What's up?"

"I won't be doing very much on the show anymore because, as you must know, they're going to hire Candace Hasey for the sub job," I told her.

"Who is that?" Sandy asked incredulously, and added vehemently, "Nobody said a word to me about a change being made."

I told her the whole story as I knew it. She thanked me and went straight to Squire Rushnell's office where, I heard, she exploded like a bomb because no one had told her and on closer inspection she thought Candace might be a prospective replacement for her at some point. Rushnell then called Richard Leibner and exploded. In turn Richard called me, and yes, another bomb exploded. He said, "Sandy went to Squire and told him the story you told her and she's mad as hell at everyone be-cause they didn't tell her anything." What surprised me was that Richard wasn't upset about what was happening to me, but rather was mad at me for telling Sandy.

"Richard," I said, "how was I supposed to know that Sandy hadn't been told? You people move us around like pawns in a chess game and it doesn't always work."

But eventually a time came when I wanted the *GMA* job, whatever the financial sacrifice, and I went out to get it.

There were two reasons for my decision. First, my contract with *Eyewitness News* was up for renewal at the end of 1979 and I could see the squeeze play coming. Channel 7 thought I was more loyal to *GMA* than to them, and *GMA* was not happy about being turned down before. In fact, Squire Rushnell proba-bly said to himself, "I hope someday she wants this job because I'd love to tell her no." There was also a new man hired as news director for *Eyewitness News* and he hadn't said five words to me in five weeks. I was apparently invisible, I wasn't getting any good assignments, and I could smell trouble. One day as I was passing his office I stuck my head in and said, with a smile and a wave, "It's been nice talking to you," and kept going. Yes, I felt that my time at the station was coming to an end.

Second, Michael and I had been married nearly a year and we wanted to have children. Street reporting is not the best job for pregnant women or for women with young children. It is a job in which you are on twenty-four-hour call, a job that gets you out on the street early and keeps you out there until all hours of the night. I didn't want a ten-hour day that would keep me from raising my children. Now was the time to take a chance.

Still, I didn't want to burn all my bridges, so I tried not to alienate the *Eyewitness News* people, in case I wanted to re-sign with them. But I faced a bigger problem in that I had to win back Squire Rushnell's support in order to get to *GMA*. I needed some good advice from someone with power so I decided to go straight to the top. I summoned up all my nerve and called Elton Rule, then chairman of the board of ABC, and asked him for an appointment. We were not total strangers because we had met a couple of times at ABC functions and I knew he was from Sacramento; I felt that sharing the same hometown might be of some help.

When I got him on the phone I said, "Mr. Rule, I'm one of your many employees and I have a problem. I'm about to be eased out of two jobs in this company and I think it would be a shame for me and the company if that happened."

He was extremely gracious and complimentary. "I enjoy you on the air very much," he said, "and I wouldn't want that to happen. I'll be glad to talk with you about it, Joan," he went on, "so if you'll just make an appointment with my secretary for three o'clock tomorrow afternoon, we can have a talk."

The next afternoon at 2:55 I walked up the front steps at 1330 with my heart in my mouth. I checked in with the guard who pointed me to the elevator and I pressed the button for the thirty-ninth floor. I had been to the ABC executive dining rooms on the fortieth floor once before (when I told Squire Rushnell no, with sweaty palms), but I had never been to the executive suite. The dining rooms are posh but the executive floor is even more so. I stepped off the elevator into carpet that seemed about four inches thick and approached the secretary, who was sitting behind a mammoth desk. I told her who I was and she picked up the phone to tell Mr. Rule that I was there. As she did so she pointed to his office. The door, which extended from the floor to the ceiling, opened with a slight "whoosh" as if it were breaking a vacuum seal, and I was inside. I have seen some nice offices, but his was spectacular. His office is bigger than some entire apartments, with windows that command an awesome view of Manhattan. The walls are done in rich wood and his marble desk sits well away from the wall. I've discovered that one of the signs of corporate power is the distance between a person's desk and the wall. The farther away from the wall a person sits, the more power the person has. Elton Rule's desk was a long way from the wall.

We greeted each other and I sat in a plush leather chair in

front of his desk. I planned to play it cool. I wanted to be strong but I wanted to evoke some sympathy for my position without breaking into tears.

After the briefest of chats about the weather, I began: "I feel caught in the middle," I said. "I don't think *Eyewitness News* has any plans for me. I thought I was going to be the first woman anchor but I was passed over for Rose Ann Scamardella. So not getting an anchor slot, I have probably devoted more time to *GMA* than the people at *Eyewitness News* would like. They don't consider me part of their team. But at the same time the people at *GMA* have asked me to come with them and I turned the offer down. I think for sound reasons. Nonetheless, I'm sure it left them with a bad taste in their mouths."

He sat there nodding and at one point said, "I'm beginning to get the picture." I wanted him to say, "God, Joan, we need you."

"I think I'm going to have to talk to the other networks," I concluded, without wanting it to sound like a threat, since he could easily have said, "If that's the way you feel, go right ahead."

Instead he said, "I'll look into the situation because it would be a shame for us to lose you. You're a delightful young woman who has worked hard. I'll call you."

He'd given me a half hour of his time to plead my case and I didn't know if I'd pulled it off or not, but I was glad I'd pressed the issue. I also have to admit that despite my best efforts I had to reach for a tissue at the end of our talk.

The next day Rule called and I was nervous when I picked up the phone. "It was nice talking with you yesterday," he said. "I've made a couple of calls and I suggest that you pursue *GMA*."

I thanked him and hung up, not exactly sure what that meant. I could interpret his advice in several ways. Was I supposed to forget all about Channel 7 because I was finished there any-way—they don't want me back, and this was his sensitive way of telling me? Or did he mean that he had smoothed things over with Squire Rushnell and set things up for me at *GMA*? No matter. I pursued *GMA* because, after all, that's what I wanted.

I finished up my contract with *Eyewitness News* and on January 1, 1980, I started on *GMA* as official reporter and substitute cohost. This time, however, there was more than a strong implication that Sandy Hill would soon be gone and the job could be mine. It was only a few weeks later that she went off to cover the Winter Olympics at Lake Placid. Pat Collins, the entertainment reporter for *GMA,* and I shared the cohost duties during that period. This was very good for me because I got to work at the job without all the pressure of being official cohost.

And this time I wasn't the new kid on the block. After all the work I'd done on the show, I knew how to handle the mechanics of the cohost's job and I felt comfortable with David Hartman and with the other people on the *GMA* staff. I thought, therefore, that I could relax a little.

It's true that I was no stranger to the job but a substitute doesn't have the same day-to-day responsibilities and worries as the regular cohost, or the additional obligations of the office work—including daily briefings, correspondence with viewers, seasonal wardrobe selections, *GMA* and network promotional appearances, speaking engagements, and all the rest. In those first few weeks, then, I had to combine my previous experience with a whole new set of responsibilities. And for what seemed like the twentieth time in my career I was getting my training on the job.

As far as being on the air, however, I hit the ground running. There was no break-in time, but as I've said before, there is always something new to be learned. The first thing I learned was that it isn't as easy to do the show every day as it is to come in a few days here, an occasional week there. The toll of those early mornings seems to add up, and the first few weeks, when I hadn't changed my evening schedule in order to get to bed early every night, I was always tired, though I'm sure it didn't show.

Next I had to learn to "put on a happy face" regardless of how I felt or how tired I might be. I had to get it into my mind that I was talking to people who had just switched off the alarm clock and switched on the television set. They weren't quite awake yet and I had to wake them gently with a smile and a short summary of what had happened while they were asleep. I had to learn to balance likability with credibility carefully. Clearly, this is much easier to do if everything is perfect in your life. Unfortunately that is not always the case with anyone. You may have a headache, a sore throat, a sick baby, or you may have had an argument with your husband that is still unresolved. There are always things to be concerned about in your life and sometimes they are more disconcerting than others.

I decided that my situation is no different from that of anyone else who has to get up and go to work, except that most people only have to pretend everything is right with the world for a few people. I have to pretend for millions. I don't consider myself an actress at all but when the red light goes on you become something of an actress: You must immediately put all of the other facets of your life behind you and talk to the viewers in a way that makes them feel that the world is still spinning on its axis and that they have a friend who's steady and reliable every morning.

Let me give you a minor example. About four days after I came to *GMA* full-time I was scheduled to do an interview that I wanted to do and had been thoroughly briefed on. Five minutes before airtime, the producer told me the interview had been switched and given to someone else. I was still feeling my way at that time and felt deflated by the news. Five minutes later I had to inflate myself and face the cameras with a big smile. The problem is not so much that the piece was changed, but that I wasn't told until I was ready to go on the air.

Despite the fact that producers should know better than to upset the talent immediately before the show, they still do it from time to time. Being on the air is stressful enough and adding to that stress makes no sense. It's like a doctor telling you, "Remember, right after breakfast you're having brain surgery." You sit a little uncomfortably after that sort of news. But the point is, the viewer doesn't want to know that I had a problem and I can't let on that things are a little off center at that moment.

Then there was the lesson of total concentration. In many interviews you're dealing with a nervous person, sometimes even when that person is a professional performer, so you have to maintain your concentration on the line of questioning in order to keep your guest or guests on the track. In theory, all you have to do is pay strict attention to the subject at hand for about four and a half minutes. The problem is that the subject can range from lawn care to piloting the space shuttle. Clearly, all subjects are not equally riveting.

Have you ever been talking with someone, standing there nodding like one of those ducks that dip their beaks in the water, but not hearing a word the person has been saying? You recognize the feeling, don't you? Well, you can't let that happen on television or you're a dead duck, because you don't know what to talk about next. Your guest may have already covered the points you plan to talk about, and you can't say, "Would you mind repeating that for the people on the West Coast?"

I'm sure that when this sort of lapse happens to you, your body immediately fires a full burst of adrenaline into your veins and you become instantly alert. You have total recall of everything that's happened for the last twenty years, but unfortunately you can't remember a thing that has happened in the last sixty seconds. At that point you're on your own.

Well, that's the way it is on TV all the time. If you let your concentration falter you're really on your own, and in front of millions of people. Talk about adrenaline—it gives you an overdose! There may be a dozen people on the set and another dozen in the control room when you're conducting an interview but they are powerless to help. You have to help yourself. This is a lesson quickly learned and never forgotten.

I have developed some tricks that help me avoid these semiconscious states. First, I write down my questions before the interview and then I read them to myself at least twice. I don't memorize them but I know them. Then I tell myself that I will be totally absorbed in ice hockey, or whatever, for four minutes, that I will truly love hockey and hockey players for those 240 seconds. Next, I pay strict attention to people's expected answers to my questions so I can skip questions if necessary or help the guest by partially filling in the answer if the guest gets stuck.

And finally, I maintain eye contact. I've found that, in a way, I hear through my eyes. This is sometimes disconcerting for guests because people aren't used to looking each other in the eye. But I have to try to make eye contact at all costs, no matter how much my guest may stray from side to side. I remember one interview in particular that illustrates this point. I was talking with a man who had been on the show before, an expert in economics, who completely blanked out on me. After we'd been on for about thirty seconds, I could see that his eyes were vacant. He wasn't hearing a word, and not only was I asking the questions, I had to answer them as well. He was sweating profusely and beginning to breathe rapidly and I knew his mouth was dry as sandpaper. We went to a commercial as soon as it was practical but he had simply been so tense that he was unable to respond.

David wasn't so lucky one morning. He was interviewing a female attorney when suddenly, when the camera was on a close-up shot of her, you could see her eyes roll back and her head slumped against the back of her chair. She had fainted dead away. And once again we went to a commercial. This is an unusual thing but it is understandable. In this case the woman knew her material and was well prepared, but the early-morning hour, several cups of coffee on an empty stomach, the bright lights, and the excitement had combined to get the best of her.

But I must admit that mastering these techniques is no insurance against fade-out. You can lose the continuity of your questions just as easily when you're having a great time and the interview is flowing beautifully. You may have gone two or three perfect minutes and then, since you've had such a nice conversation, it's hard to get back to the scripted interview and you can't figure out what's actually been covered and what hasn't.

All of this said, it doesn't mean that I can't get distracted anymore. I smile easily (my mother claims I was born smiling) and that can be a problem. I laugh just as easily as I smile, and when I'm interviewing comedians I have to be careful because it's often hard to know when they're laying a line on you and when they're saying something serious. This takes concentration. An interview I did with Bob Newhart offers a perfect example of this

problem. I am a big fan of his and I interviewed him for the first
time not long after I joined *GMA*. I wasn't really all that secure
at the time, and when I asked a question and he would answer in
his deadpan style, I had to ask myself if he was serious or joking.
I didn't want to laugh if it wasn't a joke, but when you're a
laugher that's hard to do. At one point in the interview David
Hartman came over and sat down with us; as we were finishing,
he joined in with the standard question "So where are you off to
next?" Newhart, with a perfectly straight face, said, "I'm leaving
for Chicago to visit my sister, who's a nun." When you consider
his style and delivery it could easily have been a set-up for a joke,
and out of the corner of my eye I saw David start to laugh. Fortunately he caught himself when Newhart quickly added, "My
sister runs a mission there . . ." and started a long story about it.

Bill Cosby, like Bob Newhart, is a chancy interview for a
laugher. Since he refuses to be preinterviewed (because he feels it
stifles his spontaneity) you never know which way he's going,
and it can scare the devil out of you to be faced with seven minutes of live national television time and have no clue as to what to
expect. Robin Williams is the same way. He's so free-flowing
that anything can happen.

At any rate, a good sense of humor and the ability to smile and
laugh help you survive the difficult times on the air, and your
ability to maintain that sense of humor is also appreciated by the
audience because it's a tension reliever. You often need a sense of
humor during the cooking spots on *GMA*. Because they are so
unpredictable and require a lot of rehearsal and time for food
preparation, they are usually taped. (When you come into the
studio in the morning, starving to death, you can smell whatever
is cooking, and it can drive you crazy.) Three complete sets of
everything needed in the recipe are always ready so that when
the egg whites get too stiff the first time through, someone can
come dashing in with a new bowl of eggs, or when the roast
starts to burn there is another nearly cooked roast to pop into the
oven. When these emergencies arise we start the necessary part
over.

We have had some awfully funny things happen, particularly when Julia Child is the guest chef. Julia is one of the world's great cooks but she is wild and funny—the studio crew loves it when she sloshes a lot of wine into her recipes; we always tease her about that. When her tapes play during the show and her high-pitched voice says, "This is Julia Child," the entire studio mimics in chorus, "This is Julia Child," and everyone cracks up. She has been around for several of these outbursts and got a big kick out of them, which is one of the things that makes her fun to work with. One morning she was making crêpes and she suddenly realized they were burning. She reached over, grabbed one of them to check, said, "Oh, too hot," and threw it over her shoulder. The hot crêpe plopped against the wall and slowly slid down to the floor, all on camera. Well, when something is funny, it's funny. Steve Bell, a relatively reserved man who usually does the news on *GMA,* was on the show with me that day and he completely fell apart. And yes, he flipped his crêpe over his shoulder, too. I thought he was going to have to be carried out. The entire studio was in hysterics. We got a ton of mail after that show and all of the writers said they loved it, mainly because they could see we were having fun—and besides, what Julia did is something that all cooks secretly want to do from time to time, just say what the heck and toss the whole thing over their shoulders.

Another thing that throws the studio into hysterics is something we call "verbal typos," those mistakes that occur at random somewhere between the brain and the mouth. You aren't even aware that you're making them.

For example, when I was at KCRA, I gestured to my national weather map during a newscast and said with authority, "This is the front of the position," meaning, of course, "the position of the front." This pales in the face of the verbal typo made by the regular weather forecaster a few days later, who referred to "a cold mare's ass heading our way," when he meant "cold air mass." When I was at WABC, Doug Johnson told me he once said, "Canadian Broadcorping Castration," when he meant "Canadian Broadcasting Corporation."

One of the funniest I've heard, however, was on *GMA.* Burt

Reynolds was being interviewed by David in the studio and they were discussing the image of actors. Burt remarked that he felt it was unfair for people to think of actors as not being bright. He went on to say that David was living proof that actors can be bright and intelligent since he deals with everything from heads of state to complex political and social issues.

David, finding this an appropriate place to end the interview, thanked Burt, turned to the camera, and said, "We'll be back right after this from General Fools."

More learning. As a substitute cohost I had not done much work with the scripts themselves. I was briefed on the guest, handed a script, and went out and did it. Now that I had a chance to talk with the writers every day it became clear to me that even the best writers, the people who consistently turn out the best copy, sometimes don't phrase things correctly, that is, the way I think people who watch the show are used to talking. For example, I'll pick up my script and read, "Today we'll talk with actor Tony Randall and singer Tony Bennett." If those people came to my house I wouldn't introduce them in that way. I'd say instead, "This is Tony Randall, one of the stars of TV's *The Odd Couple* and Tony Bennett, whose rendition of 'I Left My Heart in San Francisco' is a musical classic." Well, maybe I wouldn't say it quite like that either, but people's names have to come before the adjectives that serve as their credentials. Try this one: "Here's former *Saturday Night Live* star Chevy Chase." That doesn't even come close. The way to say it is: "Chevy Chase is going to be with us today. We all loved him on *Saturday Night Live* and now he's in a big new movie." Scripts need to be written the way people really talk, and I realized that more fully when I started on *GMA* full-time.

There are other script changes as well, many made at the last minute, especially in a rapidly changing story like a hostage situation or a disaster. During the TWA hijacking in Beirut in July 1985 David and I were rewriting the script during every commercial break and any other time we were off camera. At times we virtually threw the script away because even our most recent notes needed to be updated. But in essence, that's what live TV is all about—flexibility, adaptability, quick changes, being fast on your feet.

Now that I think about it, there seemed to be lessons to be learned everywhere, things not as obvious as scripts and interviewing techniques, but things that help create the total picture, like makeup, hair style, and wardrobe. As a substitute cohost I had worn my own clothes. Now my clothes would be provided for me by a chain of clothing stores in exchange for on-screen credit. This means that I can choose my wardrobe from practically any designer in the world. My dressing room is like a small store with some homey features.

Several times a year I go to New York's famous garment district where I shop for the next season's wardrobe. Although this is work for me, I realize that it is most women's greatest fantasy. We go directly to the designer's showroom, where I'll be shown the line by a salesperson who rolls out rack after rack of the next season's clothes while explaining what material they will be available in and what colors will be available in each style. Sometimes there's a videotape of that particular designer's most recent showing, and I can take notes on the clothes in the line that I like best. Then the designer's representative will take me in to see the actual samples of the clothes I've picked. At any rate, it is like being a kid in a candy store and being told you can have anything you want.

One of the most common things people say to me on the street is, "You look so much thinner in person." That's good, because I spend most of my life in person, but it points out the fact that the television camera adds ten to fifteen pounds to the average body and, therefore, if you are overweight by only ten pounds or so, you may appear to be twenty-five pounds heavier than you are "in person." There is an obvious need, then, to stay thin (no easy matter for me because I like to eat) and to choose clothes that are thinning and help to balance TV's widening effect. I constantly see good-looking clothes that would be perfect for normal wear but that can't be worn on TV. Dresses that are boxy on the top don't look good when you sit down. They may make you look great coming down the street but they make you look too big when you sit. I tend to wear a lot of knits, because they are close-fitting, or silks, which flow, and I stay away from poplin or Ultrasuede, which are stiff and add weight. As for skirts, I avoid pleats, and split skirts are totally out of the question—7:00 A.M. is too early in the day to have your thighs peeking out. I never wear layers. Since I'm usually seen from the bust up, I look for things with nice necklines and I rarely wear turtlenecks. The collar is important. If a blouse buttons and the collar is open, it is neither here nor there. It has no meaning. I never have an unbuttoned collar (I'll use a scarf or tie if necessary) because it's limp, not crisp-looking, and it can be sloppy and distracting to viewers. Because small, geometric patterns like checks cause the picture to "moiré" (vibrate) I stay away from those as well.

Since I can't try these clothes on before I buy them (there is no size selection in the showroom), *GMA* has a wardrobe person who comes in to make hems and do other necessary alterations after the clothes arrive from the manufacturer.

On the set I wear heels that are higher than those I normally wear because high heels make the legs look better. And though I'm usually not seen in full-length shots, my shoes are selected so my legs will look good even when I'm sitting down. I've also learned from looking at tapes that a shoe that is cut just right also makes the foot look thinner.

To accommodate my new wardrobe I had a special rack built in my dressing room for skirts and blouses and another for dresses and had shelves put on one wall for sweaters and shoes. There is a full-length mirror on the door and next to the door is another rack for belts. Against another wall are a sink and a mirror surrounded by lights, and a makeup counter that holds, in addition to makeup, a toaster oven and TV set. There is also a shower, which I rarely use, but it is a nice thing to have when I need it. On the wall next to the mirror I have a cork bulletin board where I tack up a variety of notes, and where I also keep personal photos, a baseball card with my picture that Jim Bouton gave me, and several lists, including my fifteen-step makeup plan. Next to this bulletin board is one of those boards you can write on with a grease pencil and it's here that I keep track of the outfits I've worn in the last thirty days. I make notes like: "Friday the 4th—Anne Klein peach jacket over silk shell and black silk skirt." This record prevents me from frequently wearing the same, or too similar, an outfit.

I've already talked a little bit about makeup but a few more details will help you understand what TV makeup is all about. In general, makeup tends to flatten the face and make it look heavier, so for TV you need more contouring, which can be created by using darker shades under your cheekbones to give them more definition. We have overhead lighting in the studio (unfortunately, it is lighting from below that makes you look thinner and younger), so I have to use more light-colored makeup under my eyes. This compensates for the dark circles under the eyes that overhead lights create. Thank goodness I don't have dark circles or puffy eyes in the morning because that would compound the makeup problem. I use more blush than normal on my cheeks because the bright light tends to wash out the face, and for the same reason I use heavier, dark shadow on my eyelids.

Because I see my face all the time and pick it apart, I know that one of my eyes opens slightly more than the other; my eye makeup has to compensate for that, so I use a darker-than-normal brown shadow on the lid and darker eyeliner applied in a thicker-than-usual line to hide this. One side of my nose is ever so slightly different from the other (I got smacked in the nose by a baseball when I was about twelve years old) and that requires extra shading as well. Whenever I have new makeup people, they say, with slight variations, "I always wanted the chance to do your face. I know just how I want it." I have to tell them to make me look exactly the way I do every day. I don't want to be a Ralph Lauren model. I have to be like a comfortable old shoe that people slip into every morning.

This wardrobe-and-makeup business isn't a case of vanity at all. Beauty isn't my business but looking "right" is. I think that the way I dress and look has a lot to do with the way people hear me. We are a society that judges by appearances. It's a tiny screen and what I wear and the way my face looks determine whether people like me and believe me and whether they respond to me.

When I finally got to *GMA* full-time I was absolutely determined to keep the job, though I knew full well that others had failed. Some of the things I've talked about in this chapter I learned quickly, and some less quickly, but I have learned how to handle almost every aspect of my role on *GMA* in the years I've been connected with the program. Of course, that's the reason I'm still on the show.

Yet—and I'm sure you find this in your own life and work—there is always new knowledge to acquire and I hope I never reach the point on the show where there is nothing more to be learned.

CHAPTER
SEVEN

If It's Monday, It Must Be _____

To say that no two days at *GMA* are the same is a gross under-statement. David and I move with seeming ease from Jimmy Carter to Lynda Carter, from natural disasters to personal disasters, from the courtroom to the tennis court, from international crises to international cuisine. I'm sure it all looks easy as you sit at home and watch, and that's the way it's supposed to look, but the problems of scheduling, the logistics of moving and assembling people and equipment, the script writing and research, and the overall coordination required to make this look easy are enormous.

Perhaps the following will give you an idea of what a busy week at *GMA* might be like.

MONDAY

Monday is usually a little wild anyway, but when you start off the week with Sophia Loren in the studio you are in for more excitement than usual. Sophia, who would be absolutely gorgeous even completely wrapped in a blanket, is extremely conscious of lighting and makeup, so it takes extra time to get all the lights placed to her satisfaction and to get her makeup applied just right.

I checked my notes one more time and underlined what the writer had said about Sophia's feeling that she has extrasensory perception and how she firmly believes that this power once saved her life when she decided not to take a plane that later crashed. The writer also noted that she had a superstition about always wearing red. This information was gathered in what we call a "preinterview," usually a phone conversation in which the writer talks at length with the guest to determine what subjects will be of the most interest to the viewing audience and the easiest for the person to talk about. The writer then formulates a series of questions for David and me to use when we interview the guest the next day on the show.

Indeed, Sophia had on a beautiful red dress that morning, which seemed to confirm the writer's information. The writer had told me in my briefing the night before that Sophia had gone on about wearing only certain colors of red (no purple hues) and had really made a big deal of it all. I underlined that too and then we were on the air.

We covered the usual subjects—how she keeps in shape, her diet, her latest projects, including her commercial products—and with about two minutes left I skipped the question about how it felt to turn 50 because I thought that had been overworked. I moved down to the "if time" section of my notes, which includes the other things covered in the preinterview that people are not usually asked on the air.

"Sophia," I said, "I understand you always wear red and that it is a color of special importance to you. Why is that?"

"Yes, I like red," she said. "That's it," I thought to myself. Yes, that was it. Okay, the pressure is on.

I continued: "It's also said that you have ESP. Is that true?"

With an absolutely straight face she said, "What's that?"

My palms began to perspire. "You know, extrasensory perception, the knowledge of what is going to happen in the near future," I said.

"Oh, I don't know," she answered.

I retold her own story about the plane crash and said that I had heard she felt ESP had saved her life, and all she said was, "Well, some people say so, I guess," and she looked at me very strangely.

What could I say? "What do you mean, you guess? It's your story." I felt like a complete jerk but fortunately I didn't have to say anything at all because we were out of time.

"Thanks for joining us this morning," I said. The interview had ended on a very weird note. When a good interview is seemingly thrown away it is very disappointing. In a case like that, after we've gone to commercial, guests will sometimes say that they're sorry or that they were thrown by the question, but Sophia said nothing. Maybe she was superstitious about talking about her superstition.

We did the news and the weather and then I had the unenviable job of interviewing Bob Guccione, the publisher of *Penthouse* magazine, not exactly a favorite on any morning but particularly not on this one. He had just published the sexually explicit pictures that forced Vanessa Williams to give up her title of Miss America, and I personally thought it was a lousy thing to do. While I usually greet all the guests on the program warmly, I had nothing to say to Guccione but "Hello." I sat down facing him and all I could think of to ask him was: "So how does it feel to have all of America thinking you're a creep?"

I was in no mood to go easy on Guccione and I began by saying, "Most people don't condone what you did to Vanessa Williams. Whether it was morally right or wrong for her to pose for those pictures is one thing, but you took it upon yourself to ruin her career. Why did you do it?"

To Guccione's credit he was straightforward. He answered, "It was strictly a business decision. We had the pictures. We determined that we could sell magazines with those photos in them and we published them."

We went back and forth on the issue for three minutes and all the time I felt that I was betraying myself and millions of viewers by not editorializing, by not screaming at him and calling him a pornographer. But I know it isn't my place to do that. My job is not to offer commentary or opinion but to elicit a story and that was what I was doing.

Finally I said, "Thanks for being here, Mr. Guccione," and then turned and looked at the camera. What I was thinking must have been clearly etched on my face. As we went to commercial the phone next to me rang. It was Amy Hirsh, the producer for the show that morning. "Boy," she said, "a picture sure *is* worth a thousand words. If you could have seen the look on your face at the end of that interview, you would have known that it wasn't necessary to say anything more. Your face said it all."

"Thanks, Amy," I said. "I'm just glad my face said it instead of my mouth because we would have been in trouble."

Immediately after the interview the phones lit up in the *GMA* offices as people called in support of Vanessa Williams, and all day long I heard comments about how well I had handled Guccione and how the message had come across clearly. Sometimes things work out well in the end, even when you can't editorialize.

After the show that morning I had to change into something special for a luncheon at Barbara Walters's apartment; she was giving it for Barbara Bush, the wife of Vice-President George Bush. I had thought carefully about what to wear, not wanting to look too businesslike or too dressy. That meant a suit was out so I picked a smashing white knit dress with suede sleeves by George Anthony. I felt it struck exactly the right note. My car dropped me off precisely at noon in front of one of those classic Park Avenue apartment buildings. A uniformed doorman opened the car door and ushered me into the lobby. There, a security man sitting behind a console with TV monitors checked my name against the list Barbara Walters had given him and, finding me on it, told me to go on up. In many of these posh older residential buildings there is only one apartment per floor, so when the elevator stopped on Barbara's floor I walked into a beautifully furnished foyer.

Barbara herself opened the door, and in her fashion as producer, she immediately introduced me to Grace Mirabella, editor in chief of *Vogue*. "The reason I'm putting you two together,"

Barbara told Grace, "is that I think you should do a story on Joan. So talk to Joan for a while." Having established the agenda, Barbara left to tend to her other guests, and the two of us were left to talk about me and not the weather or the view or the apartment. After we chatted a few minutes I excused myself because I saw Helen Gurley Brown, a former regular on *GMA* and the editor of *Cosmopolitan,* on the other side of the room and I wanted to say hello to her. She is one of the arbiters of the fashions and mores of American women and we discussed these topics for a few minutes. Then I moved over to the grand piano to talk with Liz Smith, the syndicated columnist from the *New York Daily News.* From that vantage point I was also able to look around the room, and I wanted to see who else was there. Besides Mirabella, Brown, and Smith, I recognized Charlotte Curtis, an editor for *The New York Times,* Mrs. Brooke Astor, the philanthropist; Mrs. Anna Murdoch, the wife of communications czar Rupert Murdoch; Shirley Lord, an editor at *Vogue;* Lally Weymouth, who writes for the *Los Angeles Times* and is the daughter of Katharine Graham; and Bunny Burke, the wife of Daniel Burke, whose Capital Cities Communications had bought ABC only one week before, and, of course, Barbara Bush. There were also at least six Secret Servicemen in the apartment to protect Mrs. Bush, but they were as unobtrusive as men can be at a women's luncheon, especially men who wear shortwave radios, tiny radio receivers in their ears, and button microphones on their lapels!

As we socialized before lunch, servers passed by with silver trays of tidbits, and then after about half an hour, Barbara Walters opened a set of double doors and revealed an enormous dining room with a round table set for twelve. There was a gorgeous flower arrangement in the center and in front of each plate was a place card. I found myself sitting next to Bunny Burke. In her dining room Barbara has cleverly mixed contemporary pieces with special pieces, many of them gifts she has received from foreign dignitaries.

Lunch was one of those exquisite *nouvelle* affairs. It began with a pasta salad (no bread, of course), followed by veal piccata served on a massive silver tray and snow peas. Of course, there was white wine. Dessert was a scooped-out lemon filled with shaved lemon ice, kiwi fruit, and strawberries. It was very beautifully done.

After lunch Barbara explained why she had asked this particular group to lunch. "It's my feeling that the First Lady in the U.S. gets all the attention," she said, "and I think Barbara Bush deserves to be recognized and have a chance to meet my friends in the media. Who knows, she may someday be the First Lady herself. I think you should all get to know her and she you, and that you should give her some coverage." As I said, Barbara doesn't leave much room for conjecture.

Barbara Bush responded by saying, "Barbara called a few weeks ago and said she was going to have a little lunch and could I come. I said I'd be glad to come. Then I got a lovely invitation in the mail. Last week Barbara called to tell me everything was all set and she gave me a list of the women who would be here. She also said that after dessert we'd have a few questions. Since she told me that, I've been working hard on my questions for each of you and I'm ready. Are you ready?"

When the laughter quieted the questions started coming. "What do you think of the administration's stand on abortion?" "What about the president's visit to the German cemetery?" "How do you stand on the MX missile?" "Do you have an opinion on the situation in the Mideast?"

Mrs. Bush answered, "I'm not an elected official so I don't have to give you my personal opinion on these subjects, and I'm not going to. I'll be glad to reiterate the answers the vice-president and the president would give but I don't think you want that, so let's talk about the projects I'm interested in. We can begin with adult literacy."

It was a good, gutsy response and I liked that. When Liz Smith began, "Mrs. Bush, I'd like . . . ," Barbara Bush interrupted her and said, "Please call me Barbara."

"I can't do that," Liz said, and Barbara Walters chimed in, "Maybe we should call you 'Second Lady'?"

"Second out of one hundred twenty million isn't bad," Mrs.

Bush replied. "Sure, you can call me that," she said, again show-ing her sense of humor.

The questions then turned to adult literacy and Mrs. Bush said, "I'm glad Mrs. Astor is here because it gives me a chance to thank her personally for her continued support of adult literacy programs throughout the country." Liz Smith commented: "Now I know why Mrs. Astor gets invited to all these parties." There was more laughter. Liz is straight as an arrow; she is the same with everybody, from kings to peons, and though she can cause people to shudder, she gets her stories.

The question-and-answer session lasted a few minutes more and then the formal lunch broke up. As the guests left the table, I took the opportunity to go to the bathroom. As I passed through the hallway I was aware that I was under the ever-watchful eyes of the Secret Service. I don't normally dwell on bathrooms—but this one was exceptional, all done in white. There was a stack of embroidered linen guest towels, and on an old-fashioned dressing table were perfume bottles and atomizers, and glass containers for cotton puffs and Q-Tips. It was all "ca-sually" placed and I couldn't help but think of my Q-Tip box, which I can only find with difficulty in the jumble of things in the second drawer in my bathroom. In the corner was a large sunken bathtub and, of course, huge, fluffy towels. Her apartment was meant to be in magazines (and it has been), and it was a perfect setting for this meeting of professional women.

TUESDAY

Monday had been quite a day but Tuesday was more so, a day of mixed fantasy and reality. My big interview that morning was with Baron Guy de Rothschild, of the famous French banking family. It was fairy-tale time as he gave us all a hint of what real wealth is like. The baron, a man of elegant taste and style, told how, in the past, his father had more than 100 servants, who served in all sorts of capacities. "One of these men was called 'captain of the lake,'" the Baron said. "The captain's job was to row a small boat back and forth across one of the lakes on our estate during the dinner hour." His rowing offered a special scenic effect, the family thought, though the baron commented that you couldn't actually see the lake from the main dining room. He continued, "The family also had a cook whose job it was to bake a special pastry every day just in case someone in the family wanted it. They rarely did." I suppose these are those little kicks that only the ultrarich can truly understand. They are fascinating to hear about, but the whole concept is so anachronistic that it seems to belong in the pages of a historical novel. Of course, these sorts of anecdotes are in a historical novel written by the baron, and that's why he was on the show.

The baron's final story was even more bizarre. "Of course, we had dozens of gardeners who kept the grounds impeccable, but one fall afternoon the family paid a visit to the home of some friends. When my mother got out of the car she saw leaves on the ground and remarked to the lady of the house, 'Those are beautiful. What do you call them and where do you get them?' " It seems she had never seen such things on her grounds. It is an almost unbelievable story but he told it so convincingly I formed a mental picture of her gardeners running around catching leaves before they hit the ground.

That story may be apocryphal but it hardly matters; something very much like it is undoubtedly true. When I asked Baron de Rothschild if there were any skeletons in his family closet he told of a cousin who recklessly spent all of his inheritance and was left penniless. "We took care of him," Rothschild said, "though he didn't live in luxury." I'm sure that in this case luxury is a relative term. The lives of the very rich are a neverending source of amazement.

My schedule called for me to go directly from the set of *GMA* and the fantasyland of Baron de Rothschild to the reality of the crush at La Guardia Airport, where I caught a plane to Atlanta. There I was to board Air Force One and tape an interview with Nancy Reagan about the conference on drug abuse she was hosting for the First Ladies of seventeen countries. On arrival in Atlanta my crew—a producer, a cameraman, and a sound man—and I were met and driven to another location where we would meet the First Lady's plane. Our drive through the countryside brought us to a smaller airport with an ultramodern hangar, which I was told was owned by Coca-Cola. That is apparently why as we walked into the hangar we were each immediately handed a bottle of "New Coke," which had not yet been introduced to the public.

As my hairdresser and I sipped our Cokes he took care of the ravages that travel had inflicted on me. A half hour later it was time to go to work. I walked out of the other side of the hangar, and parked on the runway were two gleaming white DC-9s with UNITED STATES OF AMERICA painted in blue and gold above the windows. It was a very impressive sight.

Before our crew boarded, the Secret Servicemen went through everything we were carrying. As they were inspecting our bags a caravan of some twenty limousines roared up, carrying the First Ladies of Finland, Belgium, Portugal, and the other countries represented at the conference. The Secret Service was there en masse and, as always, they hit the ground running before their cars came to a stop. They are a very macho bunch.

When we boarded a few minutes later, a helpful Air Force officer told me that Air Force One is not one specific plane but the plane the president is on at any given time. If the vice-president is on the plane it's called Air Force Two and if Mrs. Reagan is the passenger it's called Executive One. It may be the exact same plane, but this simple code lets everyone on the ground know who is on which plane. The officer also told me that there are two main 747s that are fully equipped for the president's use and there are several other similar 747s with less of the emergency equipment necessary to support the president and his staff; these are used for heads of state, members of Congress, and other government dignitaries when they travel in this country and abroad. This was all new information for me, since, like most people, I thought the president flew in the same plane all the time and that there was only one Air Force One. There are also a number of modified DC-9s in use as well.

Inside, in the rear section, this DC-9 is much like a regular airliner, except that there are fewer seats and they are farther apart. The front section (known as "DV" for "Distinguished Visitors") has a dining table and much larger seats that face forward and backward. For this trip the table was set with white linen, silver, White House china, with the gold presidential seal and gold trim, and a vase of gorgeous flowers. There was also a large jar of jelly beans. In an area that would normally seat about twenty people there were seats for only eight. Nancy Reagan sat on her special chair which is slightly higher than the others and swivels around.

The rear section was filled with the staffs of the First Ladies, the Secret Service, and the press—us. This time we were the only members of the media on board. There was the flight crew of four, as well as four stewards from the White House kitchen (everything is prepared fresh on this plane, no microwave specials, if you please), a White House photographer, and a nurse.

The flight from Atlanta to Washington began with lunch, an extremely light affair (nobody could overeat on this one) of watercress-and-cucumber finger sandwiches on lighter-than-air bread (without the crust, of course), deviled eggs, and assorted raw vegetables. There was lemonade to drink, served in white plastic cups with the presidential seal; I now use mine as a toothpaste cup in my bathroom at home. As souvenirs I also kept the matchbooks and the deck of cards given to all guests on the presidential plane—the jokers are indicated by the congressional seal and the aces by the presidential seal, which may or may not be a political statement.

After lunch I was told by Mrs. Reagan's press secretary to come forward to the front cabin and that I would have ten minutes with her. I went to the DV section and sat down on a small cushion, only to find myself sitting much lower than the First Lady. It was a bad position for camera angles, and sound as well, because of the jet engine noise. Nevertheless, this is what we had to work with, and work we did.

Let me say at the outset that Nancy Reagan is a gracious hostess, a pleasant person. She welcomes people and says good-bye to them beautifully. I always get the impression, however, that she is terribly uncomfortable when she is being interviewed, and I almost feel bad about putting her through it because she is so nice. Jennefer Hirshberg, her assistant at the time, had talked with Amy Hirsh, our producer, and me ahead of time. She said, "Here's what you should ask," and then ran through a series of questions on the drug conference. I said, "Okay, Jennefer, but of course we have our own questions that have to be asked."

We did ask our questions and we put together a very good four minutes of tape for use on *GMA*. We landed at Andrews Air Force Base outside Washington, where the First Ladies were met by another fleet of limousines, and we wrapped up our story. The plane ride was great and the atmosphere it offered added enough excitement and novelty to make this a very special event for *GMA*.

That evening I returned to New York from Washington and by the time I got home it was well past my bedtime.

WEDNESDAY

I was still enveloped in the glamour of Air Force One when I got to the studio the next morning. I flaunted my new knowledge of the presidential jets and showed off my playing cards. I got another boost when Phyllis McGrady, our executive producer, told me that I was flying to Boston the next day to interview Queen Noor, the wife of King Hussein of Jordan. This was stacking up as some week.

Filled with all this glitz, I hit the set running. I zipped into but not through an interview with Kevin Bacon, who was a smash in *Diner* and *Footloose,* and his girlfriend, Tracy Pollan, an actress who was less well-known than Kevin at the time. We wanted to talk about the problems faced by two young performers when one of them hits it big. They asked about the questions before we went on the air and Kevin requested specifically that I not ask any questions on that subject. We don't usually go over questions with guests beforehand, but in this case they were so nervous we did so just to try to put them at ease. Besides, this was not a controversial interview where you want to ask surprise questions to get interesting responses. Bacon bristled when he saw question

5a, which was directed to Tracy: "How have you helped Kevin handle his instant celebrity?" They were clearly very sensitive on the subject. Unfortunately, in the last-minute hubbub I hadn't crossed 5a off my list of questions and before I knew it I had asked a version of that question on camera. It just got by me. They were both clearly shocked but they got through it, and afterward Kevin asked, "Am I crazy or was that question five-a?" "It was," I admitted, "and I'm sorry, but it was a slip, not intentional, I assure you." These kinds of things happen occasionally, especially on busy and complicated mornings. And, in case you haven't figured it out yet, I'm not perfect.

My other interview of the morning came in the last half hour of the show, and it had the makings of a beautiful human interest story. Two teenage sweethearts who had gone their separate ways, married other people, grown old, and ended up in the same nursing home, had gotten back together, at ages ninety-eight and one hundred, and gotten married.

The interview was being done as a live remote broadcast, that is, it was on the air live but instead of being in the studio the guests were in the nursing home. I was told they were hard of hearing so I began in a loud voice: "Congratulations, Hank. Why did it take so long?"

He looked into the camera and didn't say a word.

"Hank, can you hear me, Hank?" I nearly shouted. Hank didn't move a muscle and I didn't know if I had a transmission problem or if he just couldn't hear because of his own hearing problem.

I switched gears. "Marilyn, how about you? Can you help me out here?" I said, trying to keep the frustration out of my voice.

Marilyn *could* hear and she turned to her husband and said, "Hank, the lady wants to know why it took you so long for you to marry up with me."

Hank said, "What did you say?"

We were only twenty-five seconds into a four-and-a-half-minute interview and there was clearly trouble on the horizon. Sometimes, when things aren't going well, or when something funny happens, you can hear the people in the control room screaming obscenities or laughing like lunatics through the head-sets of the cameramen and the stage managers. I was hearing hysterical laughter in the headsets, and the crew on the floor was also beginning to break up.

"Marilyn, how about you, then? What took so long?" I tried.

"That's a kind of long story," she answered.

I looked at my watch and said, "I don't know about you, but I've got about three and a half minutes, so go ahead." With that, the entire studio was up for grabs. I wanted to laugh too, but at the same time I was saying to myself, "Oh God, this whole thing is going down the tubes." It went like that for the rest of the in-terview. I got calls all day long from people who said they laughed so hard they cried. It was a memorable interview.

This sort of thing can happen with older people because they aren't used to television and perhaps sometimes they can get confused, in addition to the fact that they don't hear well. Each year we interview the remaining survivors of the *Titanic,* and one year I did an interview which has become a classic at *GMA.* We had assembled five of the survivors, all in their nineties, and they were sitting on the couches in the far end of the studio. I wasn't more than five feet away from any of them, but as it turned out they all had hearing problems.

"It was early in the morning," I began, "and you were asleep. Is that right?" No answer from anyone.

"What did you hear first?" I tried.

"What did I hear?" someone answered, and I was pleased.

I wanted to give them a strong hint. "Did you hear sirens?" I asked.

One woman popped up with, "Yes, I heard them."

Seizing on that, I directed my next question to her. "Then you went on deck?" I asked.

"Yes, we did," she answered.

"What did you do when you got on deck?" I said.

"Well, we went up there," she replied.

"Yes, but what did you do?"

"I remember standing there."

I decided to move quickly from the deck to the lifeboats. "Could you see the ship from the lifeboats?"

"Yes."

"Was the ship going under?"

"Yes, it was sinking."

"Did you see anything else?" I asked. No answer.

"Did you see people jumping into the water?" I asked.

"Yes, we did."

By then the entire crew was doubled over. I'm surprised the cameras weren't shaking. I could hear gales of laughter over their headsets (fortunately the guests couldn't hear it), and I'm sure they were saying that Joanie was going under with the *Titanic*. I still had two and a half minutes to go and there were no lifeboats in sight. Sometimes you can do what we call "dumping," which is closing out quickly and cutting to a commercial, but I happened to be in a time slot in which that was impossible. I said to myself, "I'm going to have to ride this baby all the way to the bottom."

None of the interviewees seemed to be able to remember anything or hear anything except the question directed to the next person and then one of them would say, "The lady wants to know how . . . ."

The writer had told me to "have fun with this one" and he had been right. I had not only asked all the questions but given most of the answers as well. I certainly don't want it to appear that I'm making fun of older people here. I only want to point out that certain guests do offer special problems when it comes to live interviews and that interviewing is an art that requires you to be well prepared and quick on your feet.

THURSDAY

The show on Thursday was uneventful, which was good because I was excited about going to Boston for my interview with Queen Noor. Queen Noor is the former Lisa Halaby, daughter of Najeeb Halaby, who was president of Pan American Airways and was at one time the director of the Federal Aviation Administration. Not unlike Grace Kelly, a girl from a Philadelphia Main Line family who married the Prince of Monaco, Lisa Halaby went to the Middle East and fell in love with a king, in a fairy-tale romance. I was intrigued because, like everyone else, I'm intrigued by royalty and power and Queen Noor is both.

I still had a show to do before the trip to Boston, though. That morning I was interviewing two celebrities, Jeff Daniels, who starred in Woody Allen's movie, *The Purple Rose of Cairo*, and Cindy Williams, who had played Shirley on *Laverne and Shirley*. Both of these interviews turned out to be interesting.

We had all heard that Jeff Daniels was terribly arrogant, much like the role he played in *Purple Rose*, and that he was a poor interviewee. But he and I hit it off from the word go, and the interview was wonderful.

I asked: "Is it true that you don't get roles because you go into the interviews looking bored?"

"That's my defense mechanism," he said. "It's the way I survive all the rejection."

"But if you act arrogant or bored, don't you think that works against you?" I asked.

Jeff said, "It may sometimes, but overall I think it works for me and I get hired because I'm already playing a role."

He had just become a father so we switched to his feelings about being a new daddy, and when we were through everyone on the set loved him. The openness he demonstrated had completely changed our perceptions of him.

I had interviewed Cindy Williams back when *Laverne and Shirley* was still a hot show, and at that time she said, "I really want to get married and have babies."

"That's a little hard with a show like yours," I said.

"Well, I'm the marrying kind," she said. "The problem is finding a guy on the schedule I work."

Well, she had found a guy (Bill Hudson, who had been married to Goldie Hawn), she got pregnant, and that was the end of *Laverne and Shirley*. I had heard that the producers of the show had opposed her pregnancy but she stuck to her guns and went ahead anyway.

Now her child was about two, and off camera Cindy told me, "I love being a mother but it does test your patience." Since this is a feeling that all mothers share, I took this line of questioning—and it turned out great.

After the program, it was off to Boston to visit the queen. I had received the following briefing on the interview: Queen Noor's full name is Noor al-Hussein; Noor is pronounced "newer"; the king gave her the name, which means "light of Hussein," as a wedding present; she graduated with honors from Princeton with a degree in architecture and urban design; Hussein had been married three times before and had seven children; together they had three more children.

Queen Noor was being interviewed because she was on a public-relations visit to this country, giving speeches at Harvard, Princeton, and other colleges and holding a series of news conferences. We caught up with her at the Ritz-Carlton Hotel in downtown Boston.

It's hard for me to imagine the kinds of pressures this woman is constantly under, not only because she represents her husband and her new country but because everywhere she goes there is an entourage, including security people, which creates a small mob scene. She is always on display but she is also completely surrounded at all times for security reasons.

We set up our two cameras and our lights in the living room of the royal suite (an appropriate spot) and sat down to wait. I was going over my notes when the door opened and she walked in. Though Lisa Halaby wasn't brought up to be a queen, I have to say that she emanated royalty as she moved around the room, shaking hands with everyone, including the production crew from *GMA*. She exuded a special quality that was innate or that she cultivated after marrying Hussein. I've noticed the same quality with other royalty, notably Prince Charles, but his case is different because he was born to his position. Had Lisa Halaby commanded people's attention when she walked into classrooms at Princeton? I don't know the answer but it would be an interesting question to follow up on.

Noor was wearing a brilliant blue crushed-velvet dress and a huge diamond brooch. ABC had made the arrangements for the room and had it filled with flowers. It almost seemed as if it had been coordinated in style and color to show her off to the best advantage. In reality she needs little stage setting. Noor is quite tall (perhaps five-feet-ten) and statuesque. She is pretty, bordering on beautiful in the classic sense, with long, naturally blond hair. Her look and personality are those of a queen.

When she finished greeting everyone she sat with me for our interview. Noor was very deliberate in her answers and somewhat guarded in her speech, and she carefully moved any questions that might have caused problems into her areas of expertise. She seems totally committed to her new country and the goals of its people and she states that case carefully.

One could look at her and envy her royalty, but she has problems like the rest of us. She married a man at least twenty years older than she, a man who is the leader of a controversial kingdom in a turbulent part of the world. She took on the responsibilities of queen and mother, and she has had to leave her past life behind her. Off camera she described herself to me as a "working mother" and explained that she tries to spend some time with her children each day. But she added, "When I can't be with them for extended periods I explain to them that the king and I are trying to make a better world for them. That's a difficult message to get across to children." Being a mother, I could sympathize with her on that point. We all have our feelings of guilt when we can't be with our children. When I can't be with my girls, I too try to explain why I'm not there, but without much success. It leaves you with a feeling of inadequacy.

FRIDAY

I'm glad that the interview with Queen Noor had been such a success because the next morning was all downhill. The Beach Boys had been scheduled to do a live remote from Los Angeles.

I've always liked their music but I hadn't seen them in years; I had some trepidations about the interview after Michael told me the story of a Beach Boys appearance on the *Today* show when he was the producer there. He said they had acted goofy and at one point he had to tell them to sit up and get their feet off the table or they were going to look foolish.

Our writer had briefed me but he had talked only to the Beach Boys' manager because they were "unavailable" for a preinterview. As a result, the writer wasn't able to construct a coherent series of questions directed to anyone in particular; he gave me some general questions suitable for any member of the group. On the surface that seemed safe enough.

Just before we went on the air I got the feeling that something was wrong with the remote but I didn't know what it was. In most cases it's usually. something mechanical like a sound problem or the fact that the satellite isn't in the right place. But that morning it was worse. What I couldn't see on our studio monitor, but what they could see in the control room, was that the Beach Boys were sitting in their chairs ready for the interview when they got into a fight with their manager, on camera. That lasted for several minutes apparently, and at that point the whole group got up and left the California set. When they came back, their manager wasn't with them. On the monitor in New York we couldn't see that he was missing. Not only that, but they sat down in different chairs, some of them wearing microphones and some without. I didn't know this was the case, and since I hadn't seen them for so long I wasn't sure who was who just by looking at them.

All of a sudden we were on, and I said, "Now joining us live from Los Angeles are the Beach Boys." I still had no idea that anything was terribly amiss and I proceeded to introduce each of them. The camera was taking head shots only, so I couldn't see that the last chair, where the manager was supposed to be, was empty. When I introduced him, the camera panned to an empty chair.

One of the Beach Boys then yelled offstage, "Hey, Jack, get in here." Jack came in and sat down. Not exactly off to a roaring start. Since I wasn't aware that they'd changed places I didn't know my seating chart was off. Therefore I didn't know I was talking to the wrong person when I asked a question. I could see that the person I thought I'd asked wasn't saying anything. I could see that one member of the group was talking but there was no sound because his mike was off. When I threw out the next question someone answered, I didn't know who. Thinking I could rectify the situation, I said, "What do you think about that, Brian?" Unfortunately, that was who had just answered the same question. He just said, "I'm Brian."

As it turned out, the one guy who I'd been told probably wouldn't talk much was the only one who had any capacity to hold a conversation this morning. There was really no way to fix things and I ended by saying "Goodbye, fellows, it's been fun."

Immediately the staff in the control room poured out onto the set, screaming with laughter. Half of them were in tears from laughing so hard. Then they told me the story of the fighting and the mix-up in seats, to which I said, "Thanks a lot, boys and girls." After that I was just about capable of saying my own name. Michael had watched the show from home and he called to give me his impression. "It was very funny," he said. "I couldn't believe anyone would do that on live television. They were more outrageous this morning than they were on the *Today* show."

But the day didn't end on that low note. In fact, it ended on an incredible high. Michael and I had been invited to lunch at the Russian Tea Room, one of New York's celebrity meeting places, by Steve Hassenfeld, president of Hasbro, Inc., a toy company for which I act as spokesperson. Our group, including Michael, had just sat down at our table when the restaurant started to buzz with excitement. All kinds of celebrities come into the Russian Tea Room and there is barely a stir, so this had to be someone extra special. When I saw the object of all that attention I could understand it. Sliding into the booth right next to me were Tom Selleck and two women, one young and the other older. I had interviewed Tom on *GMA* but only on a live remote from Hawaii, so I wasn't sure if he would recognize me.

His arrival was duly noted at our table and as we ate I couldn't help but let my eyes wander in his direction every now and then. A couple of times my eyes met his and I thought he smiled as if he knew me, but I couldn't be sure; I didn't want to be foolish and wave if I wasn't sure he knew who I was.

When we finished lunch and I was about to walk out, he looked up and said, "Joan, how are you? Saw you this morning. Hear you just got back from Morocco. That must have been a great trip."

Trying to appear cool and unexcited, I walked over to his table. Here was this gigantic star who knew me, even knew I was out of the country for a few days. I was surprised and impressed. He then introduced me to the two women, who turned out to be his girlfriend and his aunt, and in turn I introduced Michael.

I just wished there had been someone there to see all this— like maybe an old girlfriend from high school—and as soon as we got to the front of the restaurant I rushed to the phone, called my assistant, Debbie, and said, "Guess what just happened!"

I don't know if it's good or bad, but I still can't seem to accept the fact that a lot of people know me, even the very famous. That capped the day for me. Boy, I was set.

In retrospect it had been one fantastic week.

I don't want to give you the idea that every week is this eventful, because it isn't. But this is a good example of the constant variety, the kinds of highs and lows that I have every week, and the type of roller coaster I ride on *GMA*.

CHAPTER
EIGHT

~~~※~~~

"Do You Have a Day Job?"

A couple of years ago I was invited by my nephews, Danny and David Krauss, to come to a "show and tell" session in their respective classes at the Chaparral Elementary School in Woodland Hills, California. It was amusing to be part of that grammar school ritual, and as is often the case, it was a learning experience as well.

My assignment that morning was to talk to the kindergarten class and then the third grade. In the kindergarten I told the kids about the show and how it works in general terms, and when I was finished I asked if anyone had any questions. Of course they had questions, beautifully innocent and ingenuous.

One little girl asked, "Have you ever sneezed on TV?" and when I said no she asked, "Have you ever wanted to sneeze?" To that one, I had to say yes because there are many times when you feel you have to sneeze or cough and there is nothing to do but stifle the impulse.

Another child wanted to know: "How do you keep from laughing? I'd laugh all the time," and he put his hand up to his mouth and laughed as if to prove his point. I answered that I am a natural laugher and that sometimes I do laugh on the show, but not because I'm nervous, only because something is funny.

Thinking in logical terms, another child asked, "Don't you get embarrassed in front of all those people?" I explained that there really aren't any people in the studio except the people who work on the show and therefore I'm really not aware of all those millions of people looking at me.

With the third-graders I talked about the research involved in preparing for the program and compared it to doing homework for the next day in school. Then I said the show itself is a little like taking a test on my homework on the following morning. The difference is that I get to ask the questions.

Where the kindergartners had been innocent, the third-graders were pragmatic, concerned about these tests and what else I got out of the job. Relating my job to schoolwork seemed like a good idea, but when I was through, a boy raised his hand and said, "Yuck, what did you take the job for if you have to take all those tests?" It was a good question, but before I could answer, a girl piped up from across the room, "Because it pays a lot of money, dummy." I needed to say no more.

Finally, one bright-faced little guy in the back of the room raised his hand and asked, "Do you have a day job?" It was put so cutely and openly that I couldn't help but laugh. I then told the class what I do when I'm not on the air. His comment was so perfect that I continue to use it as an anecdote in many of my speeches because I've found that adults really want to ask that same question.

In fact, "How does it feel to work only two hours a day?" is one of the questions I'm asked most frequently, and it's always a surprise to me that people actually think that's the extent of my workday. I suppose they assume that since I'm seen only from 7:00 to 9:00 A.M., my day begins and ends with the live show. They must say to themselves, "Boy, does she have it knocked. In at seven and out at nine, and meeting all those interesting people besides. How does a person get a job like that anyway?"

Well, I'm here to tell you there is a good deal more to being the cohost of a major top-rated live television program like *GMA* than sitting in front of the camera for those two hours every weekday morning. So let me put this two-hour business into perspective by telling you what goes on in the rest of my day and the rest of my life outside the studio.

To begin with, when the program ends each morning, we normally stay in the studio for at least an hour, often longer, to do promos and "post-tapes." First, however, everyone needs a little time to relax from the tension and pressure of the show, so there is a ten- or fifteen-minute break. The leftovers from the green-room, the area where the guests wait before they come into the studio for their appearances, are brought to the set and quickly picked clean by a crew that has been hard at work for at least four hours. I often try for one of the bagels or muffins but they always go first so I usually end up having to choose between the remains of fresh-cut vegetables and the fruit. If I'm lucky there is a stray bunch of grapes or an apple left by the time I elbow my way up to the table.

This is actually fine because I don't need the calories anyway, but by that time of the morning I'm often so hungry I could eat my script. In fact, Debbie finds it amusing that while she is ready for toast and scrambled eggs I'm really ready for lunch and a pastrami on rye would do just fine.

This break also gives the crew time to rearrange the set if necessary and it gives me time to rearrange my face. There is a small makeup mirror and a shelf for my necessities off to one side of the studio and in five minutes or so I can replace the color that has been burned away by the lights and run a brush through my hair. Then it's back to work.

First we do the promos. You know what they are, the ten- and twenty-second announcements that are on throughout the day and during the prime-time programs in the evening. These spots tell about the next morning's guests and stories: for example, "Tomorrow on *Good Morning America,* the latest on the hostage crisis and a recipe from Jill St. John," or "Join us tomorrow on *Good Morning America* when we talk with the Beach Boys." What you probably don't know is that it may take three or four tries to do one of those ten-second pieces perfectly. If they are as little as a quarter of a second too long or too short or someone misses a cue or botches a name, that spot has to be done over completely. And though ten seconds isn't very long, each promo has to be reviewed by the director in the control room then rewound and reset along with the prompter copy. This can mean three or four minutes per take. David and I and the crew have this pretty much down to a fine art, however, and we can usually produce four or five different spots in fifteen minutes or so.

Post-tapes are those interviews and features that are taped rather than done live on the show, and these are shot next. Though we prefer live interviews, sometimes things just can't be done live. So, for example, an interview may have to be taped because the guest was available only at a later time; or a recipe prepared on tape if it is too chancy to do live. There are also personal considerations that must be taken into account. Certain guests, nightclub entertainers for instance, work until the wee hours of the morning and can't make it to the studio before 9:30 or 10:00. Other stars are concerned with the way they might look early in the morning or in the studio lighting, and they prefer—or sometimes demand—to be interviewed later in the day, usually in their hotel suite. The last time I interviewed Tom Jones, for example, we took our cameras to his hotel suite at 4:00 P.M. for a taping and he still wasn't quite ready. We had to wait until he finished his massage.

Then there are those guests whom you don't want to interview live, like an outrageous rock star or a comedian whose stage act might be risqué, because you don't know what they are going to say. I remember the first time we had Bette Midler scheduled for the show. The producers decided to tape her, as they felt she was so zany she might say or do anything, even go into the opening of her nightclub act, a thoroughly outrageous performance.

Bette comes on the stage, dressed very demurely, and says in a cultivated voice, "My manager says I'm a very big star now and I don't have to use four-letter words and do all my disgusting jokes. He says I can come out and sing and dance and act like a lady, and besides, he says, the audience doesn't expect that disgusting smut from me anymore. And you know what I say," she says, as she rips off her high-collared blouse to reveal a *bustier*, "I say if they can't take a joke, _____ them." Okay, she's very funny, but that kind of thing, which she's perfectly capable of doing on the air, isn't quite right for the audience just waking up. That time our fears were totally unfounded: Bette was prim, proper, and absolutely delightful on the show.

At any rate, these post-tapes may take anywhere from ten minutes to two hours, depending on the number of tapes and the length of the interviews. My three-part interview with Joan Rivers, actually done in one continuous taping session and then edited into three pieces of six minutes each, took more than an hour. One reason I had to tape her was that her previous appearance had caused quite a stir. Joan Rivers is an incredible talent but she can be quite risqué and very unpredictable. In her last live appearance on *GMA* some of her lines were a little strong. For example, Rivers asked, on live television: "Who dresses the Queen of England?" And she answered, "Helen Keller." That was quickly followed by this: "America is the *National Enquirer*. And when they tell about Princess Grace's daughters being tramps, that's when it's time to talk about it onstage. Princess Caroline and Princess Stephanie buy Vaseline in decorator colors. I mean these are two trampy girls." The crew broke up, but inside the control room folks were pretty upset, especially the Standards and Practices man, who's there every day to make sure that we don't say anything on the air we can get sued for. Then Rivers said, "Yoko Ono, arf, arf, arf. I went to her wedding with John Lennon. They threw Kal Kan. This woman is just not pretty. She must have a lot of inner beauty." Of course, Joan tempered it all by saying, "I think I'm the mouth of every American woman." Again, the studio crew cracked up. Joan is very funny, but her jokes can be a little heavy for morning TV.

But seriously, can we talk? Joan Rivers is not only a terrific comedienne but also a great interviewee because she is always well prepared. In this instance she was not only prepared, but up for the interview and trying hard as well, and that is very helpful to an interviewer. What is amazing to me is how many celebrities show up for their interviews unprepared or unenthusiastic or negative and therefore turn out unlikable in the final analysis. I know that I have to be up for every show and I expect my guests to be the same way. When I'm interviewed on other TV shows or for magazines or newspapers, I always prepare myself for likely questions and I try to do my best because, for God's sake, that's what people will know of me. I don't think I'm being self-serving when I say that the difference between a good interview and a poor one is usually the attitude of the person being interviewed, not that of the interviewer.

Let me give you a few examples. Dyan Cannon, who is a real beauty and an established star of long standing, is one of those who works hard at being interviewed, as hard as she would at any other role. Consequently, her interviews come out very well. Ali MacGraw never gives you a superficial answer. She digs down and gives you her feelings. Both of these stars give guaranteed winning interviews. To promote the Academy Awards in 1985, Gregory Peck had to be in our Los Angeles studios by 3:00 A.M. Though he didn't want to do the show live, he did it as a courtesy to movie fans all over the country. He gave it all he had and showed himself to be the consummate professional. This may be because he came into the movie business when promotion was part of being a star, but he is obviously still conscious of his responsibilities to his fans.

Today, it often seems just the opposite. That is, being a star gives you the license to be unfriendly. Without being specific, I can think of a number of today's crop of young stars, actors and actresses who can't carry Gregory Peck's coat, who approach an interview as if they were owed something for showing up, as if the whole thing were a terrible imposition on their time. Not long ago, one of these rising stars was in for a post-tape to promote his new movie. After we'd covered that subject, I said, "You're an intense actor. When did you first know that you wanted to be an actor?" A perfectly reasonable question, I thought. He answered, "I'm here to talk about my movie, not my personal life." That ended the interview as far as I was concerned, and though we went on for a minute, the producers never aired the interview. I know from experience that his attitude will do him no good. If people get it in their minds that some star is not a likable person, it might eventually affect that star's box-office draw. Believe me, it affects the way I feel about going to a movie.

Rudolf Nureyev gave a similar performance during a *GMA* segment when I asked him: "When you defected from Russia you had to leave your parents behind, knowing you would probably never see them again. That must have been very difficult. Can you describe how you felt at that time?"

His answer was "That's a stupid question." My mouth fell open, and everyone else on the set was astonished at his response. I felt the question was put in a very sensitive way and I replied, "No, not stupid, sensitive." Attitudes come across clearly and people can tell in two minutes if someone, even a very big star, doesn't really care a whit about the public.

At any rate, after the post-tapes are done (usually sometime between 10:00 and 10:30), I leave the studio and go up to my dressing room to make notes, for continuity purposes, on the clothes I wore during those interviews and to change into clothes appropriate for what I have scheduled for the rest of the day. Sometimes I feel very energetic at that hour and I put on my jogging clothes and grab my assistant, Debbie, for a run in Central Park. Occasionally David Hartman and I run in the park together after the show and that always turns a lot of heads. On other days I may use the limo rather than walk to my office because it saves a few minutes—I'm always trying to squeeze the most time out of each day—or because I'm just too lazy to walk.

As the elevator takes me to the fifth-floor office of *GMA,* my mind is already at work. My office is down two long halls in a quiet corner, far away from the hustle and bustle that is standard around the offices of the producers, bookers, writers, and executives. My office is really a home away from home. There is a large couch with throw pillows, an easy chair, and a coffee table that usually has fresh flowers in a large vase. In addition to a television set, a videocassette recorder, and a small library of reference books and books from authors who have appeared on the show, I also have a rowing machine and an exercise bike I try to use daily. It may sound like a lot for one room but it is comfortable, and despite my general penchant for neatness, list making, and so forth, the clutter in the office doesn't bother me at all.

Before my assistant and I sit down to work she usually orders lunch; for me it's now way past lunchtime. Sometimes it's Chinese—either sesame noodles, egg rolls, chicken and cashew nuts, beef with broccoli, or all of Column A, depending on how famished I am—but most of the time I'll order a fruit salad with cottage cheese. If I'm on a strict diet I may just have a cantaloupe or a diet soda and call that lunch, but I've found that my motor definitely begins to run down at about that time of the day and I need real food to get it going again, diet or no diet.

While we wait for the food to be delivered Debbie and I sit down with the day's mail and go over the day's calendar, which may look something like this:

10:30—Nails and mail (I can't afford the time to go out for a manicure, but my nails have to look nice for the show. So my manicurist comes to the office twice a week, and while she's at work I can do other things, such as answer the mail.)

12:00—Telephone interview with radio station in Spokane for *GMA* publicity

12:15—Luncheon briefing on upcoming trip to Ireland with President Reagan

1:15—Meet with leaders of Mothers Against Drunk Driving to discuss advertising campaign

2:15—Tape voice-over for field piece on drug-abuse treatment centers

2:45—Photo session with representatives from a national child care group

3:15—Leave for home and finish briefing in car

Because I feel a strong responsibility to the people who write to me, I spend as much of my morning as I can going over the mail. Anyone who takes the time to sit down and write a letter deserves to be answered and I can get started on these answers while my nails are being done.

The mail can run from the tragic—"My husband left me with three kids, I can't get on welfare for a month, and my mother just died"—to the frivolous—"Please tell me where you got the shoes you wore on the show last Monday."

Many times I end up getting involved in people's problems. When I get a letter like the following, I get involved: "I am writing to you because I respect you as a mother and am very impressed with your knowledge of babies, and since I am now pregnant and very worried about my baby being born normal and healthy you are the first person I thought of that I can truly trust with my questions." This woman went on to ask a number of good questions and I spent a good deal of time trying to come up with the right answers. Many of the letters are so touching they just can't be dismissed with a pat answer or a form letter in response; detailed answers take time.

I'm obviously not an authority on many subjects, but because I'm on television and people get most of their information from TV, they think I know everything there is to know about the subjects we talk about on the show. If we've done a piece on breast cancer, I'll get a small mountain of mail from women asking my medical opinion on what the best ways to detect cancer are, or what they should do if they find out they have cancer.

If we discuss the problems of working and having a family, the letters will pour in asking for information that will help women cope with the pressures of the working mother's life. These letters will get an answer, usually a referral to the appropriate agency, especially in the situations involving medical problems.

When we did a lengthy report on drug addiction I got such a sad and involved letter from one woman that I couldn't get it out of my mind for a week. She wrote: "I am married only seven months. The night we happened to conceive, my husband and I were snorting cocaine and smoking pot. I continued to smoke pot, not knowing I was pregnant, and I smoked two packs of cigarettes a day too. I am thirty-one and want a healthy baby but don't know what to do."

The problem is that you really can't do much to help in cases like this, or in most serious cases for that matter, but you still feel

Interviewing First Lady Nancy Reagan in New York City.
Mary Anne Fackelman-Miner/The White House

The lighter side of Dr. Henry Kissinger.
Fred Watkins/© 1986 American Broadcasting Companies, Inc.

Interviewing Burt Reynolds at his Florida home.
Robert S. Wiley, Jr./© 1986 American Broadcasting Companies, Inc.

Sly Stallone is a real knockout.
Leslie Wong/© 1986 American Broadcasting Companies, Inc.

On location with Michael Douglas, filming *Jewel of the Nile* in Fez, Morocco.

Bussing George Burns on his ninetieth birthday.

Interviewing Paul Newman on location for *GMA*.
Fred Watkins/© 1986 American Broadcasting Companies, Inc.

Interviewing Maria
Shriver, of CBS
Morning News, on
Mother's Day.
Michael Krauss Productions.

In 1980, the three morning shows all came live from Disney World for the opening of the Epcot Center. Pat Collins *(left)*, hosting for CBS, checks out my pregnant belly, with NBC's Jane Pauley standing by.
Walt Disney World Productions.

On the *GMA* set with
Jane Fonda.
*Fred Watkins/© 1986
American Broadcasting
Companies, Inc.*

Cohosting *GMA* with
Barbara Walters—one
of my role models.
*Steve Fenn/© 1986 American
Broadcasting Companies, Inc.*

Interviewing Diane
Sawyer on the set of
Mother's Day—a parenting
program created by my
husband, Michael, on the
Lifetime cable network.
Michael Krauss Productions.

On location at Victoria
Principal's home in Malibu,
California.
*Peter Sorel/© 1986 American
Broadcasting Companies, Inc.*

Vanessa Williams puts on a
smile after surviving some
tough times.
*Fred Watkins/© 1986 American
Broadcasting Companies, Inc.*

Dolly Parton—a real
up-front woman and one of
the nicest people I know.
*Robert S. Wiley, Jr./© 1986
American Broadcasting Companies, Inc.*

With Geraldine Ferraro on the set of *GMA*.

On the *GMA* set with former President Gerald Ford.
Mel DiGiacomo/© 1986 American Broadcasting Companies, Inc.

David and me doing a story on London cabbies while covering the royal wedding. *Steve Fenn/© 1986 American Broadcasting Companies, Inc.*

The loser gets to interview the chimpanzee.
Donna Svennevik/© 1986 American Broadcasting Companies, Inc.

somehow responsible for at least pointing people in the right direction. I try to do that by sending them to reliable sources that
will offer some measure of guidance.

I also get a good deal of mail from prisoners in jails all over the
country. Men behind bars seem to spend a lot of time watching
television. Either they want to tell me of their innocence and ask
my help in getting them out or they want financial help, like the
man who wrote: "I would like to wish you a very Happy Easter.
Also I hope you are safe and doing well. I am still in need of cash.
Hopefully you can help me in that area." Needless to say, we
can't possibly respond to these requests. Usually, however, prisoners just want an autographed picture to hang on their wall.
Typically a man will write: "Please send me an autographed
color picture of you nude." I answer them with an autographed
picture all right, but one of me fully clothed. Often their requests
for pictures are accompanied by letters with strong sexual over-
tones. "I like your legs, baby," is a typical comment, or "I fantasize about you with your clothes off," or "I'll be getting out in a
few months and I'll give you a call so we can get together." I
think these letters are basically harmless, but just to be sure I
make it a policy not to answer this variety.

Occasionally a letter is a bit more threatening—and that can
be scary. A couple of years ago I received an envelope every
week for three months from a prisoner in Michigan. Each envelope contained a picture of a part of the body, a leg or arm or ear,
and a scribbled note that said, "This is the next piece I'm going
to cut off of you and eat." As with all threatening mail, I had the
ABC security office follow up thoroughly and contact the warden
of the prison involved. ABC contacted the prison and found out
that the man writing the letters was a convicted murderer, and
the prison removed the man's mailing privileges. The letters
stopped immediately but the idea behind that kind of letter is
frightening.

When I was pregnant the normal flow of mail turned into a
flood because many women in our audience could empathize with
another pregnant woman. My public pregnancy became something of an event and I got boxes of letters telling me how proud

I should be and how proud the women in the audience were that I was pregnant and working, that I was a symbol for all working women, and that maybe now other women in less prominent jobs would be allowed to work up to the last minute with dignity. It was a rather awesome responsibility to live up to.

I also got plenty of "medical" advice during that time, including some not-so-sound advice such as one letter that urged me to eat plenty of tomatoes so the baby would have rosy cheeks. I got at least twenty letters like the one that said, "I saw you on the show this morning with your legs crossed. Don't you know that can make your legs swell?" I actually did know that, but it's very hard to sit on a chair in front of the camera without crossing your legs. Another woman wrote with a more serious and less informed warning about crossing my legs. She said, "Don't you know that you can strangle the baby if you sit that way?" But regardless of the content of the mail, it was massive. My pregnancy had apparently energized women to take pen in hand.

It was also at this time that Tina Mongelli, a very loyal supporter of mine, started the Joan Lunden Fan Club, an organization that sends out newsletters from time to time, telling the members of the club about my activities and reporting on the progress of my daughters. Tina's volunteer efforts have been impressive.

It is surprising to me that even now people still send gifts and cards for the children on their birthdays and want to be kept up to date on one or another aspect of the girls' lives. And I still get accolades from women who apparently followed my example of staying on the job while pregnant and are pleased that they did. My pregnancy, which I'll talk more about later, was a special period of my life in many ways.

And there is more mail. Some of it comes from religious and political fanatics, perverts, and people with misplaced priorities—like the man who bought me a diamond engagement ring and sent me the receipt so that I could see he had put it on layaway, or the couple who sent me tickets to Europe so Michael and I could join them on their vacation. But by far the biggest proportion of letters, at least fifteen to one, comes from "just folks" who watch the show regularly and feel the urge to write and say hello. And I have a feeling that for every person who finally decides to write, there are a hundred who think about it and never get around to it.

It may be trite, but the letters from regular people say the nicest things. Like the grandmother who after Lindsay was born wrote to tell me, "I just hope your children grow up to be as wonderful as you are." And the woman from Florida who said, "Having a family is the most important thing a woman can do. Keep up the good work." And the woman in California who said, "I admire you for having a baby and staying on the air at the same time." There are thousands of other examples and most of them carry the same message—that family is important in this country. I agree.

My nails are dry and lunch is long gone by the time we finish the mail. My hands are now free to answer some of the two dozen or so phone calls I receive every morning before I get to the office and while I'm there. A typical list includes calls from the show's producer; a radio station that wants to do an interview; my mother in California; Michael at his office; my agent; Lindsay's teacher; Morgan Brittany, who wants to find out where I got my nanny (that's a secret I'll never reveal); a speaker's bureau about a speech in Minneapolis; a congressman's office asking me to testify in support of a parental leave bill; and so on. My assistant returns some of these calls and I make some of them, but one of the things I've learned is that there is no such thing as a short phone call. That means that returning all these calls takes time.

Then the preliminary schedule for the next day's show arrives and the call comes in from the radio station in Spokane, and there are two other minor crises that need to be handled. Office meetings often take another hour or so and then there are the things that need to be scheduled for the next day or even the next year. These can include photo sessions for magazines or for publicity for *GMA*, trips to the garment district to buy my television wardrobe, out-of-town speaking engagements and other personal appearances, and the schedules for shooting my other television shows, *Mother's Day* and "Mother's Minutes."

By the time all of this is finished it's usually past 2:00 P.M. and therefore past the time I target for leaving. I've been at work almost continuously since 5:15 A.M. (really since 4:30 A.M., when I got into the car to come to the studio), and I'm ready to call it a day. I think you can see that, indeed, I do have a day job.

When I get into the car for the ride home I begin to unwind and I think about what I'm going to do with my kids. I want to play with them and find out what went on in their days and as we drive north in the mid-afternoon I can pay attention to the scenery that was invisible on the way in that morning. Suddenly four o'clock in the morning seems like an awfully long time ago.

CHAPTER
NINE

Sticks and Stones

I grew up in a relatively protected environment. My parents thought I could do no wrong, or almost no wrong. I made good grades in high school and got nothing but praise from my teachers because I got my work done on time and did everything that was required and more. I had a lot of friends and participated in all kinds of activities both in school and outside. In short, I got very little criticism from the authority figures or the peers in my life and I thought that was the way it was supposed to be. When I went to Mexico to study I did well there too. Back in California, I picked up where I had left off academically and attacked my classes with intensity and enthusiasm, again being rewarded for my work with top grades.

Then I started to work in television and things changed. Though I didn't know it at first, when you're in the public eye, you're going to get criticism, not from people you know and trust, but from total strangers. Some of it comes from allegedly qualified sources, namely, the established critics of the media, and some of it comes from the people who watch you at home and then write to say, "I don't like the way you talked to Senator Bluenose." But whether the criticism comes from the professionals or the amateurs, at the very least it causes the skin to prickle, and at worst it causes mental anguish.

As soon as you appear on the television screen you become fair game, like one of those ducks in the shooting gallery that comes up on one side and moves across a track while people take pot shots at it. If a person scores a hit the duck falls over. After you've had some experience being shot at you can usually take a hit and continue to stand up, but in your first days in the shooting gallery, that is, on-air television, you can get knocked over quite easily.

Many women who got jobs in television in the 1970s got them primarily because they were women, and secondarily because of their television experience. Most of us got our training on the job and each day brought its new learning experiences. Therefore, in my first few months not only was I learning the mechanics of broadcasting at KCRA, but being on the air was giving me an education in the semantics of current events, politics, crime, sociology, history, geography, and meteorology.

I mispronounced words and I didn't know how to pronounce all the names of the people and places that popped up in the daily script, especially those unfamiliar names from Vietnam. In short, I made some mistakes, most from inexperience, and I got criticized for them. The people at the station usually did their criticizing in a constructive way, and though I wasn't used to it, I accepted it and learned from it. But there was also outside criticism, and that was different.

. I hadn't been on the job long when I was held up to public ridicule by the television critic for the *Sacramento Union,* a man named Chris Wise. He wrote some scathing comments about me, some of which I still have in a special file that I refer to when I feel my head getting too big. But even if what he said was valid (and some of it was), Wise's remarks were embarrassing to me. After all, my family and I had lived in Sacramento for years, my father had been a prominent and respected physician, we had relatives and friends in the area and I had to face them.

Wise's columns made me angry and indignant. "How dare he say those things!" was my attitude, though I have to admit that I paid attention to a good deal of what he said. For one thing, I became a serious student of pronunciation because I saw the need and I wanted to avoid his barbs and those of others in the future.

After a while I learned to coexist with the professional and amateur critics in Sacramento. When I got letters from people who didn't like my hair, my dress, or my smile, I didn't let them bother me, at least not too much. But I did use the best of that criticism and attempted to turn the negatives into positives.

When I first came to *Eyewitness News* in New York I was faced with a new and different challenge. Now I had to please a much larger viewing audience, new and even more acid professional critics, and colleagues who weren't quite ready to accept this untested woman from the West Coast as a part of their team. As I said before, I was hired to appeal to Channel 7's suburban audience and I think my Q Scores proved that I did that. I'm not sure I ever got to the point at which I pleased my colleagues.

Their criticism wasn't just directed at my skills as a reporter, though I'm sure there was some of that, but more at the fact that I "just didn't fit in" with a group of people who considered themselves seasoned journalists. But even more than that, they considered themselves a team that represented New York to New Yorkers, and I wasn't part of that team.

The television critics of New York were another matter. In May 1977, I was a reporter and substitute anchor for Channel 7 and I was doing my short pieces for *GMA*. Marvin Kitman, media critic for *Newsday,* wrote often about *Eyewitness News* in those days. Some of his more complimentary comments included: "The quality of news journalists coming along is not what it should be. You know you're in trouble when Joan Lunden may be the best of the new crowd at Channel 7." And "Is Ellen Fleysher or Marilyn Salenger superior in doing her hair to Joan Lunden, who won the Miss Hair Spray contest last year?" But that was kid stuff compared to what I faced from another source.

At that time we occasionally had a segment on *GMA* called "Face Off," in which two people would sit facing each other and debate a topic in the news. A man named Robert Scheer was one of the six or eight people we used to call when we needed an advocate for a "Face Off" topic. He was the type who was skilled enough a debater to take either side of an issue, something of an intellectual chameleon. For example, if we were going to talk about abortion he'd say, "Which side do you want me to be on?"

One morning I was in the makeup room before the show and Scheer came in to chat. "I'm writing an article on women who are making it in TV," he said, "and I think you're a good example. Can we talk about it?"

I was flattered and I said, "Of course, I'll be glad to."

We spent some time chatting during breaks in the show that morning and after the show we sat down to finish up. Since I was inexperienced in this sort of thing at the time, I answered all his seemingly straightforward questions. He was very nice about it all and assured me that it would be a very positive article.

On a Sunday morning about two weeks later Michael and I got a call from Los Angeles from Michael's brother, Perry. Perry wanted to know if we'd seen the article about me that Scheer had written for the *Los Angeles Times*. We had not seen it, of course, but we went out to get a copy immediately. It was at that moment that I learned just how inaccurate quotes can be when taken out of context, how words can be twisted, and how a perfectly normal remark can be used to make a person sound silly. Here are some examples:

Interview question: "Did you read newspapers much as a young child?"

My answer: "Not too much because newspapers weren't a big part of my life as a young girl."

Article: "I was not an avid newspaper reader and I was bad at keeping up with current events."

Interview question: "Did they give you any kind of training at KCRA when you started?"

My answer: "Not very much. I had to learn on the job."

Article: "Joan Lunden didn't exist. She was invented by the people who run the local television news business to serve their needs."

Interview question: "Did you know much about television news when you were hired?"

My answer: "Not very much because I only watched TV for

entertainment, never thinking about actually being on television."

Article: "The real person behind the pretty blond reading off the Teleprompter for New York's *Eyewitness News* . . . couldn't have cared less about news. . . ."

This certainly wasn't the first time I'd been criticized in the press but it was the first time I'd been cut off at the knees and the neck at the same time—and on such irrelevant points. He had questioned me as an adult about my habits as a child and then he made those answers seem as if they were made by me about my adult life. To say that I was shattered is an understatement. I was in tears. I was really devastated, and mad at the same time. Michael was wonderfully supportive. "It doesn't mean anything," he said. "People wrap fish in yesterday's newspapers. Forget it, because everyone else will in a couple of days." He may have been right, but I couldn't stop my tears.

On top of everything, I had to face the *Eyewitness News* people that night because I was scheduled to do the six-o'clock news. I felt like calling in sick but I knew everyone would see through that excuse. What was I going to do? I could hardly call and say, "Hi, it's Joan. I'm sorry but I'm busy crying over an article and I won't be able to come to work today." You can't do that in the television business or in any business.

That interview has caused me more grief than any other piece of criticism I've ever received—and it still causes me grief when I think about it. Scheer made me out as a baton-twirling beauty queen who ended up, apparently by mere chance, on a major television news program.

I may have been young and naive at the time but I thought he was asking perfectly legitimate questions about the years I was growing up in Sacramento and my television experience there. And I answered with all the pride in the world, glad to tell him the things that I thought would be interesting and would add details to his story: Dancing lessons after school, performing in dance and musical recitals, and marching in parades seemed to me to be perfectly acceptable elements in a young girl's life.

To me all those endeavors were positive: They represented hard work, they put me a step ahead of the rest of the kids I grew up with. Scheer used those things against me and it hurt me deeply.

Of course, it also taught me a lesson. Today I would not give those same answers to any interviewer because I'd be suspicious. That was my first taste of an interview with a professional critic, some might say hatchetman. Take your choice. I soon found out, however, that I was in good company. This is the same writer who did the interview with former President Jimmy Carter for *Playboy* magazine in which he got Carter to say he had lust in his heart, which would haunt Carter throughout his political life. Scheer was clever. The interview with me was all done in such a way that I didn't know it was happening, and after the fact I felt violated. That column was a source of embarrassment not only for what it said but also because I knew I had been taken and used.

I was still licking my wounds the next day when I got a call from Bill Fyffe, then head of news for the ABC-owned stations. He told me to come to his office. As soon as I walked in the door he started raking me over the coals, not so much for what was said in the article, but because I'd given Scheer the chance to say it.

"How can you be so naive, Lunden?" he yelled. "If you can't give a decent interview," he said, "then the next time we'll have to send someone with you." I had no answer. "And with this guy, of all people. You gave him all the ammunition he needed to shoot you down and he used it." Finally, in frustration, he said, "You should have at least known better than to say you had been a beauty queen in high school, for God's sake."

I couldn't even answer Fyffe because what he was saying was true, beauty contests and dancing are always held against you. I left his office with my tail between my legs. I even began to doubt myself and I thought of quitting television and finding some other career.

Fortunately the people at *GMA* were more supportive, especially Woody Fraser, the executive producer at the time. Sandy

Hill was about to go on vacation and Fraser said, "Joan, we're going to fight this by putting you on the air to substitute for Sandy while she's gone. And don't worry," he went on, "that newspaper will get yellow and blow away and you'll still be on television." I appreciated his support but my self-confidence had taken a hard blow and I was concerned about going on. It's amazing how the comments of a total stranger can undermine your confidence, make you doubt yourself.

In retrospect, the really sad part about that particular piece of criticism is that it changed me. Now I'm not the same open person I used to be. Oh, I am personally, but I'm much more guarded in interviews and that's not fair to me or to the public.

People want to know about me because they see me on TV every morning and they should be able to know more than the fact that I have to get up at 4:00 A.M. It isn't the people from *Good Housekeeping* you have to worry about. They ask about mothering, parenthood, career—the important, positive aspects of life—and I still open up to such people with the assurance that they aren't going to turn things inside out. I won't do that with some other national publications that basically want the dirt and if they can't get that they'll settle for taking things out of context. Answers can always be twisted. Anyway, for that reason they get nothing but the party line from me.

I'm not for a minute saying that there isn't a place for legitimate criticism in television, because there is. We need to be kept on the right track and the good critics can help us. But here's an example of what I think really stretches the bounds of legitimate criticism. Tom Shales, a writer for *The Washington Post,* wrote of *GMA:* "[David] Hartman is definitely the star all right. There is officially no cohost on the program, unlike other networks. Hartman, the host, is, according to ABC publicity, 'joined in the studio each morning by Joan Lunden.' Hartman's female companion on the show has always been so expendably anonymous that *Today* show wags refer to her as the lamp."

Granted, David does have a detailed contract with ABC that names him host of the show and that says there will be no official cohost, but that's the way the program was conceived back in

1975. He was coming off his success in prime-time television and he was a star. But does that make his "female companions" as expendably anonymous as lamps? I think not, and it reflects on all women in television. That sort of criticism is really more frustrating and irritating than harmful because there is no way to answer it without calling more attention to it.

Those who say that sticks and stones break bones but words never hurt either lack a bit of humanity and sensitivity or have managed to grow thicker skin than I have. And when it comes to the role of women on television, my skin is still extremely thin. For despite all the real progress women have made in every area of professional life in the last ten years, women's gains in television, with some notable exceptions, have not been as great as we'd hoped.

Yes, there are more women in the newsrooms, in management positions, there are women producers and directors, there are women behind and in front of the cameras, but an attitude continues to prevail in the business. That attitude is that women (and minorities) are second-class citizens.

There is a sad but true story that made the rounds not long ago that rather vividly illustrates the point. *Cosmopolitan* described the scene this way: "Employees at ABC's Washington bureau were startled to hear on the P.A. system what was described as the unmistakably 'deep and authoritative' voice of Sam Donaldson, ABC's chief White House correspondent, warning, 'The women are coming! The women are coming!' "

In my job, one of the most glamorous in all of television, I quite often feel like the window dressing the critics sometimes accuse me of being. I don't think it's been a conscious decision on the part of management; it's just part of a prevailing attitude in the business.

In fact, this was the subject of a Phil Donahue show on which I appeared. Going on *Donahue* causes sweaty palms because you don't get asked to appear with him to talk about knitting. The topics are usually controversial. The show I did with seven other prominent women in television was no exception.

We all knew we were going to be somewhat vulnerable because we were going to talk about the perils of being a woman in the television business. And we knew that though we all wanted to be honest, we did not want to be so candid that we'd be called on the carpet by our networks.

The eight of us met in the greenroom before the show: Rita Flynn of Chronicle Broadcasting, a long-time network correspondent who is always outspoken on the subject of women's rights; ABC network correspondent Carol Simpson, who has been a leader in the fight for equality for women at ABC News; Mary Alice Williams of CNN, one of the few female vice-presidents in the industry; Lesley Stahl, White House correspondent for CBS; and the morning anchors, Jane Pauley of NBC, Maria Shriver of CBS, Connie Chung of NBC, and me. Surprisingly, this was a first meeting for most of us, even though we are often thought of and even written about collectively as if we knew each other. There was a lot of electricity in the room. We were all joking about having to look for a new job because of something we might say but we were only half kidding. And we were all a touch nervous. You might find that surprising since as professionals we're used to appearing in front of the camera. But in this kind of situation, when you're being asked the questions, and tough ones at that, you worry a bit.

When the show started, I felt we were all weighing our words carefully. Then, when things got warmed up, I found myself pinned against the wall when a person in the audience asked what I thought was the biggest difference between men and women in our industry. I answered without hesitation, "Salaries." My answer got a round of applause but that question prompted another more sensitive one. A woman asked how I felt about my role on *GMA* being secondary and even subservient to David's role.

"I'll be honest with you," I said. "I'm not always content with my status or my assignments but I knew the nature of the job when I took it. I also knew that it was one of the best jobs in television."

Actually that question came as no big surprise. I'm asked about my role in almost every interview I do, and over the years I've come to view that role as two-pronged. First, I'm paid to go out there every weekday morning and vibrantly wake up America with a smile. Second, I have to field these types of questions from the press and the public and present a good image for *GMA*.

Deep down, what am I feeling as I play these dual roles? Well, quite frankly, it's not always easy to put on a happy face, or to face up to these questions. The inequities are there, and the feeling of being a second-class citizen is always there as well. And let's face it, that feels really bad.

A good case in point. Until recently, *GMA* was always managed by male executives. When one of them would come into the studio in the morning he might give me a nod of the head but would then walk briskly over to David. The executives would talk with him and then they'd all go to the greenroom together, as friendly as clams. I attributed this behavior to one of those men's-club things.

But when the day came that a female executive was put in charge of the show, I'm here to tell you that she did exactly the same thing. After a brief hello she walked by me as though I didn't exist. Now it's clear to me that the executives gravitate to the person with the power and control. This was rather disappointing somehow, because I had expected more.

And let it be known that this isn't my imagination. When the network presented its fall lineup to the ABC affiliates at Radio City Music Hall in 1985, David and I appeared center stage with the entire *GMA* family. But people had only to look down at the program in their laps to see, "*Good Morning America,* with David Hartman." Joan Lunden's name wasn't there. Somehow, these are the things that hurt even more than not being given equal airtime or being included in important interviews.

But back to the Donahue program for a moment. It was a very positive experience for me personally and professionally, despite my trepidations going in. For months afterward, people stopped me everywhere to tell me they had liked the way I handled myself and what I had said about not being blind to the inequities but knowing how to live and grow with them.

All of this has an interesting tie-in with the way minority

groups and women are depicted on TV. Blacks are frequently portrayed as pimps, prostitutes, and muggers. Hispanics are stereotyped as stupid and slow. Orientals can't be trusted. Women are sexpots, semitough cops, or second bananas. Since a large percentage of the population gets most of its information from television in today's world, the violence, drugs, loose sex, and negative stereotypes of these groups inevitably have an effect on society. The model is there on TV for everyone to see. The screen is constantly adding data to our mental computers. Too much negative input ends up shaping the way society as a whole views minorities and women.

I said that my job is glamorous and well paying and loaded with perks. But on the opposite side of the coin is the "fluff," and like every other woman on television I have had to put up with more than my share of fluff stories—the for-women-only stories, the throwaways, and the pieces that get cut when time is a little short.

I refer to these stories with the collective name "Dog Hero of the Year," which is not to denigrate the animal world, only to characterize the type of story that usually falls to women. I've interviewed the real "Dog Hero of the Year" every year for as far back as I can remember. I've also interviewed a variety of other animals, including the cat who won the "meow-off" contest, an alligator, a baby tiger, an ape, an eagle, and many less daunting two- and four-footed creatures. These animal stories and others—the fashion stories and the weepers—fall to me and other women on both national and local TV.

Of course, these reports are not without their value, their fun, and their moments of trauma. Of all of the "lighter-side" pieces, the ones with kids can be the most fun—or the real killers. The first concern when I'm interviewing a child is whether he or she is going to talk at all. The little chatterboxes usually have a lot to say before their turn comes on the air but when the camera is on them they can just sit there and stare at you while you sweat. If they do talk, they may simply answer "Yep" and "Nope," which is just about as bad as not speaking at all. As an adult, you have to resist the urge to talk like a child and in tones that exude sweetness in order to get them to open up, because that isn't being grown-up. Psychologists tell us that if you want a child to act like a grown-up then you should treat the child like a grown-up. That isn't always easy on live television when it seems your life depends on dragging out a word here and a phrase there.

When we have kids on *GMA* it's usually because they have a huge collection of baseball cards or the world's biggest watermelon or a jumping frog, so it's a bit hard to know where to reach out and meet them on common ground. For this reason, I usually approach one of these interviews with at least fifteen prepared questions instead of the usual five or six. But as ready as I may be, those one-word answers can eat up a lot of questions. There have been times when I've used fourteen of my fifteen in one minute and still have two and a half minutes to fill. You can't ask, "What did you have for lunch yesterday, Sally?" and you can't expect any help from Mom sitting over on the side, so you have to search in your experience for something to break their silence, which can seem deafening. Count silently to four without saying a word and you have the working definition of eternity as it applies to television. As much as I love them, interviews with kids can give new meaning to that definition.

Animals are not actually as difficult to interview as children, though admittedly their "one-word" answers are less intelligible. They can be a bit more dangerous, however. One morning we had an anthropologist on the show who had studied apes for years and had determined that despite their reputation for meanness, they were really a gentle lot, hard to provoke, tending to like women more than men. He had a cute little ape wearing a diaper in his arms, and to help him prove his point I said, "Well, then let me hold this little guy for a minute." He handed me the ape and the little jungle beast promptly clamped his jaws on my arm. It really hurt a lot. I screamed. The anthropologist was shocked and quickly took the ape back. I said, "Friendly little fellow, isn't he?" I had to continue the interview for another three minutes, all the time rubbing my aching arm. Many viewers noticed that I was obviously in pain and we received dozens of calls asking if I was all right.

After the spot the producer took a look at my arm; she was shocked. I already had a tremendous black-and-blue mark along with the imprint of the ape's teeth on my upper arm. It could have been a lot worse. Fortunately the skin wasn't broken: I happened to be wearing a sweater and a lined jacket that morning, which gave me some extra protection. The black-and-blue mark developed into a giant bruise that didn't go away for weeks.

Not long after that, another animal specialist, Jim Fowler, came on the show. Jim has worked for years with Marlin Perkins, the long-time host of television nature shows. He brought a six-foot baby crocodile. The way we were sitting on the set, the crocodile's mouth was about two inches from my thigh. I was scared to death that at any second it was going to go "rumpf" and take a hunk out of my leg. Nothing happened that time, but it made for a nervous interview on my part and I realized that following my childhood desire to be another Marlin Perkins would have been a great mistake.

My encounter with the eagle took place in Philadelphia when we were doing a live show on the Fourth of July. The eagle was kept in a cage until the last minute. "We don't want to upset him," the trainer had said, and though this may have put some people at ease it only made me more alert. Just before we went on the air the bird was taken out and there he was, perched on the arm of his trainer, his imposing beak inches from my face. I turned to get better acquainted with our national symbol and found myself looking directly into these huge, unblinking eyes. I was less than comfortable. Everyone, including me, was waiting for the bird to peck my brains out. I think it was at this point that I began to think that animal interviews are not my thing, at least interviews with large animals.

The real (rather than collective) "Dog Hero of the Year" story, on the other hand, is usually a good human interest story about a dog who has done something especially brave, like save a family from a fire or find help for lost campers. These heroic dogs are always so friendly it tends to erase the memory of crocodile teeth, ape jaws, and eagle beaks.

These examples constitute some of the fluff as I see it, and they seem to be as unavoidable as the issue of equal pay for equal work. When we female TV personalities take a look at our paychecks, even though they are substantial, we know that our checks are anywhere from one fourth to one half as large as those of our male coworkers. It makes you begin to wonder when a woman in television, or elsewhere, is going to be paid what the job is worth.

Not long ago I was asked to speak to a group of bankers. I decided to use one of my favorite jokes, which rather clearly illustrates the reality of unequal pay for equal work.

When I reached the part in my speech in which I was talking about the inequality of women in the workplace, I said, "I want to ask all of you a question. Do you know why God gave women breasts?" As they looked up with keen anticipation, I said, "So bosses would know whom to give the smaller pay checks to." It broke them up and I think I made my point.

Barbara Walters and I have talked about this situation a number of times. She, of course, is, or was, the highest-paid woman on television, and though I don't know exactly what she earns today, the newspapers have reported her salary in the neighborhood of a million dollars a year. Barbara knows whereof she speaks. She came up in the business when there were only a handful of women on camera and she became a cohost of *Today* in its infancy. There is no doubt that she made it possible for other women to move into the morning shows and to get a wide variety of other on-camera and off-camera jobs in the industry. I also happen to think that she opened the way for women in other fields as well, but that isn't quite as obvious. At any rate she has been a trailblazer.

Over the years she has been supportive of me and I have learned many good lessons from her. Barbara told me some time ago that whether it's money or stories you've been shorted on, you do yourself a disservice if you get angry about what you didn't get. Her advice is to work harder, to hone and polish each little bit you are given until you make it a gem. She also told me not to wait to be given anything but instead to make myself invaluable. In other words, make your own success happen. I've taken her words to heart in the last few years. I think that my hard work, doing my homework and more, has paid off and that my role on *GMA* reflects that hard work.

Using the same basic work ethic, I also decided to work on making my own success outside the program. I have made sure my contract with *GMA* allows me to work on my own projects, where my success does not rely on what the male upper echelon at the network decides to give me. My exclusive contract at the network doesn't leave a lot of room for these projects because there are numerous restrictions about when you're allowed to be seen outside *GMA*, for how long, and in what capacity. There are also limitations on what, if any, commercial endorsements I can make.

But there are ways to work within these restrictions and build opportunities, and Michael has come up with several concepts that work within the network's restrictions and they have turned up as winners. One of these, "Mother's Minutes," is produced and packaged by his company. These short spots offer advice to parents on a variety of subjects important to the lives of small children, subjects ranging from how to prevent and treat diaper rash to how to explain birth, sex, and death to a child. Michael sold this concept to the people at Hasbro and now their Playskool Division that manufactures preschool educational toys sponsors these minutes. Michael has produced more than 200 "Mother's Minutes" and they are seen each weekday between 12:00 noon and 1:00 P.M. on the ABC network.

"Mother's Minutes" sprang from a show called *Mother's Day*, which Michael also created and which I host, seen daily on ABC's Lifetime Network. The show provides information of relevance to parents and shares my own parenting experience. Michael likes to say that it "celebrates motherhood" so that every day is Mother's Day. Our viewer response on both of these shows indicates that we are providing something parents want and need. From these two shows, Michael went on the create and develop a videotape called "Your Newborn Baby—Everything You Need to Know." Our family pediatrician, Dr. Jeffrey Brown, is the expert on the tape with me. And just to keep it a family affair, Michael's brother, Perry, who owns a TV and video distributing company, Meridian Entertainment, is handling the distribution of the tape.

Translating Barbara Walters's ideas of independence into reality has meant a lot of hard work and a lot of personal sacrifice over the last several years. But my heavy work schedule is beginning to pay off in a career which seems to be ever-expanding. It has given me an incredible sense of self-confidence and self-satisfaction and I think it's safe to say that I would not have gotten this from my role on *GMA* alone.

I now have a career that does not depend solely on the whims of one show's management. I think my self-confident attitude actually improves my performance on *GMA,* and though ABC may not always appreciate my feelings of independence, I think they do realize that my new image as an expert on parenting and host of my own show only serves to enhance my on-air presence and their program.

CHAPTER TEN

Good Morning America—
On the Road

Putting *GMA* on the air in New York every weekday morning is an enormous task. Guests must be lined up well in advance for each program (a process we call booking), they have to be preinterviewed, scripts have to be written the day before the show, and if the guests are from out of town, hotels and transportation have to be arranged. Of course, all the other elements that make up the show—the hosts, the producers, directors, camera people, the rest of the crew, film clips, tape pieces, photos, graphics, the list is endless—also must be coordinated. Then we have the *GMA* set itself, the furniture, the flowers, the cameras, sound equipment, and lights. All of this must be pulled together so that the viewer at home sees a smoothly running show with no slipups and seemingly no problems.

Think about synchronizing all of this activity in New York and then imagine taking our show on the road. All the same things have to be done and most of the same people need to be involved. It is a monumental undertaking. Making the travel arrangements alone is difficult enough when you're getting twenty or more people and all their equipment ready to go to an out-of-the-way place like Morocco or Yugoslavia. Plans for some trips are made quickly but for other trips they are made a year or more in advance. Then travel itineraries are developed (and usually changed several times), airline seats and hotel rooms are booked, arrangements for transportation need to be made at the destination, and of course, the people with whom we're going to be working in the country where we're traveling have to be informed about all of our movements.

Nevertheless, not only do we go on the road, we do it several times each year. From my point of view, *GMA* on the road is the fulfillment of all my dreams of travel. I've been to interesting, fascinating, and exotic places. I've talked with the rich, the famous, and the powerful. I've seen sights that only a few people have the chance to see. And I doubt this dream would have become a reality without *GMA*.

In the last several years, since I've been full-time cohost, I've seen most of the United States and at least twenty foreign countries; all of those trips have been memorable in one way or another. Some of them, however, have been more memorable than others, and I want to share some of those experiences with you in more detail.

In June 1984 the *GMA* crew packed up and left for a nine-day trip that had us in Ireland to cover President Reagan's visit to his ancestral homeland, and then on to France for the activities scheduled for the fortieth anniversary of D Day. We were looking to cover more than just the news aspect of these events because ABC News reports the events themselves. They get the pictures of the main characters in the drama, the handshaking, the political discussions, and so forth. In this particular case (as in most other major events) the foreign country involved is in the news for days before, during, and after the presidential visit, the conference, the celebration, or whatever. *GMA* has always tried to give the viewer the flavor of the country involved and its people. We feel we can do something special by letting the American people know more about the place they are hearing about and seeing in the news every day. In short, we try to give this kind of story some perspective. To do it we talk to the people in the street and in the countryside about their problems, their hopes, and their feelings about the United States, and we try to make what is happening more meaningful, more rounded. I'm often assigned to what you could probably call "color commentary."

This was my first long trip since my two children were born and I was a little afraid they would both forget me during those nine days. So as I started doing my background reading on the countries I was to visit, I did so with some misgivings—otherwise known as working-mother's guilt. But once on the plane I sat back and thought about what lay ahead. This would be a once-in-a-lifetime opportunity to follow the president of the United States on his journey and to see one of the most historic battlefields in the world on an occasion of great significance.

The *GMA* people did not travel on the press plane that always trails after the president. We were on our own. We spent our first four days in Ireland, three of them in the Dublin area and one in Belfast. If you recall, this presidential visit was rather delicate. President Reagan was running for reelection at the time and his visit to Ireland was viewed by some, both in this country and in Ireland, as purely political. On top of that, many of the Irish people were not the least bit happy about the administration's stance on the problems in Northern Ireland.

So in this atmosphere I was to report each morning on one or another aspect of life in Dublin and the surrounding area. We covered the major sites in and around Dublin, as well as a country wedding, a horse ranch where the finest Irish horses are raised, and other, day-to-day activities. The scenes and commentary we sent back to the States were, I thought, entertaining and informative.

Some of our coverage, however, turned out to be disconcerting. We did a series of man-on-the-street interviews in Dublin; that is, we stopped people on the street and asked them to give us their opinions on the U.S. and Reagan. What we found was a residue of discontent with our president and his policies, and as hard as we tried to balance these interviews, it was difficult to find a person with a positive opinion on the subject.

From Dublin we flew in a small private plane to Belfast. We flew low so I had a good view of the patchwork fields and small towns; it struck me that it looked very much like the States, and it seemed very peaceful, as if the strife we had heard so much about could not possibly take place here. The violence in Northern Ireland has been in the news off and on for years now, and in contrast to the tranquility I sensed looking down from our plane on the way to Belfast, as I walked through the streets there I felt cold and afraid. The roar of the engines of the patrolling tanks, the burned-out buildings, the debris, the soldiers with guns on nearly every corner were new experiences for me, and I found them absolutely bone-chilling.

As we moved through the streets with our camera we attracted a lot of children and we asked them about the strife and how it affected them. One little boy about ten years old, with curly hair and big, dark eyes that made me melt, told me, "We just want to get out of here as soon as we're old enough." Then he added, "If we survive, that is." This little boy's words were echoed in one form or another by nearly every child we talked to. Their insecurity and the losses they have suffered at such a young age had completely taken away their childhood. I was most grateful my children could still be children.

I got another feel for the problem when we took our cameras to the center of Belfast. To get there we had to go through a military checkpoint where all of our equipment, even my handbag, was inspected by British soldiers. These soldiers, all very young, looked through me as though I didn't exist, and as they frisked me with leather-gloved hands, I knew a moment of the fear that oppressed people everywhere must feel where armies are in control. Well, I can tell you that reading about this sort of thing and seeing it on TV is one thing, going through it is quite another.

Northern Ireland, for me, was a country whose physical beauty and lively people are being overshadowed by the years of fighting which have eroded its spirit and sapped its economy and energy. I had a good chance to talk with many Irish people, elicit their opinions, and see their beautiful country, but I left with a feeling of deep sadness about the prospects for Northern Ireland, and especially the future of the children there.

On June 3 we left Dublin and flew to Paris, where we stayed overnight. The time in Ireland had been trying for me, both physically and emotionally, and I was so exhausted that I skipped a night on the town in Paris in favor of a good night's sleep. The next morning we all piled into cars and drove through some magnificent French countryside to Normandy, where we stayed in a small hotel in Deauville, some distance from Omaha Beach. For the next five days the crew and I drove all around that area of France, gathering material for our stories on the D Day anniversary.

I was not born until after World War II and when I went to school we spent only the necessary time studying that period of recent American history. My knowledge of that time, then, was limited to the books, novels, and articles I had read about D Day and the war. I knew that wasn't enough, so in preparation for this trip I had read several books about World War II and had gotten a thorough briefing from our research department.

Our first piece was filmed in one of the many American military cemeteries that dot the northwestern French coast. As I looked in one direction I was struck by the serene beauty of the French countryside, green and dewy in the morning light. Then, as I turned, that serenity was broken by the stark grave markers of the cemetery. I had never seen so many: Neat row after neat row of white markers spread out on the rolling hillside. The crosses and the Stars of David on these immaculately kept graves decorated with flowers bore the names, ranks, and birth and death dates of these soldiers. I was struck too by the fact that most of them were so young when they died, eighteen and nineteen years old, and that most had died on June 6, June 7, or June 8, 1944. These were America's youth and they were killed before they had a chance to become adults. That thought deeply saddened me, yet standing there, I was surprised that this American cemetery and the others we visited were not unpleasant or depressing places at all. People strolled among the graves, laid flowers and wreaths, and the atmosphere was calm and tranquil.

GMA had contacted a widow of one of these soldiers some months before and she accompanied us on this visit. She was a lovely woman in her late fifties, with a look in her eyes that must have been in my own eyes when my father died. It's a look that speaks of vivid memories. She had gotten married only days before her nineteen-year-old husband was shipped off to the European theater with his army unit. She was seventeen then and they had planned their life together after the war. He was one of those boys who died on the first day of the battle at Normandy. It was the first time she had ever visited his grave and it was very emotional for her and all of our crew. Through her I realized the real meaning of all the young lives we lost there, the real meaning of Memorial Day.

Our next stop was a German military cemetery not far away. It was all black Maltese crosses, somber, bleak, austere, a totally different feeling for me. There were fewer visitors and the grounds were not as well kept. Yet the dates on the crosses were the same. The German boys had also been eighteen and nineteen years old and they had died in those first few days of the battle. We were there to cover a reunion of sorts between a group of former German and American soldiers who had fought against each other during the invasion. They met in the German cemetery and the Americans laid a wreath there. These veterans, all in their sixties, shook hands and talked (and even showed each other their wounds) and remembered those hellish days. But what they were basically saying to each other was: "It's all over. Let's not ever let it happen again." It was an unforgettable scene.

Then we went to the beach itself. At first we all just stood there and looked at the sand and the water. The atmosphere was so charged with those events of forty years before that you could almost hear the sound of the rifles and machine guns. We had talked to many of the thousands of veterans who had returned for this occasion, many of them dressed in their battle gear, and they had painted a stark image of the scene. When we visited the concrete bunkers that still stand overlooking the beach we were told how the men had fought for those bunkers and how many had died trying to put them out of action. We lived the invasion, we felt it, we breathed it. It was eerie. It made the skin prickle and the goose bumps rise.

One man stood with me on Omaha Beach and described in detail how his unit had been dropped from the landing boats loaded with guns and ammunition in water too deep to wade into shore. He told me how he had watched his buddies sink from sight in the water and never come up again, and how he had seen others killed and wounded on the beach as the fire came down from the cliffs overlooking the beach. As I stood there and listened to this man, bald and wrinkled now, but obviously a good-looking man when he was younger, I could have sworn I was listening to the voice of an eighteen-year-old. He was animated as he told me, with tears in his eyes, "We couldn't go back because there was nowhere to go and we couldn't go forward because the fire from above was too fierce. I don't really remember how we got off that beach, but it was an experience I'll never forget." Then he was overcome as his tears turned to sobs and he was unable to go on. Tears came to my eyes too as I imagined what it had been like for him and his young friends that day—with the noise and confusion of battle, the exploding shells, and death all around. The vivid picture he drew actually sent shivers through my body.

The books I'd read and the other research I'd done about D Day raised my awareness of the enormity of the undertaking, but they didn't provoke any of the emotions that flowed over me as I walked on the sand of the Normandy beaches. I suddenly felt that my generation is a little unappreciative. We don't really understand what it is to have our security threatened and to have to fight for it. On that beach I felt it, and our *GMA* audience must have felt it too. In the last segment on Omaha Beach, I walked through the sand, talking about those feelings. On camera I said: "David, the walk on this beach and my talks with these veterans give me a whole new sense of appreciation for what our country is all about, what we have, what we almost lost. I think there's a whole generation of American young people who would be strengthened by bringing them here, to walk through these cemeteries and on this beach." I had to shoot that final segment at least half a dozen times because I kept getting a lump in my throat. I just couldn't talk. And while the other pieces we did from France were interesting, while there was history in every story, people remembered the scene on the beach and the real emotion in my voice.

My ten-day trip to the Winter Olympics in Yugoslavia in 1984 was also emotional and it too raised goose bumps—but a different kind from those I experienced at Normandy. This time I was seeing a different kind of history, a happy, peaceful slice of history. I remember standing on the side of the ice rink where the speed skaters were racing. As I watched these great athletes from around the world glide so gracefully across the ice, as the ice shavings thrown by their skates peppered my face, I was thrilled and excited. Then when I saw the flags of the winners raised in the arena and heard the anthems of their countries and saw the pride in the faces of the competitors and the crowd alike, I was moved.

On this trip we had flown directly from New York to Paris and had then made two other stops in order to get to historic Sarajevo. This little town, the scene of the assassination of Archduke Francis Ferdinand of Austria, the event that served as the spark which ignited World War I, has changed little in those seventy years and I suspect it has changed little in the last 300 years. Sarajevo is a town, not much more than a village really, out of the Old World. It is as picturesque as a postcard but it is still extremely primitive by American standards, even with all the preparations for the Olympics. The people live in tiny houses with outhouses behind, there are more horse-drawn carts than cars (the farmers driving these carts look as though they'd stepped out of old *National Geographic* photographs), and electricity is scarce and unreliable. The air in the town was always thick with the smell of burning coal, since coal is still used for heat in most homes. But inside the public buildings and restaurants the dense cigarette smoke made the outside air smell like a garden. In restaurants, in fact, it was often so smoky that I couldn't see across the room. The press decided that the country's national pastime was smoking cigarettes. Our executive producer, Susan Winston, asked an older Yugoslavian man why the people of the country smoke so much. "Statistics show," she said seriously, "that smoking causes cancer, and people in America are very concerned about it." The old man looked at her for a moment and then said, "We don't have to worry about that, ma'am, because we don't have statistics."

To accommodate the influx of tourists, athletes, and press, the government of Yugoslavia had built new housing in several sections of Sarajevo. Our *GMA* crew was put in one of the press buildings, part of a group of six-story apartments. Each apartment had a main room that served as living room, dining room, and kitchen, and two tiny bedrooms and a small bath. There were no phones in the rooms so we had to go to a central telephone exchange to make our calls. The facilities were a bit minimal compared to what we were used to. After the Olympics all these new buildings were to be turned over to the town and the townspeople were expected to move in. But it was hard to see how a family of four or five could live with any comfort at all in such cramped quarters.

On the streets there were soldiers everywhere, all carrying loaded submachine guns. Whenever we came out of our apartment building there was a soldier with a gun pointed at us, and on every corner in the Olympic Village there were soldiers with guns. It was an uncomfortable atmosphere but unfortunately these are security measures necessary in today's world. I kept thinking to myself, however, "Those guns are real and they could go off."

The security was even tighter at the Olympic events than in the Olympic Village. To get into an Olympic event a member of the press practically had to strip down for a search, and if you didn't have exactly the right credentials to enter a certain door you couldn't get in that door. The guards were polite but firm, and they would say to you in their thick Eastern European accents, "Yes, these are the right credentials but not the right ones for this door. You have to go to the next one." Then they would point to a door thirty feet away and we'd go through the same process all over again.

There had not been much snow prior to the Olympics, and that had been a cause for concern among the Olympic committee and the athletes. But three days after we arrived it started to snow, and it snowed solidly from that day on. Not only was it snowing but it was freezing cold, and we had to wear layers of ski clothes all the time as we trudged in our heavy boots from the site of one event to the site of another.

The mild discomforts of our living arrangements and the weather aside, it was an exhilarating experience for me to observe the Olympics in person. The events themselves were fascinating to see, and I got to talk to many of the athletes. But most of our attention was focused on the people of Sarajevo and on some of the thousands of tourists who were there from all over the world. We filmed from early morning until late at night, and sometimes even into the middle of the night, during our entire stay.

At the end of five days it was still snowing hard and the rumor was spreading that the airport was going to close indefinitely. It was becoming clear that in a day or two it would be impossible to leave Sarajevo. My work was essentially done at that point and I very much missed Michael and Jamie and Lindsay. I didn't want to be stranded on the other side of the world so I said to our unit manager, Bill, who also wanted to leave, "Let's get out of here before we get snowed in permanently."

He said, "I'll go with you, but I heard that the airport is already closed. I'll check the railroads." It turned out that we could have gone by train to southern Yugoslavia, then on to Turkey, and then could have flown out through Istanbul if weather permitted. But it was chancy, the railroad personnel said, and they were reluctant to sell us tickets.

"Let's rent a car then," I suggested to Bill.

"I'll see what I can do," he said.

I was in my room packing when I heard the sound of an airplane taking off in the distnce. I ran to Bill's room, told him I had heard a plane, and suggested we head for the airport. With that we threw our bags into one of the rented ABC cars and roared through the snow to the airport. When we got there we were told that no flights were leaving.

"But I heard a plane," I said.

One of the clerks answered: "That's only because we're trying to get the planes that are on the ground here to other airports so they can fly elsewhere in Europe. We don't want them to get stuck here for perhaps days."

I didn't want to get stuck for days either, so I said in a determined voice, "We want on one of those planes." It took some more fast-talking but we made arrangements to get on one of the Yugoslav Airlines planes that was being ferried out. As we sat in the plane waiting to take off, the maintenance crews were deicing the entire plane and when we looked out, we couldn't see more than ten feet past the window. These weren't the best of circumstances in which to be flying, to put it mildly.

There were extra airline crew members on the plane who were being sent to other cities, but we were the only passengers. After what seemed like several hours on the ground, the storm let up for a few minutes and our plane finally took off. We didn't really know where the plane was going to land because of the weather; a short time later we landed in Zagreb, still in Yugoslavia. There we had to try to get another flight. The two of us ran from one end of the airport to the other and finally managed to squeeze in on a flight to Frankfurt. From there it wasn't difficult to get another flight to New York. I was back home within twenty-four hours of the time I had decided to leave.

The Olympics themselves had definitely lived up to their reputation for athletic excellence and international spectacle, but the distance from home, the work schedule, and the weather conditions had combined to take the edge off things for me until a bit later, when I had time to sit and reflect on the beauty of it all. In retrospect it was a thrilling show, a journalistic challenge, and a valuable experience. Not a bad combination.

In the spring of 1985 I got another travel assignment that sent me on the road to Morocco to interview the stars of Michael Douglas's film, *Jewel of the Nile,* which was being shot on location. The travel arrangements were complex and tiring, though I guess it's hard to complain about a half-day layover in Paris that allows you time to eat in a bistro and take a whirlwind tour of the Louvre Museum. At least I felt that I had done a little bit of Paris.

Royal Air Maroc flew the crew from Paris to Rabat, the political capital of the country, and then on to legendary Casablanca, which still seems to be full of the intrigue one remembers from the movies. Unfortunately we had no time to spend in Casablanca; we were to catch a small plane chartered by 20th Century–Fox, which took us to Fez. We landed in Fez at an airport that was one in name only. There were no people and no other planes in sight and only a small building that served as the terminal. It was more like a bus stop than an airport.

A few minutes after we landed, however, a car appeared out of the heat waves and stopped in front of us; we all climbed in for the last leg of the trip. As is the case with Yugoslavia, I'm sure Morocco hasn't changed much in the last 300 years, and certainly not since Bing Crosby, Bob Hope, and Dorothy Lamour made *Road to Morocco.* There are few cars on the roads (though every one you see is a Mercedes) and the people walking on the side of the road are dressed, for the most part, in traditional Arab garb—especially the women, who wear veils covering their faces and henna on their hands, the same way their ancestors did in ancient times.

Our driver took us into Fez through the ancient wall surrounding the city, which has served as protection for centuries, and then wound his way through the narrow, winding streets, impossible to navigate without a guide. When we arrived at the hotel we were exhausted and after a quick dinner we all headed to our rooms to try to get some sleep.

After a night's rest we were driven to the shooting location, about an hour's ride from Fez. The site included a series of catacombs, large underground caverns, where at one time slaves and horses were housed for protection. We spent most of the next two days in these catacombs, filming the filming of the movie, and talking with the stars, Kathleen Turner, Danny DeVito, and of course Michael Douglas, who also directed the film.

Despite my being from California, where movies are king, and despite my one movie appearance in *Macho Callahan,* I had never really seen a major movie being made before. It isn't at all like live television. For one thing, there are dozens of technicians involved and dozens (sometimes even hundreds) of extras, plus the stand-ins for the stars. But for me the major difference is that everything seems to take forever. One small part of a scene, a line or two, can take hours to prepare for and more hours to shoot. Because moviemakers are creating illusions, retakes are the order of the day in the film business, and this process consumes massive amounts of time. Watching this snaillike pace made me appreciate live TV all the more.

I have to admit, however, that the whole filmmaking process is fascinating. The scene we were watching them make was to be near the end of the movie, but it was actually being filmed before some of the scenes that would precede it in the movie. In this particular scene Michael Douglas and Kathleen Turner are hanging from a scaffold, with their hands tied over their heads and a "bottomless pit" filled with rats underneath them. The bottomless pit is actually only a couple of feet deep; the rats, however, are real (just as they used real alligators in *Romancing the Stone,* one of Douglas's big hits), but they are drugged so they aren't dangerous. Still, rats—ugh. On this day the rat trainer had drugged the little beasts a little too much and they were just lying around instead of scurrying like proper rats, so the shoot had to be delayed repeatedly. When it was finally finished and we got the film we needed, we all went back to the hotel in Fez for dinner. We had a dish that is considered a delicacy in Morocco, quail pie with all the trimmings.

The next morning I had a chance to interview the stars and

one of the questions I asked both Kathleen and Michael was something that has always intrigued me. The question, directed to each of them, was: "How do the sexy love scenes in your movies affect your husband or wife?" They were both candid. Michael said, "I don't want my wife around during those scenes, even though I think she has learned to deal with it. I just don't want to press the issue." Kathleen felt the same way, saying, "I definitely don't want my husband around because it's very distracting. I have to think about too many things if he's here." I thought these were sensitive responses to a difficult question. I also thought it would also be interesting to know how Michael's wife and Kathleen's husband felt, but they weren't there to ask.

Then, lo and behold, later that day, when the others from *GMA* and I took a break and went to the pool to cool off, who should lay their towels down next to us but Kathleen Turner and her new husband, Manhattan real estate developer Jay Weiss, who had just flown in from New York. When I had the opportunity, I asked him the question, and not surprisingly, I thought, he said he was very uncomfortable about the whole thing. He said he could never be around when Kathleen was doing a "hot" love scene because it would really get to him. He had never seen her in her provocative role in the movie *Body Heat* until after they were married. He told me that as he watched it was difficult to believe that it was his wife up there on the screen.

Later I asked Michael Douglas whether making movies, living and breathing movies as he does, and being on the road so much is hard on a marriage. "We all know when we go into these marriages that our time together is going to be limited," he said, "and we know that family just can't be around because there is never enough time for both family and moviemaking. If that is understood at the outset, then there shouldn't be a problem."

Perhaps it's this total dedication that made *Romancing the Stone* such a box-office smash. But Douglas said, "We had no idea the movie was going to be such a gigantic hit and we certainly had no thoughts of making a sequel when we finished it. I think it would be arrogant of me to think there would be a sequel before the first movie was even finished."

One interesting little sidelight to this trip was running into Joel Douglas, Michael's brother, on the set in Morocco. Joel and I had been on World Campus Afloat when the ship had stopped in Morocco eighteen years before and we hadn't seen each other since. The two of us had a nice chat and then he had to go take care of some movie business, something involving Moroccan customs officials who didn't want to accept the machine guns and the jet fighter plane that were needed for a scene in the film. As we parted, I said, "Joel, we have to stop meeting this way."

The next day was spent shooting pieces for *GMA* in Fez. We wanted to capture as much of the flavor of an ancient culture as we could. As we walked from our hotel, we passed through the spice district, the brass district, the cloth district, and several other areas that specialize in certain products. It all seemed a bit mysterious and the heat and the smells permeating the air added to that sense of mystery. We also passed scores of buildings that have survived from the ninth century—houses, beautiful mosques, fountains, and public baths.

With our guide and translator we shopped the brass market; over mint tea we bargained emotionally for some inexpensive jewelry (I learned that in Fez you bargain for everything, even a tomato), and we toured the food market. While we were walking the streets, Michael and I happened to notice a little girl leading her smaller sister by the hand and carrying her baby brother on her back as she made her way toward the market. So different from home was this scene that it shocked us. We Americans are very protective of our children and we don't give them enough credit for being able to fend for themselves, but this sort of life for a child is very foreign to most Americans. What we don't seem to be able to get straight is the fact that the way life is lived today in Morocco is common to most of the world; we are the ones who are different, not they.

That night, as we had dinner on the terrace of our hotel overlooking Fez, I couldn't help but think that the trip was one of those special things that happen when you have a job like mine. After all, how many times do you get the opportunity to see the world and get paid for it too?

Interestingly, I've found that you don't have to go halfway around the world for thrills in the TV business. In 1980 I was sent to cover the presidential inauguration in Washington, D.C. We flew down from New York the night before and by 5:00 A.M. the next morning the crew and I were at the Capitol, where the inauguration was to take place.

Even at that early hour, when we got out of the car we were in the middle of a frenzy of activity. There were painters putting the finishing touches on the announcing booths, the bands were already out setting up their music, technicians were testing microphones, chairs were being arranged in the main visitors' area, and tapes of the presidential march were being played over the public address system to make sure it was all in good working order.

At that moment the sun started to come up and its rays were shining directly on the inaugural podium. Not only was it beautiful, it seemed like a good omen as well. A few hours later people started to gather on the Mall, and as we settled into the announcing booth members of Congress were starting to file into their seats.

When the time approached for the inauguration itself, all the members of Congress and the Supreme Court were seated, and then the two First Ladies, the outgoing and the incoming, took their seats. By that time there were thousands of people on the Mall. The swearing-in ceremony is very brief but very impressive. Then, as the crowd starts to disperse, you realize that the torch has again been passed and that, unlike what happens in many other places in the world, it has been passed peacefully.

As with all the other events I've mentioned, seeing this impressive display in person is very different from seeing it on the nineteen-inch TV screen. There is electricity in the air and that familiar skin prickle starts up. When you know that you're the one who's going to be describing all the activity to the people at home, you can't help but feel a combination of pride and responsibility.

My first inauguration really knocked me off my feet. I think —and hope—everyone in the broadcasting business feels the majesty of it all the first time around, whether it's the Olympics or the presidential inauguration or whatever. It's important to have emotions about those events in order to convey a sense of immediacy to the people who aren't there in person. If you don't feel the importance of something yourself, the audience can't possibly feel it either.

There are other thrills closer to home than Morocco or Yugoslavia, as well. I have made two trips to Arizona in recent years, trips that were both educational and remarkable in their own way. The first was to another inauguration, only this time the man being inaugurated wasn't the president of the United States but the chief of the Navajo Nation.

We had flown to Phoenix to cover the story and had dressed for the hot weather there without thinking that there were places in Arizona that weren't quite as warm as sunny Phoenix. So when we got on the plane to fly to the Navajo reservation that evening, we were dressed for heat. When we got off the plane in the northern corner of the state there was snow everywhere. Not only were our summer outfits useless, but they looked foolish.

Since the Navajos live on a reservation, the only place to get substantial clothing was at the general store, a place that would have been called a trading post in the old days. There we bought parkas, heavy pants, and boots which served us well for two days in the cold, snow, and mud, but we didn't look much like fashionable New York City.

Initiating a new chief for the Navajos is a rare and fascinating event. During the course of our short stay we were able to visit with many Indians, see the houses of the tribe and the tribal ceremonial areas, and sit in on their campfires and ritual dances, and we had a chance to hear the new chief's hopes and dreams for his people. The chief told me that his most profound hope was that the Navajo Nation and its people would be able to hang on to their traditions and their culture as they moved into the modern age. He is not the first leader to have this desire, and I wished him well.

My second Arizona visit was a trip to cover spring training with the Chicago Cubs. My husband, Michael, joined me on this trip and when the Cub management brought out my official Cub uniform he turned green with envy. As he watched me put it on in the hotel he said, "You know, every boy in America, and that includes me, dreams of someday seeing himself in a big-league baseball uniform. We see ourselves putting on the pants, the shirt, the long socks, the spikes, the hat. It's a dream. The next dream is sitting in the dugout, waiting to take the field, and the last dream is hitting a home run to win the crucial game in the bottom of the ninth inning. And here I am in a spring training camp in Arizona, watching my wife put on that big-league uniform that I've always dreamed of wearing. It's not fair!"

Fair or not, I wore that uniform and I played shortstop (even caught a couple of ground balls), batted, did the team exercises, and lived every American boy's dream, if only for a little while. The Cubs gave me a warmup jacket, a cap, and an official baseball card with my picture on it, but unfortunately I had to give them back the uniform.

As I said, I did exercises with the team; when I got back to New York I was so sore it was almost too painful to smile. That, however, was a small price to pay for my big-league experience.

One of the biggest thrills I've had in my job was my interview with Prince Charles when he was in the States for a tour that included a visit to the United World College in New Mexico, which was founded by Lord Mountbatten, his favorite relative. The college is located in a rather barren part of the state and the crew and I stayed in a little hotel just like the small hotel you would envision in the middle of nowhere. This was not a *GMA* exclusive interview, but it was exciting that Prince Charles had agreed to do only three American television interviews, and they went to the three morning female anchors—myself, Jane Pauley of NBC, and Diane Sawyer of CBS.

The first night there, we were all invited to dinner at a local restaurant with the entourage that accompanies Prince Charles wherever he goes. In essence we were there to be interviewed to see if we were acceptable, but more than that, we had to be instructed on what we could not talk about and how to conduct ourselves in the presence of the prince.

As it turned out, it would have been easier to tell us what we *could* talk about because as they ran down the list of don'ts— don't talk about royal finances, don't talk about the Prince Andrew–Koo Stark incident, don't talk about the personal lives of Prince Charles or Princess Diana, and all the other don'ts—it appeared there wasn't much left. Then they had to teach us how to approach and address royalty. We learned that the prince would extend his hand first and we were not to extend ours until he did; he was to speak first and then we could speak; he would sit first and then we could sit; we were to call him "Your Royal Highness" when we were introduced and then either "Sir" or "Prince" thereafter. What this meant for the three of us was that when we went in to the interview we figuratively had to try to pat our heads and rub our stomachs at the same time, as we remembered the rules and tried to get our interviews in order. We had also been limited to talking essentially about what he was there for, that is, to promote the school, which was the least interesting of the possible topics.

The interviews were scheduled for the next morning and Diane, Jane, and I had flipped a coin to see who would go first. Jane won, Diane was to go second, and I was to go in last. As the three of us watched from a room nearby, the prince came up the stairs into the room where the interview would take place, and as he ascended those stairs you could get a feeling of royalty, you knew that you were looking at the next king of England. He looked every inch a royal person. His carriage and his manner, everything about him, bespoke royal breeding. The room itself, with its high ceiling, large fireplace, and two elegant high backed leather chairs, also looked like a royal setting.

Jane's interview went well enough. But as my producer, Susan Winston, and I watched from the library (we couldn't hear what was being said but we could see), Diane Sawyer asked the prince something that made his face change completely. Susan said, "Uh-oh, she must have asked about Koo." That was what happened, all right, and at that point the prince became very guarded in his responses to Diane. I must say that I think it's perfectly all right to ask tough questions but for maximum effectiveness they should be saved until last if you're going to ask them.

Unfortunately, I had to walk into that rather tense atmosphere after Diane was finished and win him over, and I was nervous. But I had one big thing going for me at that point, and it was sticking out right in front of me. I was seven months pregnant. The prince is the man who once shocked feminists around the world by saying of women, "Keep them barefoot and pregnant," and in this instance I planned to use my pregnancy to my advantage. Princess Diana had just given birth to Prince William and I thought I could use that to lighten his mood. Of course, the prince immediately noticed my condition and he congratulated me. Before we sat down we exchanged some parental chitchat; I could see he was warming up and I began to relax.

The rule established for these interviews stated that as soon as we both sat down there would be ten minutes for the interview and that was all. In that ten minutes I was able to get some very warm and personal thoughts from him about his wife and his new child, though I had to work within the restrictions mentioned above. I started in a general way by asking him about his schooling, and then we discussed the kind of schooling he wanted for his children. From there I moved on to Princess Diana and their new son, Prince William. Among his answers was an admission that he missed his wife and child very much and for that reason this particular trip had been a hard one. I could certainly sympathize with him on that score (I feel the same way when I travel without Michael and the kids), and it was this level of empathy that helped me get a good interview. In fact, I'm sure *GMA* got the best interview of the three networks because I went for his humanity and I got it. Later, the prince sent word back that he had liked our interview very much and that pleased me immensely.

Keeping in the royal vein, more recently I flew to California to interview Prince Rainier of Monaco, his son, Prince Andrew, and his younger daughter, Princess Stephanie. Prince Rainier had taken a whole floor of suites at the Beverly Wilshire Hotel in Los Angeles and that's where the interview took place. The rules in this case were roughly the same as with Prince Charles. Prince Rainier was to be addressed as "Sir" and "Prince," and the children as "Prince" and "Princess." If all three of them were together in the same room I was supposed to address Prince Rainier first, Albert second, and Stephanie last, as that is the order of the monarchy. I later accidentally called the children by their first names because they had been in the *GMA* studios before and because they are so personable and young it's hard to address them formally.

Here too, our questions were limited. There were to be no questions about the accident in which Princess Grace was killed and no questions about Prince Rainier's romantic affairs or those of his children. Again, not much left to work with, but I think we got a good few minutes of tape, which included Prince Rainier telling me that his greatest wish for his daughter Stephanie was that she find a nice man to marry.

After we had finished I called home and told Jamie I had just been with two real princes and a princess, just like the ones we read about in our books. She was very excited because, like all little boys and girls, she loves prince and princess stories.

My biggest royal event—and possibly my biggest thrill since I've been in television—was the wedding of Prince Charles and Princess Diana in London. Jamie was only about a year old at the time and I wasn't too happy about leaving her for two weeks. Fortunately I had pregnancy clauses written into my contract so that ABC and I could agree on a compromise. We decided that I would go to London for one week alone prior to the wedding if ABC would pay for Jamie's ticket; she would come over the second week with Michael, who would pay his own way.

Almost the entire show went to London for this event, and the first week I was out with the crew from morning until night. We taped interviews with dozens of Londoners and visited nearly every tourist spot, and some not so touristy spots, in the city. I was filmed in a turret of the Tower of London, at Buckingham Palace, at Big Ben, at Westminster Abbey, in Trafalgar Square, and riding around the city with a London cabbie. It was all tremendous fun.

You're absolutely overwhelmed with a sense of history when you visit London. We think a building that is 100 years old is a relic, but there people live and work in a city built many centuries ago. One night Michael and I stopped for dinner at a small inn on the outskirts of London. As we stood waiting for a table, we were marveling at the historic quality of the building, so as the owner took us to our table he said he was sorry, he would have to seat us in the new part of the inn. That seemed a little disappointing so I asked him, "When was the new part built?" With typical British understatement, he said, "Oh, around 1640." That seemed historic enough for us so we stayed and had a wonderful time.

During the wedding I was broadcasting live from a booth in front of Buckingham Palace. The crowds were huge throughout the event and I've never been so aware of the spirit of a large crowd. I think one of the reasons for everyone's good humor was that the wedding was one of the few major news events in recent memory that was a completely joyous occasion. It didn't seem that there was an unhappy person in London at the time and that added enormously to the tenor of the event.

Although we weren't able to get a personal interview with the royal couple (no one did except British television), we were very close to all the pomp and circumstance that could be mustered by a monarchy, even one known for its pomp. From the mounted guards and gilded carriages to the smiles of the members of the royal family assembled on the balcony of the palace following the ceremony, it was an event I'll never forget.

This is a taste of what it's like when *GMA* goes on the road. Often, when we're out in the field—in Normandy or Yugoslavia, in New Mexico or Arizona, for instance—there is really no glamour to the job, at least not the kind of glamour one normally associates with the television business. It's just plain hard work. We're up with the sun and on the road constantly. We usually eat in the car, if we have time to eat at all, and we're always down and dirty. It's not a place for your good knits, and in fact, pants, shirts, and boots are often the order of the day. I do my own hair and makeup when I have the time and if I don't have the time I'll go on camera without it. These trips are often difficult, long, and trying, and there is a good deal of tension, but they are truly rewarding and they represent some of the high points of my career at *GMA*.

CHAPTER
ELEVEN

The Giant Grape

Like most couples, Michael and I had discussed when and if to have children many times even before we were married in September 1978. About a year after we were married the discussion continued with a greater sense of reality. In principle we both wanted to start a family but in practice we weren't certain about the whole idea. My career was beginning to flourish at *GMA*. I was doing more spots on the show and subbing regularly for Sandy Hill as cohost while continuing to report for *Eyewitness News*. The possibility of eventually becoming permanent cohost at *GMA* was a real one. Quite frankly, I was just becoming successful and part of me wanted to wait until my career really took off before committing myself to a family. After all, a pregnancy would mean I would have to take time off, I could suffer a decline in popularity, or a substitute might come along and do the job well enough to take my place on a permanent basis. These were all real risks that I had to consider.

For Michael's part, he had just decided not to renew his contract at *Today* because he wanted to bring to reality his dream of forming his own production company. He did so and soon Michael Krauss Productions was under contract to produce several important programs, which consumed most of his time and energy. Our jobs kept us both completely occupied, often from early morning until late at night. All too often we were going in opposite directions and our schedules were very unpredictable. On the positive side of the coin, both our careers were going well and, more important, neither of us wanted to wait too long and wind up being the oldest parents in the car pool. When we put all this together, the positives definitely outweighed the negatives and we decided to go ahead and start our family as soon as possible.

At the very time we made this decision, the fine points of the contract that was to bring me to *Good Morning America,* not as cohost but as a regular member of the *GMA* family, were being finalized. As fate would dictate, one week after we'd made a verbal deal (no contract had yet been signed) I had an appointment with my gynecologist for an examination. Later that day I was in the newsroom, putting the finishing touches on a story I had covered about leakage in a chemical plant, a story I was going to do on the air less than an hour later. Michael was at a music session and was supposed to come by the newsroom after it was over. As I looked at the clock, I suddenly realized it was 5:30. I was supposed to call for my test results before 5:30! I quickly dialed the doctor's office. The nurse who answered said, "Let me see. Oh, yes. Here's your name. You're positive."

"Positive?" I said. "You mean I'm pregnant?"

"Yes, ma'am, I mean you're pregnant," she responded. I just sat there with a big stupid grin on my face for a minute, but my impending deadline snapped me back to reality. As I began to type Michael walked in.

"Looks like we can celebrate tonight," I said with a big smile on my face.

Michael just looked at me in disbelief for a second and then said, "You're kidding?" He gave me a big kiss and then I went in to do the six-o'clock news. Michael stood in the corner of the studio during the whole newscast just staring at me.

The next morning I wanted to shout to the world, "I'm pregnant, I'm going to have a baby," but before I could do that I had to call my lawyer and talk with him about what effect my pregnancy was going to have on my contract with *GMA*—it had been worked out in a long series of meetings between my lawyer and the ABC lawyers. I thought the contract could be in jeopardy and I was suddenly certain that this very-much-wanted pregnancy was going to undo all that work—and possibly my television career as well.

I had always liked children and had always dreamed of having my own, but I had also dreamed of a top job in television and had worked hard to get where I was in the business. I didn't want to see all that work wasted. I knew that family and career could be mixed but I wasn't so certain that my type of career and my idea of how a family should be raised would mix all that well. What I'm trying to say is that I was filled with mixed emotions and I realized, possibly for the first time, what all the fuss about working mothers was really about.

I called my lawyer. "I'm pregnant," I said.

"That's wonderful," he said. "When are you due?"

"Sometime in July," I answered, aware that he didn't seem to be making any connection between the *GMA* contract and my getting pregnant.

I gave him the details and then said, "Do you think they'll still hire me?"

"They absolutely have to," he said calmly and reassuringly. "All the details have been ironed out. The deal has been cut and, besides, in today's business world a company couldn't back out because of a pregnancy."

As it turned out, my lawyer was right and my concerns were ill founded. The people at ABC didn't seem to be upset at all. They congratulated me on my contract and my pregnancy and that was all there was to it.

I still had a contract to fulfill at *Eyewitness News* before going over to *GMA,* however, and it wasn't long before everyone there knew I was going to have a baby. I wasn't visibly pregnant yet but there wasn't any point in trying to keep that kind of secret in a business that thrives on gossip.

As soon as possible I met with the news director and told him that I would not be able to do any more reports about leaking chemicals or reports from hospitals, where I might catch some thing, or ride in unpressurized helicopters to cover stories (which we did a lot of in New York), or go out on any other dangerous assignments. "There's also the problem of covering remote stories where we use microwave TV equipment," I said, "because there is concern that it can be dangerous to a fetus." (This has since become a national issue among female news reporters.) When I was finished with my list he looked at me and said, "Joan, why don't you make it easier and tell me which stories you can cover?"

Then, on January 1, 1980, I left WABC-TV and went to work at *GMA,* subbing for Sandy Hill and doing more stories. When Sandy left shortly thereafter to cover the Lake Placid Olympics, my cohosting became more frequent in her protracted absence. Then the word came down that Sandy would not be coming back to *GMA.* It was fairly common knowledge that she was unhappy with her role on the show and her assignments. And she apparently decided that her Olympic assignment offered her a good chance to exit on a high note. She worked it out with *GMA* to be a "special correspondent," responsible for only a few reports a month, until her contract ran out. For that period she must have been the highest-paid part-time person in all of television.

Nevertheless, Sandy's departure signaled my entrance and I became a full-time semipermanent substitute cohost, growing stomach and all. This meant that I began to receive the buildup accorded to a new person on the program, and as I was going to go through much of my pregnancy on television, there was growing attention paid to that as well. There were stories in all the major magazines—*Time, Newsweek, Redbook, Woman's Day,* and *TV Guide*—as well as most of the daily newspapers in the country. I had become the subject of enormous public attention.

Frankly, I had no idea that the American public would be so excited by something so common, so everyday that it hardly causes a stir in most circles. But cause a stir it did. My daily progress and the way I was going to handle my career after the baby was born became the subject of scores of radio and TV interviews, thousands of pieces of fan mail, and uncounted phone calls to the *GMA* office.

Believe me, the whole thing was not a publicity stunt. If it had been it wouldn't have worked as well. In fact, Michael and I originally planned to keep everything a secret until I began to show, around the fourth or fifth month, and then for me to keep working as long as my pregnancy was proceeding normally and I wasn't so large as to distract the audience. That plan was quickly dropped, probably because I looked pregnant as soon as I was diagnosed so. So David announced on the show that I was pregnant but that I would continue to work as long as I felt like it and return four or five weeks after delivery.

David was truly helpful. He is a devoted family man with four children of his own and he was supportive of me from the beginning. I think it was his positive approach as much as anything else that convinced me to stay with the show until I was ready to go to the hospital.

Although other women who were pregnant had continued to appear on television, I was among the first women to be publicly pregnant for practically the entire term. Interestingly, Florence Henderson, who appeared on *Today* in its early days, was pregnant while she was on the air, but it was never announced and she was always shown sitting behind a desk. On the day before she was to leave the show she stood up so everyone could see, and that was the first the public knew about it. Since my pregnancy, however, Jane Pauley has been pregnant on the air, as have a number of local newswomen I know of, so that today it's a relatively common and little-noticed event. Without taking too much credit for blazing this trail, I do think my pregnancy put the stamp of approval on continuing to work on camera while pregnant. The feeling of women in the industry seems to have been, "If Lunden can do it, it's clearly all right for me," and I think this positive attitude forced management to take another look at the whole issue. I certainly didn't have that in mind but I feel good about it.

I don't think things were ever quite normal on *GMA* during

that period because everyone who came on the show had to make a comment about my condition. Instead of, "Nice to be here," it was, "How do you feel?" In truth, we all had fun with it on the air. Bill Cosby gave me some tongue-in-cheek advice for after the baby was born. He quipped, "Walk softly and carry a big stick." When Dom DeLuise was on we compared stomachs and he said, "I think I'm due before you." It was all lighthearted and it made that period a special time for me and, I think, for the audience as well.

And of course, my condition seemed to give me special medical qualifications as well. I was doing stories about normal and problem pregnancies, natural childbirth, postpregnancy problems, early childhood diseases, nutrition for children, and maternity clothes for working women. I became the resident specialist on all subjects related to my being pregnant. And my condition gave me a very high profile: By the eighth month, my profile, on which I was carrying an extra fifty-five pounds, was so high it could be seen a block away.

It was at that time that I was sent to do an interview with Burt Reynolds and everyone around the office was kidding me about interviewing America's number-one sex symbol with my extremely obvious stomach. You've got to admit this is a real case of bad timing. It doesn't seem that there's much justice when you're sent to interview Burt Reynolds and you look like a Sherman tank.

And speaking of Burt Reynolds, he offers the perfect example of how unfair it is to have a preconceived notion about someone. I had never been a big *Smokey and the Bandit* fan, and I'd only seen and read about Burt in magazines and watched him a couple of times on *The Tonight Show* on Friday nights. With Johnny Carson he assumes a role—a cocky, arrogant, sexy guy. Therefore, I approached my interview with him with my mind set on the idea that I wasn't going to like his "God's gift to women" attitude.

At any rate, what I found during my interview was a charming, sensitive, gracious, lovely, open man with a great sense of humor. I was pleasantly surprised. He was nice and I felt comfortable with him, so I said, "How do you feel about your reputation as a ladies' man?"

He answered: "I think the image is partly because I'm single. It makes for terrific reading in the bathroom and you know that's what it's meant for. The magazines follow you around and they would love to get a shot of you and me right now, especially in your condition. It would make a terrific shot."

About two years later, I was preparing to fly down to Burt's home in Florida to interview him a second time. The day before I was to leave, my doctor told me I was pregnant with our second child. I was very excited and I immediately called Michael to tell him. That night we celebrated, and the next morning I took off for Florida.

As before, Burt was perfectly charming, and during a break in our interview, he and I were standing by his swimming pool. I said with mock seriousness, "Burt, we have to stop meeting this way."

"What do you mean?" he asked innocently.

"You know the last time we met for an interview I was pregnant, and . . ."

"No," he said, "are you?"

"Yes, I am," I said, "and I just found out yesterday. In fact, you are only the third person to know. The people on *GMA* don't even know yet."

He congratulated me warmly and we went on with the interview that was partly to promote his movie, *The Best Little Whorehouse in Texas*. He later sent me an extra-large *Best Little Whorehouse* T-shirt with a note that said he hoped it would accommodate my future figure.

But let me tell you that being pregnant and keeping my working schedule wasn't easy, although it may have looked easy from the other side of the camera. Picture trying to put on panty hose at 4:15 A.M. when you can't see your feet. And there were mornings when the normally smooth ride to the city felt as if I were on a sailing ship caught in a typhoon. On those mornings I got very little work done in the car because I spent most of my time munching saltines and trying to get the crumbs out of my pockets. I even started carrying bags like the ones used on planes for airsickness. That thirty-minute trip often seemed to last three hours and when the driver finally pulled up in front of the studio I'd drag myself out of the car and rush (did I say rush) up to my dressing room to either collapse or throw up.

On those mornings, and on less trying ones as well, my makeup person had to perform major miracles. I mean, what's the color combination you use to change murky green skin to bright, healthy-looking skin? I don't know what she used but her magic worked. The same was true of my hair. It was always limp and damp and needed serious help.

My morning sickness was usually in full swing by the time I got to the studio. There were mornings when I thought it was going to be impossible to go on the air. But somehow I managed to make every show; in fact, I never missed a day during either pregnancy.

Here I was five months along and getting very large. At first I had worn jumpers and blouses from several maternity shops on Madison Avenue, but I soon got tired of the little-girl look. I then asked my friends at Lillie Rubin to figure out something that looked more businesslike. They found some regular clothes in generous sizes—tailored pantsuits, skirts and tops—and cut the side seams and inserted stretch material that would expand as I continued to gain weight. As I continued to grow I decided that dark blue, almost a purple, was one of the more slimming colors for me to wear on the air and I got several maternity outfits in various shades of blue.

One of these outfits was a marvelous knit dress that didn't look like a maternity outfit at all; I wore it often. But the first time I wore that particular dress on the set, David took one look at me and said, "Joan, don't take this wrong, but you remind me of a giant grape." And thus was born the nickname that followed me for the rest of my pregnancy. It didn't help matters when I had my hair cut shorter either. It emphasized my girth even more and made me look as if I had a tiny little head and this tremendous grapelike body.

I got so much mail during those months, literally thousands of cards, letters, and telegrams, that it was difficult to go through it all. But I eventually managed to answer every single piece of correspondence. Viewers wished me luck, offered advice, and sent special recipes for during and after the pregnancy, and at least half the letters contained suggestions for naming the baby. School classes sent long lists of possible names and some teachers turned the whole thing into a classroom project. They would send the children's guesses on the day and the time the baby would be born.

It was a very exciting time for me and I was enjoying my pregnancy thoroughly—until I did an interview on the show that changed my entire thought pattern for the next four months, right into the delivery room.

A Catholic priest who was also a handwriting expert was booked for the show and I got the interview. This man had helped police departments by analyzing and identifying handwriting and was considered an expert in the field. He also claimed he could tell the sex of an unborn child by analyzing the mother's handwriting, since, he said, pregnant women go through a hormonal change which affects their handwriting and that change differs according to the sex of the child.

I sent him a sample of my handwriting before the interview and had no idea what he was going to say on the air. The day he was on we went through the interview and at the end I said: "You've had time to analyze my writing, Father. What sex do you think my baby will be?"

He said, "Joan, you're going to have a girl."

"If you're right," I said, "we'll have you back on the show in a few months."

At that point we broke for a commercial; I was about to thank him for coming, when he put his hand on my arm and said, "Joan, I have to tell you something."

He was very serious. "What's that," I said.

"I'd be remiss if I didn't tell you that I noticed something else in your handwriting," he answered. "There is something wrong

with your pregnancy. I don't know what it is but you should tell
your doctor that there's a problem."

I was trying to remain calm but I'm sure my mouth dropped
open. "What kind of problem?" I asked.

"I really don't know, but it's serious," he said.

I don't normally put much stock in fortune telling, and to me
this fell into that category, but when you're pregnant you're not
quite as rational as usual and I was suddenly scared to death. I
picked up the phone on the set and called Michael to tell him the
story.

He was outraged. "I can't believe anyone would say a thing
like that," he said, "but there's nothing to it, there can't be, so
just put it out of your mind." I didn't put it out of my mind; in
fact, I could hardly think about anything else for the rest of the
show.

As it turned out, Michael hadn't been so cool about it either.
He had called the doctor and set up an appointment for me as
soon after the show as I could get there.

My doctor, Hilliard Dubrow, is certainly not an alarmist. He
took me in immediately and sat me down in his office. "You are
having a perfectly normal pregnancy," he said, "so don't let
some stranger—a handwriting analyst, for God's sake—tell you
any differently."

"I want you to run some tests," I said, completely uncon-
vinced.

"All right," he said, walking over and putting his hand about
an inch above my stomach. "If my hand turns right it's a boy and
if it turns left it's a girl. Or do you want me to dangle a penny on
a string and see which way it spins?" he said rather disgustedly.
"If you want to believe in witchcraft and quacks who foretell the
future, go ahead; but if you want to believe in science, then believe that your baby is absolutely healthy and so are you. People
should not give medical advice unless they are doctors."

As I left, Dr. Dubrow, who is the kind of obstetrician every
woman wishes she had, said once more, "There is nothing
wrong. Everything is perfect."

Despite his reassurances, I couldn't help it, I remained uncertain. I know it was irrational but that creep of a handwriting expert had planted a seed of doubt in my mind that ruined the rest of my pregnancy. I never again felt as secure as I had before that interview. From that point on, I went out of my way to do everything according to the book. I ate the right foods (one reason I gained so much weight), I ate extra protein, I didn't drink alcohol (I don't smoke so that wasn't a problem), I drank milk, I wouldn't take an aspirin if I had a double migraine. I was a fanatic.

Then, even in the delivery room, I was scared. When they said the baby had ten fingers and ten toes I relaxed a little but I kept my eye on her for weeks, looking for signs of problems. Later, Michael wanted to wreak some kind of revenge on that man for putting us, especially me, through all that agony. We didn't do anything, of course, but you can bet the man will never be on *GMA* again if I can help it.

I left the show at the end of June and Jamie was born on July 4, 1980. Pat Collins, another regular on the show who had just had a baby of her own, filled in for me in July and part of August, and when I came back on August 24 I was officially named cohost of *GMA*. That morning there were balloons and banners on the set and the press was there in force. David made a formal announcement about the job and the baby was brought in from backstage. It was all very nice, if a little reminiscent of *Queen for a Day*.

About six months into my pregnancy it had become clear to me that the pregnancy itself, even if it was difficult, wasn't going to be as big a problem as the first few months after the baby was born. I planned to breast-feed and wanted to be with the baby as much as possible. On the other hand, the executives in charge of *GMA* didn't want me to miss too much time on the air; a compromise was worked out and my contract was revised to cover some of what I considered the important points. Specifically, they agreed to set up a nursing area next to my dressing room and another one at the *GMA* office and to provide a nanny for me when I traveled for the show during the first six months after the baby was born. They really came through.

The first thing ABC did was to turn the dressing room next to mine into a nursery. They even put Jamie's name on the door. There was also a nurse, whom I provided, to take care of Jamie while I was working. She certainly didn't suffer from a lack of attention, because a baby on the premises was a novelty.

One day I was putting Jamie down for an early-morning nap (and I do mean early-morning), I looked up to see Barbara Walters standing in the doorway marveling at the scene.

"How wonderful it is that you're able to do this," she said. "When my daughter was a baby they would have laughed me out of the studio if I'd asked to bring her to work with me. It would have been like asking to bring my puppy to the office."

Sammy Davis, Jr., was in the studio for an interview not long after Jamie was born, and he came up to me and said, as everyone did, "How's the baby?"

"Just great," I said. "In fact, she's right upstairs in my dressing room."

He said, "Really, bring her down."

So I got Jamie and brought her to the studio. Sammy took her in his arms and cuddled her for a couple of minutes and a photographer who happened to be on the set that day took an impromptu picture. It now hangs on a wall at home and we refer to it as a picture of "Uncle Sammy."

Not only was the nurse on duty at all times, but my assistant, Elise Cohen, spent a lot of time entertaining the baby in the nursery and, later in the day, in my office.

In fact, traffic control in my office became a real problem. Trying to coordinate breast-feeding time and office appointments eventually required a sign on the door that read, "Stop! Please Knock Before Entering. Breast-Feeding Mother Lives Here." Needless to say, when a male writer came to brief me, Jamie had to wait a few minutes for lunch.

Jamie had cribs all over the place. I carried her to the studio in the morning in a basket. There she was put in a crib in the nursery. From there I took her to my office, where she had another crib. When I left to go home she went back in her basket and when I got home I had a basinette downstairs so she could be with me while I made dinner. At the end of the day, of course, she went to sleep in the crib in her room. After observing the bed situation for several days, Michael said, "You know, this kid has more beds than Conrad Hilton."

In addition to the letters and cards I received while I was pregnant and after the baby was born, I also received so many presents it's hard to imagine. There were literally hundreds of baby blankets, hand-crocheted bibs and booties by the score, a huge stack of afghans, and dozens of dolls. There were so many gifts that we couldn't store them all, and those we didn't use we passed on to the appropriate charities, who assured me that the gifts would get into the hands of people who couldn't afford to buy necessities for their newborns.

About a year and a half later, I got pregnant again. I knew that the first time had been different and interesting and kind of cute to the people on the show and to the audience, but I felt certain the second time would be a big bore. Susan Winston was executive producer of *GMA* at the time and she and I had gone to see a screening of a new film in preparation for an interview with one of the stars. The movie had to do with family and children, and as I sat there watching I thought to myself that I really had to tell Susan what was going on. I was already three months pregnant and if I didn't say something soon she'd eventually say, "Joan, don't you think you ought to lose a little weight?" After the screening we stopped for a cup of coffee and I said, "I have something to tell you, Susan."

"You're pregnant," she said without a pause.

"How did you know?" I asked. "I thought I was hiding it pretty well."

"I didn't," Susan said, "but after that movie it seemed logical that if you wanted to tell me something it was about having another baby. Anyway, I think it's great."

It was good to have a woman for a boss at that moment. I said,

"I would like to keep this one low-key if we can. I don't want the audience to start gagging over the whole idea."

Susan agreed, and this time around I didn't do all the stories about pregnancy, childhood diseases, and all the rest. But about a month later David said on the air, "If you've noticed Joan has put on a few pounds, it's because she's pregnant, and we all want to congratulate her."

That was it for public announcements but the congratulatory mail, the baby-naming contests, and the presents started all over again. Still, we did manage to keep everything low-key until the very end, when I went into what I thought was labor on a Sunday night. I called the producer and said, "I won't be in tomorrow because I'm going to have my baby." That was fine and David went on the next morning and said, "Joan's not here this morning because she is in labor. Don't worry, we'll let you know what happens." The problem was that it turned out to be false labor and I ended up going home from the hospital that noon.

I called Susan Winston to tell her, saying, "For some reason I'm not good at figuring out when babies are actually due."

"I don't know why it's so hard to figure," she quipped, "just figure out which weekend it was. You're the one person that I know who didn't get pregnant during the week."

Since it would have been a bit anticlimactic to come back on the program and tell people, "Only kidding, folks," I decided to stay home, even though I wanted to use my maternity leave after the baby arrived and not before. That whole week went by with my doctor advising me that it could happen any minute. Every morning at some point in the show David would say, "No, she hasn't had the baby yet, but we'll let you know when she does," and the producers at *GMA* were saying, "Do it already." By the time the next weekend rolled around, I called the doctor and told him, "I want to have this baby already."

He said, "Okay, if you don't go into labor this weekend we'll induce you on Monday morning."

That Monday I woke up with contractions and called the doctor. He said, "If your labor has just started why don't you wait until after the rush-hour traffic is over and then come on in and I'll meet you at the hospital."

I said that was fine but as soon as I hung up the phone something inside told me that it wasn't fine. I don't like to be late for little things and I didn't want to be late to the hospital for this big thing.

"Michael, I want to go now," I said. "I'd much rather wait on the other end because if it isn't all right to wait then I'm there instead of here."

We packed the car and left for the hospital. As we got close to the highway we could see that it looked like a parking lot with no vacancies. This was very unusual even at rush hour. Nothing was moving toward the city and we couldn't figure out what was going on. Michael turned on the radio and we heard the news that there was a transit strike and there were no commuter trains running. The first morning of a transit strike is no time to try to get anywhere by car, especially to the hospital in a hurry. As we crept along, my contractions were increasing. When we got near the city, traffic stopped completely and as we inched toward an exit Michael decided to take drastic action. Since there was almost no traffic coming from the city he crossed over the median and started south in the northbound lane in order to attract a police car. It worked. Inside of two minutes there was a patrol car, all lights flashing, signaling us to pull off on the shoulder.

When the officer got to the car Michael pointed to me and said, "My wife's having a baby."

"Okay, we'll take her to Women's Hospital," the officer said calmly, "it's only a few blocks from here."

"No," Michael said. "We have to get her to Lenox Hill. Special case! Special doctor!"

The officer said, "Let's go."

With the siren screaming, the police led us across town, weaving through all the traffic, and dropped us off at the hospital door. It was 10:05 A.M. At 10:40 Lindsay was born. I was very glad we left earlier than we had planned, for we hadn't anticipated a transit strike.

That same afternoon I got a call from one of the *GMA* producers. He wanted to know what I thought about the idea of a live remote from my hospital room the next morning. I talked it over with Michael and we decided to go along with the idea because it would give people a chance to see the baby—not only the regular viewers, but also all our relatives and friends who otherwise wouldn't be able to see her for some time.

Everything was arranged with the hospital and the next morning, at about five, there was a knock on my door and in walked the camera crew to set up for the shoot. I had insisted that they all wear surgical masks, so it was quite a strange sight to see all these technical people running around with white masks on. When it was time, the baby was brought in, we went on, and everyone had a grand time. Later, someone from the *Daily News* came to photograph the baby, Michael and me with the two policemen who had escorted us to the hospital.

I was off the air for only three weeks after that hospital scene because I felt a personal responsibility to get back to the show. Returning to work that soon is not something I would recommend to anyone else. It was hard. I was still heavy and I was constantly tired from lack of sleep. In fact, emotionally and physically, I felt as if I'd been hit by a speeding truck.

And to top it off, I'd been back only about two weeks when I got word that the executive in charge of the show had said he thought I was looking too fat and ought to get busy losing weight and getting back in shape. I was mad and I exploded. How could he say such an insensitive thing to a breast-feeding mother who'd come back to a very demanding early-morning schedule less than a month after giving birth? In all fairness, however, I was in a state in which I would explode or cry when anyone looked cross-eyed in my direction, but this explosion was beyond postpartum depression.

I told him I'd be glad to take the rest of my maternity leave to get back in shape and I'd see him in two months. At that point he realized it wasn't such a hot idea since a rating period was coming up and I was important to the show. So he backed off.

Now just between you and me, while he didn't do the right thing, his remarks did give me the kick in the pants that I apparently needed, and within an hour I'd signed up for an exercise class. It's not easy to lose weight when you're combining nursing and an exhausting work schedule, but I started to get back in shape and as soon as possible I started dieting as well.

In all of this talk about balancing children, marriage, and career, I've said very little about our home life—so little, in fact, that you may think that the four of us lack both the highly touted quality time and the much-maligned quantity time together. That isn't the case at all; because of my schedule we probably have more time together than most families with two working parents.

The disadvantage of getting to work so very early is balanced on the other end by the fact that I get home by mid-afternoon on most days. That means I'm usually home when Jamie gets home from school and occasionally I'm even early enough to pick her up at school myself.

When I do pick her up, Jamie usually wants a treat after school (and so do I) so she and I sometimes stop for ice cream or cookies on our way back home. I've discovered, as most working mothers have, that you must rather quickly change your emotional and intellectual gears when you get home. In a working situation you are organized, you're able to deal somewhat unemotionally with your colleagues, you give orders, and so forth. These are essential attributes for the working woman, but at home things don't work that way; in fact, they are quite the opposite. You have to be flexible, to change your schedule repeatedly, to take orders, and the last thing you can be is unemotional.

In my own case my gears are switched from federal deficits and crises in the Mideast to My Little Ponys and Candyland. In the wider world Candyland may not be as important as federal deficits, but it is important in the small world of a young child.

From the time I get home until my telephone briefing from the office at around 6:00, the girls and I do things everyone else does. We color, we paint by number, we bake our Shrinky Dinks, and we play with Barbie dolls. I find it all incredibly relaxing and therapeutic.

Of course, the girls really get a big kick out of playing Let's Be Safe! They call it "Mommy's game" because my picture is on the box. It's a Hasbro board game for young children which helps them learn about safety at home and in the neighborhood, the dangers presented by strangers, the problems of sexual abuse, drugs, and alcohol. It may be a game but it is a teaching device as well, and as far as I'm concerned, it's never too early to learn about these types of modern-day hazards.

Around 6:00 I go up to the study to call the office for any late briefings on the next day's interviews. The briefing may take anywhere from thirty minutes to an hour (rarely longer) and during that time I can't be interrupted. The girls know this, though they don't quite understand my need for complete privacy just after the three of us have had such a good time together. This is one of the tradeoffs I've had to make as a mother. True, I'm home, but each weeknight there is work to be done. Then, after my briefing, all three of us do something together until Michael gets home.

Since Michael usually gets home around 7:30, I wait to eat with him, but I always sit with the girls while they eat, at 5:30, and unfortunately for my figure I all too often eat something with them too.

Jamie and Lindsay are always anxious for their daddy's arrival and there is a general commotion when he hits the front door. He is then the center of attention while the girls tell him the same things they've already told me. When the hubbub subsides the girls sit down with Michael and me and have cookies and milk while we have dinner. This is a very important family time for us, a chance for Daddy to catch up on all the events of the day.

Of course we don't stay at home every night but since I absolutely must get to bed early on weeknights, we can't do anything much more adventurous than go to dinner at a local restaurant. We try to do this at least once a week.

The weekends are different. Both Michael and I make a real effort to keep them free for the girls and ourselves, for visiting friends or having them at our house. We sleep later on Saturday and Sunday but when your body is used to getting up at 4:00 A.M. it's hard to sleep in really late. I usually wake up at 5:00 and panic because I think I'm late, and then again at 6:00 and again at 7:00. Then by 8:00 I find myself wide awake, looking at the ceiling.

We try to plan things for the weekend that keep us together as a family group. From time to time, my other commitments— speeches, personal appearances on various shows, and traveling for *GMA*—throw a crimp into these family weekends but I try to keep these interruptions to a minimum. If there is a real choice between being with the family and doing something extra that isn't an absolute necessity, I always opt for the family. Both Michael and I are very conscious of our responsibilities as parents and I think Jamie and Lindsay will realize that as they get older.

I freely admit that I'm in a privileged position. I have a good, glamorous, high-paying job. I have help to clean the house and a nanny to help with the children. Few working mothers can afford these luxuries but few working mothers have the same level of job responsibility that I have. My job follows me home during the week and it even follows me on weekends. The question of work and family is one that I continue to examine closely. I love my work but I will not let it stand between me and my husband and children. I am a career woman—but I put my family above my career.

CHAPTER
TWELVE

——✦✦——

"Mommy, What's a Celebrity?"

On the weekends I often take my kids with me to the local supermarket to shop for groceries. Invariably, I'll be stopped several times by strangers who recognize me and want to say hello. One morning, a woman stopped me in the aisle and in the course of a short conversation she said, "It must be hard to be a celebrity."

As the girls and I walked toward the checkout counter, I felt Lindsay's hand pulling insistently on my skirt.

"What is it, honey?" I asked.

She looked up at me with that honest inquisitiveness that is so beautiful in little children, and asked, "Mommy, what's a celebrity?"

I laughed and answered, "A celebrity is a person whom a lot of people know, a famous person, like the president of the United States or a movie star or a TV star."

"Well, you're on TV. Are you famous, Mommy?" she asked.

"Well, kind of, I guess. A lot of people know me because they see me on TV every day."

"Then you're a celebrity, right?" she asked.

"Uh, I guess I am," I answered.

Lindsay's question was a good one and I can hardly blame her for asking because I still have some trouble with the concept myself. Of course, I realize I'm well-known, but a celebrity, that's a very hard handle for me to grasp. A celebrity is someone else. Elizabeth Taylor is a celebrity. Henry Kissinger is a celebrity. Reggie Jackson is a celebrity. Johnny Carson is a celebrity. Joan Lunden is not a celebrity, at least in the eyes of Joan Lunden. I'm not being coy or self-effacing here, it's the truth.

It is abundantly clear to me, however, that I've achieved a certain level of public recognition. People stop me and say things like: "It's so nice to see you" or "You look much thinner in person" or "How old are the kids now?"

These are not the greetings of good friends nor colleagues at work. These are common questions from total strangers and I get them wherever I go. Television personalities, like all other celebrities, are public property and when twenty-five million people see you each week, you are bound to be recognized almost everywhere. I have, therefore, become public property. I get stared at, I get familiar hellos from grandmothers and muscular handshakes from tourists from Grand Forks, and I get asked questions. I know that nearly all of these are people's well-meant attempts to get close to someone they are used to seeing and figuratively having coffee with every morning and I'm used to these attempts by now. I also realize that most of these greetings are impersonal, but some people (again, probably well-meaning) have no hesitation about crossing the thin boundary line that separates a casual question from a very personal one.

It's not unusual at all for people to ask me how Lindsay and Jamie are doing in school, whether I have problems finding good household help these days, what kind of deodorant I use, and where I buy my clothes. Or, like the woman who stopped me on the street in Manhattan and asked without any qualms, "With your schedule, how do you and your husband find time for sex?" The friendly questions I don't mind at all, but when someone starts to probe my children's grades, my shopping habits, the condition of my armpits, or my sex life I want to respond with something like: "Hey, how would you feel if I asked you that question?" But I can't say that, of course.

Prying aside, the questions people ask most frequently are:

1. What time do you have to get up in the morning? There is a tremendous fascination with the fact that I get up every weekday morning before the sun.
2. How are the girls? Since our regular viewers saw me pregnant they have a special attachment, and when I tell them how Jamie and Lindsay are doing, they react just like old friends. They usually say, "I can't believe it. I remember when they were just babies."
3. Do you get to keep your clothes? The answer to that one is "No, unless I pay for them myself."
4. Who writes to you and what do they say? That's a tough question to answer in a few words, so I usually say something like: "People just like you and they ask me the same question you just asked."
5. Do you answer all your mail? The answer to that is, "Yes, I answer all of it, and it's a big job."

The comments people make most frequently are: "You look so much thinner in person" and "You look so much prettier in person." Of course both are meant as compliments, but when you think about it they are a bit backhanded. No matter, I take them at face value because I know people are being nice.

These questions and comments come from every angle. I get them on the street, in the gas station, in restaurants, and in places like Bloomingdale's; they sometimes catch me off guard. Not long ago I was shopping for towels in Bloomingdale's when a familiar-looking, elegantly dressed woman came up to me and said, "Joan, I just want to tell you I think you're great on the air." I said thank you and we chatted for a few moments. I have to admit I wasn't paying much attention because I was intent on what I was shopping for. The woman left and when I got to the cashier's desk the two women working there were chattering excitedly about Eartha Kitt buying towels in their department. I realized immediately that this woman I had been so casual with had been a guest on GMA a number of times and I felt so dumb I went running around the floor, looking for her so I could make amends. I had to give up after a few minutes of searching because she was nowhere in sight.

Obviously you have to be ready for people to greet you at any time, and although it isn't always a joy to be recognizable and accessible, it is a part of the job that has to be accepted. You're fair game whether you're ready or not. One Sunday morning I rushed out to a nearby convenience store to get a quart of milk for breakfast. I had hardly done more than run a comb through my hair and throw on a sweatshirt. There I was, leaning over the milk case, when a man tapped me on the shoulder and said, "You're Joan Lunden, aren't you?" I said, "Yes I am, just doing a little shopping." When I got to the checkout counter, the woman at the register asked the same question. Again I said, "Yes, just needed some milk." What was surprising to me was the fact that these people were able to recognize me at all, the way I looked. I certainly didn't look anything like the way they see me on television.

I mentioned earlier about being recognized by Tom Selleck in the Russian Tea Room and that is a perfect example of what I'm talking about, that is, my problem with accepting the fact that people recognize me in public. I immediately knew him, as did everyone else in the place, but I was surprised and pleased when he recognized me and called me by name. I was even more surprised that he knew what was happening on *GMA,* even that I'd just been to Morocco.

Not long after that encounter I took the girls and Shelley, our nanny at the time, to see the Ringling Bros. and Barnum & Bailey Circus at Madison Square Garden. The circus people keep a section for special guests and we had seats in that section right on the aisle. We were just getting settled when I saw Larry Hagman (who plays J.R. on *Dallas*) coming up the aisle. Like a teenager, I leaned over and whispered to Shelley in an excited tone, "Here comes J.R. Ewing." When he got to where we were sitting he saw me and said, "Joan, how are you? It's great to see you," and he threw his arms around me and gave me a big hug. It's still a new experience for me when people I consider "big stars" recognize me.

It so happens that I had interviewed Larry Hagman a few

months before. The morning of the interview he came on the set with his ten-gallon hat and western boots, looking very imposing and powerful, like his character on *Dallas*. He seemed a bit intimidating to me before we started talking but then he relaxed and we had a good interview. After the program we talked and he told me that he used that imposing personality to psych himself up and get him through interviews, which still made him nervous.

Over the years I've found that many of the stars we interview on *GMA* are uncomfortable with live interviews. Art Carney, an established star of stage, movies, and television for decades, came into the studio one morning to talk about his new movie and I could tell he was nervous. Seeing his discomfort, I introduced myself and we chatted for a couple of minutes as I tried to put him at ease. "I'm a big fan of yours," I said. "I still enjoy the reruns of *The Honeymooners*."

He thanked me and said, "You know, I've been scared about this interview for three days and I can't help it." Then he added, "I thrive on being a character, on playing a role on the set or onstage because what people see is that character, not Art Carney. When I have to be myself and talk about myself I get very nervous." And he stayed nervous until we were actually on camera.

The more prominent people you meet, the more you understand that celebrity is not an easy thing to handle, especially when it hits you out of the blue. We had Tony Geary, best known for his role as Luke Spencer on *General Hospital*, on the show when he was in the first flush of his stardom. He and his TV girlfriend Genie Francis, Laura on *General Hospital*, were there to discuss their upcoming "wedding" on their show. It must have been one of his first appearances on a talk show because he was so nervous he was sweating as if he had just stepped out of a sauna. There was sweat coming out of his hair and pouring out under the cuffs of his shirt. Genie was holding his hand so tightly I thought she'd either cut off his circulation or break his fingers. Interestingly, Tony came on again about six months later and this time he strutted around like a peacock, seemingly without a trace of nervousness. He had quickly gotten used to his celebrity.

Henry Fonda, who certainly had plenty of time to get used to celebrity, once said on the show, "As far back as I can remember I was shy and self-conscious and I'd cross the street rather than pass somebody and have to say hello. I'm just too self-conscious. That's why I'm an actor. And I discovered, fifty-four or fifty-five years ago, that when acting, I could put a mask on and I wasn't self-conscious."

And Clint Eastwood told David in an interview: "Sometimes you feel people are disappointed because you're maybe not that guy [on the screen]. They really would like to say, 'Hey, that's the way he really is.' "

Even Mary Tyler Moore, certainly no beginner, seemed nervous one morning as she was waiting to go on, though she turned out to be a wonderful interview. Now to me, MTM is a genuine celebrity. I watched her show and she was one of my big role models. That morning she told me, "I always watch *GMA* and I feel like I know you, Joan. I'm a big fan of the show." She's a big fan? Come on. I truly tend to forget and it's probably a good thing—it could make me nervous if I remember that a lot of famous people are out there watching.

But I have to admit that, although the thought of famous people watching the show—or, in fact, millions of people watching—doesn't make me nervous, speaking in front of live audiences does get my stomach churning. In the last several years I've made at least a dozen speeches annually to groups ranging in size from several hundred to several thousand. I clearly have plenty of experience in front of those live groups but I'm still plenty worried before each live appearance. That's one of the reasons I prepare my speeches so thoroughly. Each one has to be tailored to the audience, and stories and anecdotes have to be changed to appeal to each group; so I always like to know as much as possible about the makeup of the audience. Delivery is another matter. Anyone who has approached a podium knows that all the preparation in the world isn't enough to fortify you at that moment when you're introduced and you actually have to stand up in front of a group. Despite the fact that you know your material and the fact that the audience is friendly and came to hear what you have to say, it's still a nervous time.

Apparently my audiences aren't able to detect my nervousness, however. I remember speaking to more than 1,000 members of the chamber of commerce in a midwestern city and being as nervous as always before and during the presentation. But afterward, one of the officers of the group came up to me and congratulated me on the speech and my calmness. "Your experience in front of an audience really shows," he said. I didn't tell him that the main reason I appeared calm that day was that the spotlight from the balcony was hitting me in such a way that I really couldn't see the faces of the people in the audience, even in the first row. I think I may request a strong spotlight at all my speeches in the future.

Public recognition also has its down side and one entry on that side of the ledger is the problem of personal security. I began to be aware of this when I was a street reporter for Channel 7 in New York, and ever since then, though I'm not obsessed with it, I've been worried about security for myself, and now for my family as well.

As I said, when I came to New York I found an apartment very close to the WABC-TV studios, and I was able to walk to and from work at all hours. In the beginning, I was completely carefree about walking the streets of New York, even though I had heard all the horror stories of assaults, muggings, and rapes that natives are so fond of telling newcomers. I believed those were things that happened to other people, not to me. But there were two times in those years when I felt physically threatened and I know it was only because I was being seen regularly on the news. My face was becoming known and I learned my first lessons about the price you pay when that happens.

In the first instance, I began to take notice of a man hanging out on the corner whenever I came out of the *Eyewitness News* building. I couldn't help but notice him after a while because he was always there. He was youngish; he wore a hat, had long hair, and looked a little strange to me, though I didn't actually take the time to examine him closely. And he was there at all hours. If I came out at noon he was there. He was there at 10:00 A.M., at 9:00 P.M., whatever the hour. He never said a word but I could see him following me around the neighborhood and he gave me the kind of stares you don't want to get when you're walking down the street in New York, or in any city. Then one day the doorman in my building told me that a man had asked if I lived there and when the doorman described the fellow I knew it was the same person.

That, I felt, was serious. It was clearly time to do something about this eyeballing so I went to ABC Security to ask them to take some action. They aren't the police so they don't have any real power outside the building but they wear uniforms and they look official. Two of the security guards went out and tried to persuade my "fan" to move along. It didn't help a bit. When one of the guards asked him to move, the young man told him, "I'm a student interested in communications and an admirer of Joan Lunden. This is a public street. Leave me alone." The guards were powerless.

Finally, my paranoia got the better of me and I called the police. Two very nice officers came to the newsroom that same day to investigate my complaint. They understood the situation perfectly, they told me, but they said that unless he actually did something to me, threatened me, or attacked me, there was absolutely nothing they could do.

"You mean I have to wait for the guy to stab me or rape me before you can help?" I said, a bit irate.

One of the officers said, "Unfortunately, lady, that's the way it is. There are thousands of crazies on the streets and we can't throw them in jail for standing on the corner."

"That's just great," I said. "So what do I do?"

"Just keep your eye on him," the policeman said, "and if he makes any kind of a move, scream your head off and we'll come running."

For weeks afterward I had to live with this creep following me and staring at me, and I expected him to leap on me with a knife and slit my throat at any time. Then one day I stopped in a little delicatessen across the street from the studio to pick up some yogurt. I was a regular customer so the owner and his helper knew me. I was standing in front of the refrigerator case, trying to choose between strawberry and apple-raisin, when I felt someone standing right up against the back of my body and breathing on my neck. I turned quickly and it was the creep. When he smiled, a crazed sort of smile, I could see that his front teeth were missing. I screamed and in one second the owner jumped over the counter and grabbed the guy from behind. The counter man came to help and they both held him until the police showed up a few minutes later and arrested him. It's the kind of experience that leaves you a little rocky. But nothing had really happened to me so after they took him away I went to work.

Later that day I had to go to the police precinct station to sign a complaint (he was charged with harassment) and one of the ABC couriers, a man named Tony, took me there. These couriers used to drive reporters and camera crews to and from assignments, rush film back to the station (in the days when we used film), and they were usually on hand when someone needed any kind of transportation. All of them are members of the Teamsters union, and though I don't want to categorize an entire group, they are tough as nails. At any rate, I felt better with him along.

When Tony and I got to the precinct the arresting officer took me aside and said, "This fellow we're holding is an illegal alien from Bogotá, Colombia, and he has three warrants out on him for sexual abuse."

"And he's been following me around?" I said, unbelieving.

"He's already been through the psychiatric exam," the officer said, "and though you would be perfectly right to press charges, I think you should know it really doesn't pay to prosecute this kind of case because nothing is going to happen. This guy is going to be right back on the street."

I was shocked. "Can't you deport him?" I asked.

"Not likely. We barely have enough manpower to take care of felons," the policeman said.

"You mean I had to wait for him to make a move on me and when he did he still doesn't go to jail?" I said indignantly.

"I'm afraid that's about it. For guys like this it's a revolving door," he said.

As it turned out, on further checking the police found that my "assailant" was wanted for assault in another state and they were able to ship him off. That worry was ended, though a tinge of anxiety stayed with me for some time.

The second incident was even stranger. I started to get passionate letters from a man who professed his undying love and devotion. Then the same man began to phone me almost every day. I ignored both the letters and the calls but then he started coming to the station and asking for me. When I left the newsroom to walk the block to the studio he would be waiting for me on the street and would walk next to me, saying, "I'm the one who has been writing and calling. Talk to me, please talk to me." This happened over and over again and I always tried to appear nonchalant while examining him closely out of the corner of my eye. He looked like the straightest man alive. He was thirtyish, well-dressed, decent-looking, and absolutely average in every way—except that he was following and talking excitedly to a woman he didn't even know.

Again I told ABC Security and the guards tried their best— but when their uniforms and badges can't discourage someone, they have used up all their power. Finally, one day my husband was at the studio when my admirer came to visit; Michael went out and told this fellow in no uncertain terms to stop bothering me. I don't think he phrased it delicately.

Apparently unabashed, the man responded, "I know she's not in love with her husband, she's in love with me and he's just keeping her against her will."

Taken aback, Michael said, "I am her husband and she wants you out of here now."

The man looked at Michael and shook his head. "You're not her husband," he said. He then took a thick stack of articles and photos out of his pocket and said, "Look, I know everything there is to know about Joan Lunden and you're not her husband."

Michael couldn't help but notice a picture of Cheryl Tiegs in the pile of clippings in the man's hand. Pointing to the picture, Michael said, "That's Cheryl Tiegs."

"No it's not," the man said.

"Yes it is," Michael insisted.

The man said, "Of course that's Joan Lunden. If you were her husband, you'd know that."

Michael tried to explain to the man that Cheryl Tiegs and I were not the same woman but he couldn't convince him. When Michael left, the man was still standing in front of the studio. We both knew we were dealing with a troubled person.

Later that week, I got a call from the ABC security desk on the first floor, saying I had a visitor who claimed to be my husband. Not all of the guards knew Michael so it could have been he, but it so happened that Michael was in the newsroom right next to me. He had come to meet me for dinner after the show so I knew that the visitor wasn't Michael. "That can't be my husband," I said, "so you better get rid of him."

I thought no more about it until I left for the studio. As I was rounding the corner, my admirer came up to me and without so much as a "Hello" said, "I know that you're in love with me and I'll help you get away from your husband."

That was it. I ran back to the security desk and called the police. In a few minutes there was a big scene in front of the studio. The police came, they handcuffed the man and put him in the car to take him to the station. As they were ready to drive away I gave him one more chance to say he'd stop bothering me. Instead he just threw me a kiss from the window of the police car as it drove off. The police fingerprinted him and let him go, because, again, there wasn't much to hold him on. I hadn't expected such a scene and I had some minor guilt feelings about making such a stink but you can't help but feel threatened by that kind of behavior.

I never saw either of these men again (though the second man left me little presents at the studio for months) but these incidents are illustrative of the kinds of things people in the public eye must expect.

And that public eye rarely blinks. When I walk down the street in New York, it makes no difference if I'm going to a business meeting or just for a walk around the block, I have to be aware of the way I look. All that needs to happen is that someone sees me with a run in my pantyhose or my makeup a little out of place and the next thing I'll see is an item in a gossip column that says, "Joan Lunden's not looking so good these days. Does this mean there is something wrong at *GMA*?"

It's also hard to realize how incredibly observant television viewers can be. A couple of times over the last few years I've appeared on the show with a Band-Aid on my finger and once with a small bandage on my knee. The number of calls and letters I received in each of those instances was amazing. "Is Joan okay?" was the gist of those inquiries. The same people who called or wrote about my bandaged finger probably wouldn't notice a Band-Aid on a member of their own family, but they are sharp-eyed when it comes to celebrities.

Occasionally they are not only observant but opportunistic as well. That's one of the reasons celebrities have to be aware of who they are in public. The things that ordinary people can do with impunity are forbidden to celebrities. If I were to get upset with a salesperson in a store a good part of the world would know about it the next morning. Gil Gerard, probably best known for his TV role as Buck Rogers, told me the kind of story that drives celebrities crazy. It seems he and his wife, Connie Sellecca (from TV's *Hotel* series), and their son went grocery shopping. While they were shopping, their son displayed all the normal characteristics of a three-year-old. He was in and out of the shopping cart, he brought his mommy the boxes of sugar-coated cereal he wanted, and he protested when she put some of them back on the shelf. Any mother will readily identify with this perfectly normal situation, and it was perfectly normal as far as Gil and Connie were concerned, too. But the next week, in one of those weekly newspapers that feature aliens from outer space and crash diets,

Gil happened to notice a headline that said something like, "Star's Son Is a Terror in the Aisles." Gil and Connie were outraged, and I would have been, too. For one thing, absolutely nothing had really happened. But more important, their son had been held up to ridicule for one reason only: His parents are celebrities. It's one of those cases in which you want to say, "They can say anything they want about me but they'd better not bring my kid into it." Gil later found out that a woman had recognized them in the store and decided to make some money by selling a story to one of the weekly scandal sheets. It was a mean thing to do, but not all that uncommon.

Since I'm conscious of public scrutiny when Michael and I go out to eat, I always take a chair that faces the wall. If I face the other direction I know I have to be extra careful because people watch me eat. It's a voyeuristic pastime, of course, a little like looking at the victim of a traffic accident. They secretly hope that I will squirt myself in the eye with the grapefruit, splash catsup on my yellow blouse, or just sit there and drool. Then they can tell their friends they were so surprised to see Joan Lunden sitting there with a long strand of spinach hanging between her teeth.

The other problem with restaurants is that when you're there you're trapped, that is, people have unlimited access to you. It's like being on an airplane and having an empty seat next to you. It's an open invitation to company. You can't make an excuse and get up from your seat in a plane and you can't leave the dining room when you're sitting in front of a plate of food. It's a perfect opportunity for people to come over and chat. They ask about my daughters' health, about *GMA* and our parenting show, about David Hartman, and then they don't know how to break off and leave. I have to figure out a way to give them an easy exit. Usually I'll say something like "Thanks so much for stopping by," and that will do it; but if that doesn't work I say, "You'll have to excuse us while we finish dinner," which, though it is a little bit rude, gets the job done and is worth it. I know in my heart (but not in my head) that these "greeters" are all well intentioned, and believe me, it's nice to be recognized. But it can make going out to dinner, the movies, or the theater more like part of the job than a romantic night out with my husband.

Easy access in public places brings up another aspect of celebrity and security. In today's world, the real negative side of public recognition is the remote but real danger of personal attack, kidnapping, or worse. Let's face it, the Sharon Tate murders committed by Charles Manson and his gang of drug-crazed misfits still haunt a lot of celebrities. Very few people enjoy living the reclusive life of a Howard Hughes, and you have to accept a certain amount of personal risk. But Michael and I do take precautions and when it comes to Jamie and Lindsay, we're very cautious.

Since I had two very public pregnancies (everyone who followed *GMA* at the time knew the exact birth dates of both children), the girls have, in a way, always been public property. Even before Jamie was born I got dozens of requests from magazines and newspapers for pictures of me with her, and when Lindsay was born, I got the same requests for pictures of me with both girls. I was pleased to agree to those requests then because I felt it was important for women to see that I was surviving as a new mother, a wife, and a career woman and that therefore they could too. At the same time, I was aware that because of all this publicity the girls would be easily recognizable. Since the girls often appear on our "Mother's Minutes" and *Mother's Day* programs too, their public exposure is far greater than that of the children of most television personalities.

Michael and I have had a number of long discussions about the pros and cons of public exposure of the children. And as the girls get older and more recognizable we are becoming more and more protective.

We have had to make some other adjustments as well. Since the girls have been old enough to go to nursery school Michael and I have had to consider the choice of schools very carefully. We decided that though the public schools in our area are very good, a public school would not serve our purposes. Certainly a public school would offer Jamie and Lindsay the advantage of meeting all kinds of kids, but the girls might also have the disadvantage of being singled out as special. If the teacher asks the class, "Did everyone see Lindsay's mommy on TV this morning?" it tends to point a finger. We felt the girls would be objects of either envy or ridicule and possibly both. This has meant finding a private school that is especially sensitive to our special needs for security and privacy. Michael and I visited half a dozen schools, talked with the administration and the teachers, and finally chose one that has proved to be good educationally and extremely conscious of the security and privacy of its children. The teachers there have also been responsive to my requests to keep the girls' school life and my television life completely separate.

Don't get me wrong. Michael and I don't sit around wringing our hands over safety and privacy, we aren't that way, but we are being prudently careful, as all other parents must be today.

If it sometimes seems as if the price of celebrity is high, it has its positive payoffs as well. It is the mixture of celebrity and motherhood that has opened the door to all kinds of other nice things for me. In 1982 I was named "Outstanding Mother of the Year" by the National Mother's Day Committee, an honor shared that year by Lynda Bird Johnson Robb, Erica Jong, Judy Blume, Geraldine Ferraro, and other women prominent in their fields. I was the guest speaker at the committee's annual luncheon and for the next twelve months I was a spokesperson for the organization. In 1981 I was named "Today's Mother" by the Council of Cerebral Palsy, in 1983 the National Institue of Infant Services named me "Career Mom of the Year," and in 1985 I was presented the New Jersey Division of Civil Rights annual award because the organization felt I represented an inspiring image as a working mother.

I'm also invited around the country to speak to all kinds of groups, including college students, women's and other professional organizations, chambers of commerce and other business groups, and civic groups. When I started at *GMA* I got few if any opportunities to speak to the public but the number of invitations has grown rapidly over the years. Now I receive several hundred every year. Obviously, I can't possibly attend all or even a major portion of these events and still have time for *GMA,* so

I'm very selective when it comes to speaking engagements, awards ceremonies, and so forth. If it means taking a day off from the show or taking away part of my precious weekend time with my family, I'll usually turn an invitation down, no matter how prestigious the event or how large the fee.

There are exceptions, of course, the most important being the Disney parades at Christmas and Easter. Since 1983 I have been hosting these parades, and they have turned into major events for our family: We all make the trip together and the children have the opportunity to be around their favorite Disney characters during our stay. This is one job I couldn't turn down if I wanted to because my kids would never forgive me. And the Disney image fits so perfectly with all our parenting and family projects.

When I do go on a speaking engagement, I'm generally asked in advance what I'd like to speak about, and I have an extensive list of important subjects that I suggest to every group. These topics—violence on television, children's programming, drunk driving, parenting, the responsibility of the news media—are usually rejected. Everyone wants essentially the same speech. They want to know what the television business looks like from the inside, how I mix motherhood and career, and what my daily schedule is like. Issues, unfortunately, don't usually make it, though I always try to work one or two into every speech I make.

I've learned that people want to be entertained more than enlightened, whether they are executives attending a convention of the National Association of Savings and Loans or students at Baylor University. They want you to share a little bit of yourself with them. I always do that because I know that if a speech isn't entertaining the information I include won't be heard either. Over the years I've developed a good basic speech which I modify extensively for each occasion. But no matter what I may say in the body of my speech, I begin by saying, "Before we get started here, the answer to your question is: I have to get up at four every morning. Now that's out of the way." It always gets a laugh, breaks the ice for me and the audience, and disposes of one of the questions everyone wants to ask.

These speaking engagements, of course, involve much more than giving a speech and hopping on the next plane out of town. I always allow time to chat with people after I speak and time for autographs for everyone who asks, often hundreds of them. The group sponsoring the event usually holds a luncheon, dinner, or cocktail party in connection with my appearance and I attend that as well. Then, more often than not, I have interviews with local television and radio stations, perhaps with the local newspaper, and I'll end up doing a series of promotion spots for the ABC affiliate in the area. All of this, including the travel, usually takes place in twenty-four hours or less. Then there is a rush to the airport for the plane back to New York and, far from hopping on the plane, I often feel that I need someone to carry me to my seat.

While in New York I also get many requests from out-of-town newspapers, magazines, and radio and TV stations for interviews and articles. Since part of my job is publicity for *GMA* and ABC, this is something of an obligation, though it can also be enjoyable. It does, however, mean a good deal of extra work. Magazines always need photos of me, of Michael and me, of me and my mother, of me and the whole family, and so on. So there are photo sessions connected with each commitment and the selection of clothes to wear at those photo sessions. Then there are proofs and slides to go through, all of which is added to my regular schedule at *GMA*.

This may seem like a lot to cope with, but in an age in which many celebrities are also corporations, I fall into the category of a small business. Most stars have publicists whom they pay $1,000 a week and more primarily to say no to most requests and to select those two or three things the star decides to do each year. I don't have a publicist because I've never felt the need for one, but I do have an assistant who handles most of what would be a publicist's work. Debbie screens the requests for speeches and public appearances, for magazine, radio, and television interviews, and for personal endorsements of products and causes. Together we go over those that seem worthwhile and I'll select the ones that are the most appealing and interesting. She also makes all my travel arrangements and plans the publicity for my appearances. Quite often she will even negotiate the fees I receive for these appearances.

I do have agents who handle offers for commercials and various other offers of a business nature that are made to me. Either through my agent or directly, I get a dozen or so commercial offers each year and the chance to endorse products of every kind. During the toxic-shock scare a few years ago, I got an offer from Tampax to do their tampon commercials because they felt they needed a "news" image to calm the public and restore trust and they thought my reputation would help them out of a delicate position. I turned that offer down, as I do with other offers for bathroom and household products, not because I don't like or approve of the products, but because I have to be as careful of my image as the companies are of their own.

But I don't need publicists or agents to seize some of the other opportunities that come my way because of my position. These opportunities include the endorsement of good causes, and in the last few years I've gotten very involved in two that I think are vital—the search for missing children and Mothers Against Drunk Drivers, or MADD. And one issue that gets a lot of my attention on a less formal basis is the campaign against violence on television.

In a larger sense, it's my feeling that the American people simply don't need to see a lot of what is shown on television. I use television as the example because I know it better, but the same is true of radio, newspapers, and magazines. The news has been mega-sensationalized to the extent that there are cameras and microphones everywhere and the smallest event can be blown up into an international incident. Frankly, I hate to be a party to this. It seems that the first three stories on any local newscast are almost always violent—murder, rape, and kidnapping.

As I said before, I was working for Channel 7 during the "Son of Sam" murders and I was sent out to interview people, family and friends of the girls who were killed by David Berkowitz, the man convicted of those senseless murders. For some reason the station thought that viewers wanted to know exactly how these poor people felt about the deaths of loved ones and friends. I thought it was unnecessary, an invasion of people's privacy at a most tragic moment, and I resented doing it. I did my job but I'm not convinced that's what people want.

But it's not only adults who see news they don't need to see. Children are exposed to it as well, and to my way of thinking this is even more dangerous. The news is not one of those programs that advises "parental guidance," though I'm not at all sure violence isn't more damaging to young psyches than some of the movies that carry PG or even R ratings. Children see more violence and death on the average thirty-minute news program than in any *Dirty Harry* film, and on the news it's the real thing. There is always footage of the dead and dying, the blood on the ground, the bodies being wheeled out. Sometimes if we're unlucky enough, we can even see somebody gunned down right in front of our eyes. We are being desensitized to the sight of dead bodies, and violent death has become an almost meaningless, commonplace occurrence. I think we are systematically lowering the value of human life and diluting our natural sense of outrage.

The entire *GMA* staff has become sensitive to the feelings of our early-morning viewers. We consider it so much a family time that we try to avoid the "damns" and "hells" and the suggestive scenes from movie clips whenever possible. But when you're doing live TV, you can't always avoid it. During an interview with the foreign minister of Nicaragua, Miguel d'Escoto, David asked him about building a military force more powerful than all the countries of South America. D'Escoto answered, "This is a sheer lie, hypocrisy, and bullchit. Pardon my English."

Or the time I interviewed Susan Baker, cofounder of Parents Music Resource Center, and wife of Senator Howard Baker. We were talking about putting warning stickers on rock-and-roll records aimed at the teenage market that contain explicit lyrics.

I asked Mrs. Baker, "Specifically, what are the kinds of lyrics that concern you?"

Without hesitation, she began quoting sexually explicit lyrics from the Rolling Stones album *Undercover of the Night*. In fact, they are so explicit I'm not including them here. Mrs. Baker then went on to say that her group felt labels should warn parents about the lyrics on the records their children are listening to every day.

Both of these were live interviews and nothing could be done. But these kinds of situations are rare; usually we have a little more control. We aren't The Playboy Channel and as free TV we must be responsible, particularly in our morning time period.

One of my other causes is the search for missing children. This has also become important news because the media have made it important, and in this case the results of media attention can be positive. Every week on *GMA* we show pictures of missing children, and some of them have been found alive because of that exposure. I am not thick-skinned and when I hear of cases of missing children, and worse yet must report them, I can hardly bare it. I get such a lump in my throat and sometimes tears in my eyes that it takes the utmost self-discipline to get me through. My husband responds in the same way, only he wanted to do more than sit by and feel terrible. He decided to produce TV spots, called "The Lost," that would really make an impact around the country. He's used popular celebrities to make dramatic appeals for information on missing children. The idea is to capture people's attention and, when you've got them, to give them the vital information so it will really make a difference.

Child abuse is another issue that is so much a part of the news these days, and it is another area in which the media have had a voice. There have always been abused children in this country, but suddenly child abuse became big news. Thanks to media coverage it now has been labeled as the epidemic that it is. Again, the media served a very useful function. Too bad we weren't doing this years ago. This is what I feel is the most important purpose of mass media. I don't mean to take away from the value of entertainment programming, but improving the quality of people's lives is a vital function that we should serve. This is my personal opinion, but it's one of the *privileges* of celebrity that I'm taking advantage of here.

Now let me talk about one of the *myths* of celebrity. It's a common misconception that people in television, the movies, the theater, and the music world are involved in a mad social whirl of cocktail parties, glamorous theater openings, and intimate dinners with other celebrities. It's thought that we all know each other and that when we're not working we must be out with our friends in the field in which we work. People often ask if Jane Pauley and I are friends, if Dan Rather is as handsome as he looks on TV, what it's like to spend a quiet evening with Jill St. John and Robert Wagner, and so forth.

The truth is, I have never even met most of my colleagues on other networks and I don't socialize with the stars on ABC or run in the jet set. It's not that I'm not a social person, because I am, it's simply that those sorts of things, for me at least, don't happen. I don't pick up the phone to find Victoria Principal on the other end of the line asking me to lunch at La Caravelle and John Forsythe doesn't pop into my office for coffee and doughnuts in the morning.

Sure, I do have contact with celebrities but it's generally for professional reasons only. Jane Pauley and I have talked a few times and I've had chitchat conversations with scores of other celebrities and politicians, but the type of intimate socializing people imagine isn't part of the business for me. In fact, I worked with Kathleen Sullivan, who does "World News This Morning" and often does the news on *GMA* from Washington, for two years before I met her in person, and that was in Yugoslavia when we were both covering the 1984 Winter Olympics. It's a long way to go to meet someone you so often see on the screen.

People associate being a celebrity with glamour, haute couture, parties, drugs, and the high life for vicarious reasons, but I want to point out that if I wore high-styled or trendy clothes, hung out with rock stars, danced till dawn, jetted from here to there, and used drugs, I wouldn't be on a program like *GMA,* on a national news show, or even on a local news program. I don't know of anyone involved in the news or entertainment business, as we are at *GMA,* who leads the kind of life the gossip columnists and fiction writers create for us. Besides not having the time or the inclination, we can't afford to take the risks involved and we're smart enough to recognize that fact.

If you are at all involved in reporting news events, credibility is everything, and establishing and maintaining credibility places limits on your activities. If I'm arrested for drunk driving, how do I interview the head of Mothers Against Drunk Drivers? If I cheat on my income tax, how do I talk with the director of the Internal Revenue Service about the latest tax legislation? If I openly support a candidate for public office, how do I fairly interview his or her opponent?

On the other side of this coin is the fact that we newspeople are supposed to be able to sit down and talk intelligently and calmly with the beautiful, the chic, the avant-garde, the zealous, and the criminal, in short, the people who do all of the things that we aren't supposed to do. We also have to be able to assimilate enough information to make these public figures sound interesting or sympathetic, or at least credible.

For example, how am I supposed to relate to the beauty and glamour of someone like Victoria Principal? I did a five-part interview with her when she came out with a beauty book called *The Body Principal*. It was December when we set up the interview at Victoria's Malibu Canyon home. I had interviewed her in our *GMA* studios but did not know her personally. We all know what a beautiful woman she is but I didn't realize what an absolutely perfectly groomed physical specimen she is. Just being with her gave me a heavy dose of inferiority. Part of the interview was taped on the beach at Malibu, and when I got there and took off my shoes I was horrified to discover that my toenails weren't polished, while hers were perfect, like the rest of her. My New York pallor extended all the way down to my feet, which had been in boots all winter, and contrasted rather sharply with her cultivated tan. The cameraman took one shot of the two of us walking on the beach and before we started I whispered to him to get on her side so her feet and legs would show more than mine.

I don't know if Victoria actually uses the apricot scrubs, mint facials, and tea leaves on the eyes that she recommends in her book but her arms look so incredibly smooth and hairless it's almost unnatural. But beauty is Victoria's job and she is bright and business-minded.

Thinking of being on that beach reminds me of another trip to California to interview Jane Fonda about pregnancy and exercise, which certainly applied to me at the time—I was six months pregnant. On location at her Workout salon, dressed in a leotard stretched to its absolute limit, I felt like a blimp in the midst of all those Hollywood starlets.

Then there is the other end of the scale to which we have to adjust, and this is about as far at the other end as you can get. I was once sent to a New Jersey prison to interview a child molester, a man who had committed acts that are completely beyond my comprehension. As a parent who understands the incredibly precious quality of a child, it was disconcerting to sit and talk to this man who had violated children, his own included, and to have a sense of what destruction his act caused. As I listened to him I noted that he looked very average, like a neighbor, and he said, "You know, people make a mistake in cases like mine. They look for the guy with the raincoat who exposes himself in the alley or attacks kids on the street. Our type is invisible. We're teachers, gymnastics instructors, scout leaders, camp counselors, all the people that parents tell their children to listen to and to trust. As parents we say to kids, 'Listen to the teacher,' 'Be a good boy for Uncle Harold,' 'Do what your scout leader says.' Kids listen to what their parents say more often than we think they do."

He told me that he never forced a child to do anything and never was mean to a child in any way, another statement that was hard to stomach. "I have relations with a child because I like them," he said, "and because I don't feel accepted by people my own age. Children like me and they look up to me and I'm important to them. I tickle them, pat them on the knee. It's all very gradual. Then I say, 'You better not tell because we'll both be in big trouble.' "

As I sat and listened I realized that he was right. I wouldn't be able to tell the man was sick just by looking at him; that's a very frightening realization. As you pry into the brain of a man who sexually abuses his own daughter you get scared, defensive, and angry. I hated this man and pitied him at the same time.

I cite these two extremes to emphasize the point that as broadcasters we must maintain credibility and that celebrity, with all its glamour, also has its limitations. I cannot bounce from interview to interview—from Victoria Principal to a sex offender—if people don't believe me.

For me believability and trust are achieved by a combination of a number of things—a high level of empathy, interest, sincerity, directness, humor, intelligence, and a certain charisma. And none of these traits is based on good looks, the way you do your hair, the amount of makeup you use, the clothes you wear, or the people who are your friends.

Of these traits or qualifications, probably the most difficult to maintain is a level of empathy. You just can't be empathetic with Bob Guccione, whose treatment of Vanessa Williams is a classic case of exploitation for profit, or with Cathleen Crowell Webb, who was on the show after she recanted her story of being raped by Gary Dotson after he had served a lengthy prison term. In her case I tried to put myself in a man's position and from that perspective I thought she did a horrible thing. On the other hand, I know that many men get away with rape because the law enforcement system often works against women in rape cases, so I had the inclination to be nice. Webb's attitude made that difficult. I felt she was very cold, even nasty, and that instead of assuming an adversary position she should have been apologetic. I weighed every word in that interview because I didn't want people to think that I was being nice or that I was essentially saying, "Well, good luck to you in the future."

But it's easy for me to empathize with all kinds of people on all kinds of subjects because that's the way I am naturally. I quickly get involved in other people's stories, their problems and hardships, and that involvement gives them the feeling that I'm in their camp.

Maintaining your level of personal interest day after day can be as difficult as being empathetic because you have to show concern for things that don't normally interest you. When I'm talking to a soccer player I have to be totally interested and excited about soccer for three or four minutes. The day before that interview I don't know anything about soccer but I am briefed by the writer and given enough background to sound interested for the length of the interview. Neither the audience at home nor the soccer star knows that my knowledge of the game is limited to that briefing. And that, if you'll permit me, is the kind of ability it takes to make *GMA* work. It took long practice to learn how to do this, how to concentrate and project real interest, and when I first came to the program I didn't have this ability. In fact, it used to be the hardest thing for me to do, to concentrate totally right in that tunnel between my eyes and the interviewee or the camera. There are a lot of things in the studio and in your mind that can distract you from that basic job.

Directness, another of the qualities that makes for trust and credibility, is closely related to sincerity. But to my mind there are two kinds of directness, the blunt, Mike Wallace variety ("You mean to say that you murdered twelve people and have no remorse?") and the kind that asks questions people sitting in the audience would themselves like to ask. I've found myself asking people things that I wouldn't want to answer if someone asked me the same questions, but the medium of television, especially live television, seems to induce people to answer questions and express feelings they wouldn't reveal to their most intimate friends. For example, during a live interview I said to Kenny Loggins, "Tell us about those painful weeks in your life following the recording of your first album with Jim Messina."

He said, "My hands started shaking, my eyelids started fluttering. I realized I was losing my mind . . . I think I was just burned out."

"But you had found so much success," I said.

He replied, "After so much success it was like a big empty pit. Where do I go? Hitting bottom and clawing my way back out of the abyss has influenced my writing."

I knew he had had emotional problems during that time and had wondered about bringing it up. The question is: Just because you make good music or do anything in the public eye, do you have to bare your soul? And do the majority of people really want to know these intimate details? The truth is that after asking a question like "What did you do after your breakdown?" I sometimes want to say, "Hold it. Don't answer that question. I take it back." There are many times when I pry that I have to do a lot of self-examination first.

Clearly a sense of humor helps you at these times, and in general, because the constant pressures of the news business can bring your spirits down with a loud crash. I've found that comedy is one of the ways to deal with the tragedies of life and I pride myself on my extensive repertoire of tension-relieving jokes. I'd love to share some of them with you but discretion, not to mention our Standards and Practices people, dictate otherwise.

A lot has been said about the importance of charisma in television and I think it certainly plays a part in how much an audience trusts and believes a TV personality. The persona, the image, the aura created by anyone in the public eye is crucial to success. I don't think charisma is something you can learn; you either have it or you don't. But it is something you can cultivate and polish and that's what I've tried to do. First, however, you have to recognize that you've got this intangible quality and unless you have a gigantic ego, you don't know until people start to say things like "Your personality seems to come right into the room" or "You project a human feeling that I can't really describe" or "You make me take notice." I apparently have a measure of this strange power, and though I don't know where it came from, I do know it has been a positive factor in my career.

Finally, there is no doubt in my mind that you have to be intelligent to be effective on live television. The day of the "vague on the inside, *Vogue* on the outside" television personality is long gone. As you can tell by now, there is a good deal more to being a television host than reading the TelePrompTer. A pretty face and an expensive wardrobe won't cut it alone. Assimilating a small mountain of research material each day and handling a wide variety of subjects and people takes more than straight teeth. A talk-show host needs to be bright, creative, a quick study, swift to react, and adaptable, and it all takes brains.

CHAPTER THIRTEEN

Looking Back and Looking Forward

I've been fortunate in my career and I know it. I've often been in the right place at the right time. After all, I owe my first television job to a weatherman who just happened to hear that I was being interviewed for a job in the news department at KCRA at the same time he was looking for a woman to assist him. But I don't really believe in luck. I believe in opportunities. I recognized that opportunity and grabbed it. Then it was up to me to make my own breaks and create my own good fortune. After that first chance in KCRA-TV, where I learned a lot, I've been in the right place at the right time because I worked to get into that place. When the opportunity came along to move from Sacramento to New York, I grabbed it. I gained invaluable experience at WABC-TV and used that experience as a stepping-stone to *Good Morning America.* I've learned a lot at *GMA.* I've grown in the job and I'm now at the top of my profession. And all along the way I've gotten support from people whom I care about and who care about me.

As I look back on my career at *GMA,* I can hardly believe that it all began such a short time ago. I can only hope that the future will be as stimulating, exciting, and rewarding as the past has been.

Now a little about that future.

As I'm sure you know, a lot has been happening in the morning-ratings battle in the past year. Until early 1986, *GMA* has been the number-one morning show for years and in those years we really overwhelmed the competition. In fact, being number one was something we almost took for granted; we never really experienced the ratings pressure that is felt on most television shows. It may seem strange, but I hardly bothered to look at the ratings when they came across my desk during that period because it wasn't necessary. A tenth of a point here or there didn't make a bit of difference.

Well, those days are past. These days a tenth of a point *does* make a difference because NBC's *Today* show mounted an all-out attack on *GMA* and we have been battling each other ever since.

Why? Many things came into play, but first I'll talk about the obvious—the time of day that we're on the air. I'm referring to the fact that any show on television is affected by the show that precedes it. But what you probably don't know is that even an early-morning program is affected by the shows that precede it in the previous evening's prime-time and late-night lineup.

How does that translate? It's simple. Think of what you do at night. You watch the prime-time shows and maybe the late news and then you turn off your TV. You may have been watching any of the regularly scheduled evening programs but you didn't switch the dial to another channel before you snapped off the set. Since viewers usually leave their sets tuned to the channel they were watching when they went to bed, they usually turn on the TV to that same channel the next morning. That is why the evening schedule is so critical. If more people are watching NBC at night, more people may well be watching *Today* the next morning. When our ABC evening schedule is strong it has a positive effect on our ratings. And when it's weaker, it can have a negative effect.

Another factor in the success of a TV show, or any product for that matter, is advertising, or what we in television call on-air promotion. In the last several years, with *GMA* riding high, ABC has not wanted, or needed, to promote us because we were

so strong. They needed to promote other shows that weren't
doing as well, and that's what they did. Meanwhile, at *Today,*
they pulled out all the stops and plugged the show hard, with
bright, zippy promo spots featuring both cohosts throughout
their evening schedule and during such prime-time winners as
The Bill Cosby Show. How much more of an audience can you
reach than that? This has resulted in introducing *Today* to a
whole new audience.

I mention the fact that both cohosts do the promos on *Today*
because that hasn't been the case at *GMA.* This has been a cause
for which the female cohosts on our show have campaigned for
years, long before I arrived on the scene.

Another reason for *Today*'s surge has been the travel that
show has done in the last year. They've gone to Moscow and the
Vatican (where Jane Pauley and Bryant Gumbel had an audience
with the Pope); they've taken a train trip across the United
States and spent time at Carnaval in Rio, and so on. It's hard to
gauge how much a show's travel swings the audience to a particular program, but it seems that travel does attract viewers. If
you're at home, you may very well tune in to see what Rio looks
like—it's exciting and interesting to see places you've never seen
before. And the ratings suggest that special features like travel
do draw attention to a program.

I regularly hear comments and suggestions from people who
stop me on the street, in the supermarket, in restaurants, when
I'm on the road making speeches, and even when I'm at the local
gas station. They seek me out to give me the benefit of their
thoughts.

It turns out that many of our fans, not to mention the critics,
are speculating about the format of the show. Some feel we've
gotten away from one of our original concepts—the *GMA* family. In the beginning, *GMA* consciously developed a "family" of
personalities, and people tuned in to watch the members of that
family. They wanted to see what Rona Barrett, Jack Anderson,
Geraldo Rivera, Howard Cosell, and Cheryl Tiegs had to say.
They watched not only to see what was going on that day but to
see what the members of the family were doing and how they

looked and felt. Other viewers speculate that there is too much inside talk about a particular piece of legislation or the newest economic theory. They're home making toast and getting the kids off to school. They want to stick to the basics and know how they will be affected.

One other thing I find myself doing constantly is defending my role on the program with the viewers, not to mention with every newspaper and magazine reporter who has ever done a story on me. Not being billed as cohost (in fact, sometimes being referred to as subhost, which sounds something like subhuman) and the constant struggle to get important interviews are personal issues for me. But the real question is: How does the woman's role on a program such as ours influence whether or not a viewer will tune in or turn off. People ask me about this, men as well as women, partly because of the women's issue involved, but also because they think it would be nice to see two people who relate to each other and who look like they're having fun.

For instance, one of the most frequent comments I heard for four years was "Why don't they let you say hello at the opening of the program?" It's true that for four years I wasn't allowed to join in the hellos at each half-hour opening. But progress has been made. I now join in these greetings at two of the four openings. That may not be revolutionary but it's certainly a step in the right direction. And as I've always said, I take every little bit they give me and I build on it.

Only time will tell which approach is best for *GMA*. One thing is certain, however. *GMA* has been putting a terrific show on the air for years and we'll continue to be the best by responding to the viewers' needs and tastes.

By now you know that I am a very optimistic person and I've tried not to let these things get me down. My positive approach has been a big help, but, aside from my wonderfully supportive husband, what has gotten me through many tough times is this thought: When I look back on my career, I realize that I've really done all that I set out to do, and much more. I've met kings, queens, presidents, world-famous athletes, and almost every celebrity you can imagine. I've traveled to foreign countries, I've been on magazine covers, and I'm asked for my autograph on the street. If I walked away from it all right now, I could do so with wonderful memories and a feeling of enormous personal fulfillment. It's a fortunate position to be in.

And looking ahead, I also feel very fortunate. I feel that not only have I come a long way from Sacramento but that my career has just begun. All sorts of opportunities are opening up for me, and my two pregnancies have sent my husband and me down a path we both love—programming for parents. This path too is expanding and there is so much more we want to do. It's exciting, it's challeging, and it's all out there ahead of us.

Of course, central in my life is my family—the source of all of this love, happiness, productivity, and hope. And just between you and me, as they say in show biz, we're in preproduction for next season's big hit.

AFTERWORD

I'm going to leave you with some thoughts about what went into the writing of this book because it wasn't an easy thing for me to do. I must admit that the idea of writing a book seemed great in the first blush. But going through the process was, besides being incredibly time-consuming, almost like going through therapy, but without having to pay the psychiatrist. Getting my thoughts onto paper turned out to be an exercise in introspection and self-realization and the kind of self-examination that I would never have undertaken otherwise.

I know that I have grown from, and through, the experience and that it has changed me as a person. It helped me find out what makes me happy and unhappy, what things are truly important, what really makes me tick, and many other facets of myself that I had never voiced, nor would probably have ever voiced. In the final analysis, I feel it's been a positive experience; I've found some weak points and some strong points in myself that I never knew existed. It is this kind of self-knowledge that makes it possible to change.

Acknowledgment

I want to give special thanks to my assistant Debbie Bergenfeld. Her attention to detail, her moral support, and her constant good humor during the preparation of the book were invaluable.